Approaching the
Hunger Games Trilogy

Approaching the
Hunger Games Trilogy

A Literary and Cultural Analysis

TOM HENTHORNE

McFarland & Company, Inc., Publishers
Jefferson, North Carolina, and London

LIBRARY OF CONGRESS CATALOGUING-IN-PUBLICATION DATA

Henthorne, Tom.
  Approaching the Hunger Games trilogy : a literary and
cultural analysis / Tom Henthorne.
      p.   cm.
  Includes bibliographical references and index.

  ISBN 978-0-7864-6864-5
  softcover : acid free paper ∞

  1. Collins, Suzanne — Criticism and interpretation.
2. Collins, Suzanne. Hunger Games.   3. Young adult fiction,
American — History and criticism.   I. Title.
  PS3603.O4558Z6845 2012
  813'.6 — dc23   2012022250

BRITISH LIBRARY CATALOGUING DATA ARE AVAILABLE

Front cover images © 2012 Shutterstock

Manufactured in the United States of America

*McFarland & Company, Inc., Publishers
  Box 611, Jefferson, North Carolina 28640
    www.mcfarlandpub.com*

Table of Contents

Acknowledgments

I want to begin by thanking my sister Nancy for recommending *The Hunger Games* to me years ago and my sister Susan for sharing her own young adult fiction with me. The rest of my family has also been critical to the project in ways that are not always so obvious, so I want to thank them as well, namely Samuel, Amy, and Madeleine Henthorne; Mathew and Jack Pivarnik; Philip Mostic; Shaelyn, Kai, and Zoe Ransome; Eden, Holden, and Talia Way-Marcant; Katie Way; and, of course, Paul Way-Henthorne. Special thanks go to Juliet Way-Henthorne for her careful work as a research assistant and to Zane Way-Henthorne as a copy editor. And to Patricia Way, of course, for everything else.

Richard, Christine, Danny, Tommy, and Marco Nardi have also been very important to this project, as have my friends, students, and colleagues Sarah Blackwood, Kathie Cheng, Carol Dollison, Martha Driver, Dara Feldman, Amy Foerster, Kathryn Gau, Qian Hua Ge, Sandra Gonzales, Brittney Hagan, Stephanie Hsu, Karla Jay, Lindsey Lee, Victoria Measles, Tony Murphy, Cody Osterman, the Scaleras, Andrew Theori, Lee Transue, Catherine Zimmer as well as historians-at-large Nancy Reagin and Bill Offutt. I also want to thank Karlene King, Mona Khaldi, Megan Maule, Noelle Tennant, and the other members of OUT House for their assistance, support, and humor.

Special appreciation goes out to Kristen di Gennaro, Agie Markiewicz, Sid Ray, and Jonathan Silverman for their usual assistance, which I fear I take for granted and can only hope to return when they are similarly over-whelmed. And thanks to Gwendolyn Limbach for her invaluable help in the early stages of the project. The students in my literature and women's and gender studies classes at Pace University were also of tremendous help, not only because they shared their insights but because they continually remind me to not take myself or my work too seriously.

I also have great appreciation for the Pace University library staff, particularly those working in the interlibrary loan office, Amernel Danton, Chloe Pimera, and Editha Wilberton, who are always so kind and efficient. Pace University's Scholarly Research committee also deserves thanks for granting me released time to work on this book, as do Nira Herrmann, dean of Dyson College, and Associate Deans Adelia Williams-Lubitz and Andres Villarga for their continued support. I am also grateful to Students Against the Pacetriarchy for making the university a better place.

Additional thanks go to Has Beans, Sit and Wonder, the Velvet Peach, the Tea Lounge and various other places in Brooklyn that provide coffee, bathrooms and wireless to people like me, as well as places like the Coffee Bean and the Goleta Public Library in Goleta, California. Starbucks deserves special mention for being just about everywhere, including airports and grocery stores, and for being open late and on most holidays.

Preface

"Now I'm not a person who cries easily when she reads something, particularly something for kids. Yet as I was taking a train to Long Island I found myself tearing up over significant parts of this story [*The Hunger Games*]. It's good. And it's so ridiculous that a work of science fiction like this could even be so good."
— Elizabeth Bird, "Review of the Day: *The Hunger Games* by Suzanne Collins," *School Library Journal*

"...the *Hunger Games*, like *Harry Potter*, *His Dark Materials*, and *Twilight*, is a series written for young readers but heavily colonized by adults. Why do these books in particular grip adults? What is it about the *Hunger Games* that allows me to read them without shame on the subway?"
— David Plotz, "*Mockingjay* Left Me Sated, Not Satisfied," *Slate Magazine*

The *Hunger Games* trilogy has become a literary and cultural phenomenon. People are reading it on trains, in restaurants, and even while walking. "Down with the Capitol" tee-shirts can be purchased at Hot Topic. Fansites with names like "The Hob," "Jabberjays," and "TheGirlon-Fire.com" are drawing thousands of users daily. *Mockingjay*'s light blue cover can be seen poking out of children's bookbags. People can go to *InStyle* magazine's website to see what they would look like with Katniss Everdeen's signature braid. Millions of copies of the books have been purchased for Kindles, Nooks, and iPads. The books are referenced in mainstream media, taught in schools, and have even been the subject of academic conferences. And all of this happened before the first movie was released.

To an extent, the *Hunger Games* Trilogy phenomenon can be understood as being part of a larger cultural trend, one that became visible when the *Harry Potter* books went to the top of the *New York Times* bestseller list in 1999 and stayed there until the *Times* created a separate list for children's books to "clear some room" for books written for adults (Smith). Like the *Harry Potter* series, which was published between 1997 and 2007, and *The Twilight Saga*, which ran from 2005 to 2008, the *Hunger Games* trilogy appeals to a very broad demographic, as evidenced by overall sales in the millions: the books are popular with readers of all ages and marketed accordingly (Springen 2010). But the *Hunger Games* trilogy is markedly different from the other two series in the nature of its appeal, Suzanne Collins's work being cynical and ironic in ways that *Harry Potter* and *Twilight* are not. As Rebecca Cusey points out in an article for *The Daily Caller*, Rowling's series is essentially conservative, affirming traditional values as the title character comes "to believe in justice, freedom, and basic decency, to identify the trustworthy, and to take responsibility for fighting evil in his time." The *Twilight* series is even more conservative, possibly even reactionary, in its heteronormativity, its attitudes towards authority, and its celebration of traditional American values. For Katniss Everdeen, in contrast, "[j]ustice doesn't exist and freedom is an illusion" and the trilogy ends with her being "used up psychologically and emotionally, thoroughly disillusioned" (Cusey).

The *Hunger Games* trilogy, of course, is a product of its era, just like every other cultural artifact. The appearance of the first volume of Collins's series coincided almost exactly with the beginning of the world economic crisis that began in late 2008. Although critics could hardly argue that *The Hunger Games* represents a reaction to the crisis — the volume having been completed before the crash — the mood of the time shaped its reception; the book's biting irony matched the mood of the times as a population, which was already weary of the ongoing wars in Afghanistan and Iraq, and suspicious of its political leaders, faced a very real prospect of economic ruin. *The Hunger Games* is a dark book for a dark time, as are *Catching Fire* and *Mockingjay*, which appeared 2009 and 2010 respectively.

Recognizing the importance of Collins's work both as literary texts and as cultural productions, this book addresses the *Hunger Games* trilogy from a number of literary and cultural perspectives in an effort to better understand both its significance and its appeal. It takes an interdisciplinary approach to Collins's work, drawing from literary studies, psychology, gender studies, history, media studies, and cultural studies. Although it is an academic text, being more analytical than evaluative, it is written so as to be accessible to general readers, dispensing with extended theoretical discussions, academic jargon, and even footnotes. Because this book assumes that readers are familiar with all three volumes, it also avoids plot summary and character analysis, instead focusing on the significance of the story and its characters.

Most chapters begin by introducing a theoretical approach and then applying it to the trilogy in order to address issues that might be overlooked by the casual reader and demonstrate why Collins's work warrants careful analysis. Chapter Two, "The Importance of Being Katniss: Identity, Gender, and Transgression," for example, explains how gender can be understood as a social construct and then analyzes how gender relations are both structured and represented in the trilogy, addressing topics such as how the Capitol uses gender differences to position people against one another; how romance is figured both inside and outside of the arena; how heteronormativity is promoted by the Capitol in order to affirm its own patriarchal power; and how Katniss ultimately challenges the authoritarianism of both the Capitol and District 13 by refusing to perform any of the roles they assign her. Because this book defines its terms as it goes along rather than assuming readers are conversant with them, readers who are unfamiliar with literary and cultural theory should not only be able to follow the arguments but come away with a better sense of how various theoretical approaches work and hopefully be able to apply them to other texts they encounter.

This book also includes a biographical essay on Collins, one that not only details her life and work, but also identifies the ways in which the two are interconnected. In addition, it provides a glossary of concepts and terms employed by Collins in the trilogy as well as a glossary of characters. The volume also includes a series of discussion questions for the *Hunger Games* trilogy, *The Hunger Games* film, and Collins's previous series, *The Underland Chronicles*. The questions are designed to help readers come up with new ways of thinking about Collins's work and the issues they raise. Finally, the volume offers an extensive bibliography that provides information on both primary and secondary sources, including books, essays, interviews, reviews, and commentary.

Although the intent of the present volume is to analyze the *Hunger Games* trilogy rather than celebrate it, the fact that it can be approached in so many ways serves as a testament to the quality and depth of Collins's work.

Introduction

"Most of the things we normally have to deal with understanding are complex, fuzzy, messy, changing, and in fact poorly delineated. We don't actually know where the boundaries of them are, let alone whether we are able to make clear questions about them. We spend a lot of our time as ordinary human beings navigating through complicated situations with one another that require constant negotiation and constant new attempts to understand."
— Brian Eno, "A Big Theory of Culture" [64]

The Hunger Games, *Catching Fire*, and *Mockingjay* are complicated texts — messy, even — moving in one direction and then another, doubling back or jumping ahead, and sometimes going nowhere at all. Of the three volumes, the first is the most linear, events being presented for the most part as they happen by a first-person narrator who uses the present tense almost exclusively. Things soon become messy, however, not just for Katniss, who must sort out her feelings for Peeta while trying to out-think the Gamemakers who have pitted her against him in a fight-to-the death reality show, but also for the readers, who must figure out what is happening from a narrator who herself is overwhelmed and confused. Things become messier still when Katniss finds a way to win the Games without having to kill Peeta, only to quickly learn that the Games are not over for her and are likely never to be with President Snow insisting that she continue her showmance with Peeta indefinitely.

It is in *Catching Fire* and *Mockingjay* that things become messiest for Katniss, however, as she tries to sort out not only her personal issues but her own interests as an individual, as a member of a family, as part of a community, and as a citizen of a nation involved in a civil war: at times she become so confused that she literally has to remind herself who she is and what she knows to be true, beginning with her name (*Mockingjay* 4). She also must constantly contend with other people's expectations of her,

5

which include being not only a daughter, sister, lover, and friend but "the girl on fire," a "love-crazed schoolgirl," and the Mockingjay (*Hunger Games* 70; *Catching Fire* 21). Finally, she must cope with various forms of physical and emotional trauma, drug addiction, disorientation, and the guilt she feels for being responsible for the deaths of so many people.

The trilogy is also messy in terms of genre, Collins herself commenting, "People view the books differently — as romance, as dystopian, as action adventure, as political" (Jordan, 9 December 2010). She might easily have added that it is a *Bildungsroman*, a science fiction novel, and a survivor story as well. Although Collins partakes of all these genres, she adheres to the conventions of none, confounding the expectations of readers and critics alike as the story continually changes direction. Some readers, of course, find the trilogy frustrating for this very reason: they expect their romances to end romantically, their dystopias to end hopelessly, their adventure stories to end triumphantly. For other readers, however, this is one of the trilogy's strengths: because it is so unconventional, it is impossible to predict what is going to happen from chapter to chapter, making the story that much more engaging.

Finally, the trilogy is complicated thematically. Even though Collins considers the novels to be "first and foremost, war stories," the war against the Capitol begins only in the third volume, the first two concerning themselves with themes such as family, friendship, love, trauma, gender, governance, personal responsibility, and ethics (Margolis 2010). The fact that she considers *The Hunger Games*, a novel that never even mentions the possibility of a war against the Capitol, to be a war story indicates just how complicated her thinking about the subject is: war cannot be separated from themes such as family, friendship, love, and everything else because they are all interrelated. In order to understand war, she seems to suggest, we need to understand what it is to be human since war is a very human thing. And the same goes for all of her other themes: none can be understood in isolation since they all connect with everything else.

This volume plays in the Collins mess rather than trying to clean it up. It makes no attempt to sort out Collins's ideas because they do not need sorting out. Indeed, one of this book's underlying assumptions is that messiness is a good thing, at least when it comes to fiction, since it reflects the way life really is. If Katniss's story were easy to follow, if the novel were easy to classify, if Collins's themes were easy to discern, then the *Hunger Games* trilogy would tell us little about the world we live in or how we might go about changing it. What makes Collins's work worth discussing is its difficulty. Not that it is difficult to read, of course: many readers report finishing it in one sitting. But it is difficult to process and digest.

This book is designed to help with the digestion process. Rather than offer a definitive reading of Collins's novels — as if any reading could ever be definitive — the present volume considers the various ways that that the *Hunger Games* trilogy can be approached so as to arrive at a better understanding of it in all of its complexity. If no single approach could ever adequately explain the trilogy, or any complicated text for that matter, perhaps a combination of them can begin to do so. That is what this book attempts: it is interdisciplinary not only because each chapter addresses Collins's work from the perspective of a different discipline or field of study but because every chapter is itself interdisciplinary, drawing from a number of methodologies and approaches simultaneously. In the chapter on war, for example, approaches Collins's representation of war through an area of the social sciences known as "Peace and Conflict Studies." Its discussion of war in both *The Underland Chronicles* and the *Hunger Games* trilogy, however, draws from literary studies, gender studies, history, psychology, and cultural studies as well as the social sciences.

Chapter One approaches the trilogy as a literary and cultural production. Following a discussion of how young adult fiction emerged as a genre in the 1960s, it considers the process by which certain texts are accorded literary status and others are not. Although book reviewers and critics would have us believe that the literariness of any particular text is established through the application of objective aesthetic criteria, as Alan Sinfield argues, it has more to do with power and politics (35). According to him, texts that are designated "literary" tend to "reinforce prevailing understandings," that is, the beliefs and values of those in power (36). This is not to say that aesthetic criteria are not an important factor in judging a text's literariness: they clearly are. The point is, rather, that aesthetic criteria are set by a literary establishment that serves the interests of those in power, and that these criteria are used to justify judgments about literary quality that determine not only which books are produced and in what volume, but how they are promoted and distributed. With all of this in mind, this chapter discusses the trilogy in aesthetic terms, exploring its structure, its narrative mode, and its use of various literary devices. The primary question this chapter addresses is whether the *Hunger Games* trilogy has aesthetic qualities consistent with literary text as they are defined today. If it does, then it is more likely that the trilogy will be deemed culturally significant and worth preserving by the literary establishment. If it does not, then the trilogy will likely be classified as genre fiction, that is, a text that strictly conforms to the conventions of a particular genre and therefore has limited cultural value.

The second chapter focuses on issues pertaining to gender and sexuality and therefore falls under the rubric of women's and gender studies. After discussing the ways in which gender can be understood as a social construction, the chapter explores how gender functions in Collins's text, addressing the relationship between gender and power in particular. The chapter also considers how masculinity and femininity are defined in Panem, how heteronormativity is used by the Capitol to reinforce patriarchy, and how gender boundaries are policed. Finally, it addresses how Katniss's continual transgression of gender boundaries makes her a radical figure, someone capable of challenging the social order from the outside, effecting change in a way no other person can. At the end of the novel, Katniss, Peeta, and, arguably, all of Panem enter into a third space of possibility, to borrow Margorie Garber's term, that is, a space that by its very existence challenges the legitimacy of binaries such as male and female, masculine and feminine, heterosexual and homosexual, that until then govern their lives.

Chapter Three focuses on Collins's representation of war, considering not only *The Hunger Games* trilogy but Collins's earlier series of novels, *The Underland Chronicles*, the first volume of which was published in 2003, the same year that the United States invaded Iraq. As Collins indicates in interviews, she is very much concerned with the ways in which children are acculturated to war and violence through television, video games, and other popular forms of entertainment (Margolis 2010, Hudson). In an interview with the *School Library Journal*, Collins states that she writes about war because she thinks "the concept of war, the specifics of war, the nature of war, the ethical ambiguities of war are introduced too late to children (Margolis 2010). In addition to addressing questions about when, if ever, war is justified, in both *The Underland Chronicles* and the *Hunger Games* trilogy, she considers the effects it has on combatants and non-combatants alike both physically and psychologically. She also seems to offer indirect commentary on the wars the United States became involved with following the September 11th attacks, suggesting that it may not be so easy to discern the good from the bad since both sides do unconscionable things. As Susan Carpenter of the *Los Angeles Times* observes of *Mockingjay*, "Much of the action takes place on a battlefield akin to Iraq — where innocent civilians are murdered to further a cause and each side resorts to unsavory tactics that could lead to a terrorist label." Carpenter goes on to observe that the novel is "overtly antiwar" in a way that the preceding novels are not, suggesting that Collins's attitudes towards the war became increasingly negative as the war continued into the second decade of the 21st century. A careful reading of the war novels Collins produced since the United States' wars in Afghanistan and Iraq began — that is, *The Underland Chronicles* and the *Hunger Games* trilogy — seems to bear this out, Collins coming to doubt whether war should ever be resorted to as a means of addressing conflict.

The fourth chapter approaches the trilogy through philosophy, arguing that Collin's work can be understood as a study in pragmatism. At the beginning of *The Hunger Games*, Katniss makes a critical decision, choosing to fight for the survival of herself and her family rather than remain passive in the face of starvation. More than that, though, she engages in what John Dewey might call "intelligent practice," applying the scientific method to everyday life in an effort to achieve her goals. Although she faces numerous setbacks, sometimes behaving impetuously and even engaging in conduct that is counterproductive if not dangerous, as the trilogy proceeds she becomes increasingly adept at making initial hypothesis, putting them into practice, observing the results, and then, based on those results, refining her hypotheses so that she can proceed intelligently. She is, in short, a pragmatist. The chapter also explores Katniss's actions in relation to pragmatist ethics as articulated by William James, arguing that Collins rejects "ends justify the means" types of arguments as being morally insupportable since "ends" are abstractions that have no legitimate standing in the real world. As an alternative, Collins proposes evaluating potential action in terms of reasonably expected outcomes since this allows for concrete analysis and even testing. In addition, Collins considers the ethics of inaction, suggesting ultimately, as James does, that the decision not to act is itself an action and therefore subject to ethical analysis. Finally, the chapter examines pragmatist ethics in relation to law, focusing on Katniss's insistence upon determining right and wrong for herself and acting accordingly.

The fifth chapter takes a media studies approach to the trilogy, considering how the Hunger Games broadcasts and related programming are used by the Capitol to maintain control over the people of Panem. In addition to discussing the Games' social and ideological functions, the chapter explores how Katniss effectively subverts the Games, forcing the Gamemakers to change the rules so that two victors will be allowed. In a sense, she becomes the Gamemaker, taking control of the Games and altering them forever. The chapter also considers the relationship between the Hunger Games and contemporary reality programming, arguing that contemporary shows like *Survivor*, *Extreme Makeover*, and *Project Runway* are not so different from the programming offered by the Capitol, at least in principle, and that their real-world consequences should be examined. Although Collins's primary concern seems to be the ways in which reality television desensitizes viewers to violence, she also addresses the ways in which it promotes violence as a means of resolving conflict. Moreover, she suggests that reality programming — like both the Hunger Games and the Roman circuses Juvenal refers to in his Tenth Satire — prevents viewers from fulfilling their civic responsibilities, not only through distraction but by promoting the idea that people only have a responsibility to themselves.

Chapter Six analyzes *The Hunger Games* and its sequels as dystopian novels, arguing that they break with the conventions of the genre in important ways. Rather than make a dystopian future the novels' subject, the trilogy makes a dystopian future its setting, keeping its focus tightly on Katniss and her experiences. By presenting Panem through Katniss, Collins provides readers with a means of experiencing dystopia themselves to the extent that they are able to identify with her. More than that, though, because Katniss relates the story in the present tense, we learn about the world outside of District 12 at the same time she does and therefore process information simultaneously with her. This ability to see for ourselves, so to speak, becomes critical in *Mockingjay* when, because of the various forms of trauma she has been subjected to, Katniss becomes an increasingly unreliable narrator. Because she relates events as they happen, we can interpret the dystopian world she enters upon relocating to District 13 for ourselves, connecting it to our own world in ways Katniss cannot since she lives in our future. Constructing the text in such a manner seems to serve

Collins's didactic purpose, which, as she indicates in an interview with National Public Radio, is to induce readers to "look at governments and situations throughout the world and wonder if they are moral or not" (Neary). She continues: "You have to have that, You have to at some time in your life begin to question the environment, the political situation around you and decide whether it's right or not and if it isn't, what part you are going to play in that."

Chapter Seven takes a psychological approach to the trilogy, focusing in particular on trauma and its effects upon Katniss. The trilogy itself, I argue, can be read as a survivor story, that is, as an attempt by Katniss to narrate her own story in a way that will enable her to better come to terms with it. Over the course of the trilogy Katniss faces not just the trauma of losing her father at an early age but severe physical and emotional injury. Refusing to be a victim, she retains agency as best she can, repressing much of her pain and distracting herself with her duties as the Mockingjay. Engaging in such strategies gives her only limited relief, however: she is only able to move beyond her trauma once she accepts that there is no going back to the person she was before she participated in the Hunger Games and that, therefore, she must move on. Collins also represents survivor stories as fulfilling a vital social function to the extent that they enable communities to come to terms with shared trauma and to "prevent the enactment of similar horrors in the future" (Tal 121). Telling her story is a "transformative experience," not only for Katniss but for society at large (Tal 119).

The final chapter circles all the way back to the beginning of the book. Like the first chapter, it considers the the *Hunger Games* trilogy as a literary and cultural production. Rather than address Collins's work in terms of established concepts and categories, however, Chapter Eight discusses the trilogy in terms of concepts and categories that are coming into being as digital culture changes the very nature of textuality. As Pierre Levy, Donald Tapscott, Alan Kirby, and others suggest, digital technology has fundamentally changed the ways in which people engage with texts. In particular, readers increasing regard texts not as words on a page so much as worlds that can be entered into, participated in, and even changed. Not surprisingly perhaps, works such as Collins's that are constructed so as to accommodate readers' desires to participate in the meaning-making process develop large fan communities where readers can both explore and expand fictive worlds together. Such works have what may be termed a digital aesthetic, that is, formal features that are characteristic of digital-age texts. In the case of the *Hunger Games* trilogy, these features include 1) the construction of an immersive, internally-consistent world that combines the familiar with the unfamiliar so that readers do not become estranged from the text; 2) the strategic placement of gaps in the narrative so that readers can contribute to meaning-making in significant ways; and 3) the privileging of expressiveness over originality so that the narrative reads quickly while remaining compelling. Judging by both sales figures and reader response to the trilogy on numerous fansites and blogs, Collins has succeeded in creating a narrative that is fully contemporary in terms of both style and content.

Literature, gender, philosophy, television, dystopia, war, psychology, digital culture: in the *Hunger Games* trilogy, things are messy, just like a teenager's dirty room. As this book tries to demonstrate, however, messiness in a narrative can be a good thing, at least when it induces readers to think about things in new ways rather than just confuses them. Collins accomplishes the former by creating a text that is messy but not disorderly: the trilogy may appear untidy, but, as it turns out, everything is in its place. With this in mind, it is no wonder that the series has received both popular and critical acclaim: the *Hunger Games* trilogy is not only worth reading but worth thinking about.

Suzanne Collins

A Biography

Suzanne Collins was born on August 1962 to Jane and Michael Collins. The youngest of four children, she spent her early childhood near the United States Military Academy in West Point, New York, where her father, a career Air Force officer and military historian, taught for the Army temporarily. Her earliest memories include watching cadets drill on the parade grounds where her father worked. She also recalls her father, who, having grown up during the Great Depression, regarded hunting as a means of surviving, gathering wild mushrooms in the woods to eat, adding that her "mom wouldn't let any of us go near them!" ("A Conversation").

In 1968 her family moved to Indiana, and soon afterwards her father was deployed in Vietnam. Although her mother tried to shield her and her siblings from coverage of the war, Collins remembers some of the evening news reports, commenting, "I would hear them say 'Vietnam,' and I knew my dad was there, and it was very frightening" (Margolis 2008). She goes on to observe that many American children are going through a similar thing today because of the ongoing fighting in Afghanistan and Iraq (Margolis 2008). Her father returned from a one-year tour of duty traumatized by his wartime experiences, suffering from "nightmares ... that lasted his whole life": Collins recalls sometimes awakening herself to the sound of his crying out (Dominus).

Following Michael's return from Vietnam, the family moved again repeatedly as Michael was assigned to various military installations in the eastern half of the country, including the Pentagon in Arlington County, Virginia, and the Air Command and Staff College in Montgomery, Alabama. As a result, Collins reports knowing personally "what it feels like to be a stranger somewhere," just like Gregor, the protagonist of *The Underland Chronicles* ("A Conversation"). Fortunately for Collins, as the

13

youngest child she had siblings to help her adjust to new places and parents who kept her engaged and active wherever she was. She remembers enjoying gymnastics when she was Gregor's age and playing with her friends in the woods ("A Converstation"). She also learned sword-fighting, another activity that seems to be reflected in *The Underland Chronicles* ("A Conversation").

Collins was an avid reader even as a child, returning repeatedly to Margaret Evans Price's *Myths and Enchantment Tales* and *D'Aulaires' Book of Greek Myths*, both of which she credits as sources for the *Hunger Games* trilogy. She counts the myth of Theseus and the Minotaur as a particularly "significant influence," describing Katniss as "a futuristic Theseus" ("A Conversation"). She also developed a taste for adult literature early on, participating in an open classroom in the fifth and sixth grades where her English teacher, Miss Vance, would read Edgar Allen Poe stories such as "The Telltale Heart" and "The Mask of the Red Death" on rainy days. According to Collins, her early exposure to adult themes such as "death, loss, and violence" helped shape her later conviction that children can benefit from stories with serious subject matter and frightening themes (Hudson).

While in seventh grade, Collins moved to Belgium with her family when her father was assigned to NATO. She lived just outside of Brussels for three years, attending an American school, where, though instruction was primarily in English, she began to learn French. She also learned some Flemish, though she had no formal instruction in that language. While in Europe she travelled extensively with her family, visiting battlefields and military installations, and historic sites, her father telling Collins and her siblings about what caused a particular war, "what led up ... to this particular battle, what transpired there, and what the fallout was" (Hudson). She was also exposed to literary perspectives on war, recalling, for example, thinking about *The Wizard of Oz* as she looked across a poppy field in Belgium, only to have her father recite John McCrae's "In Flanders Fields," a poem in which the speaker, a recently killed soldier buried beneath poppies, beseeches the living to continue the fight so that he and the other dead soldiers can rest peacefully. Collins describes the event as "transformative" since it made her realize that any field could be a graveyard (Dominus).

As an adolescent, she preferred books written for adults to young adult fiction, though she very much enjoyed Jaap ter Haar's *Boris*, the story of two children who struggle to survive the Nazi siege of Leningrad, as well as Madeleine L'Engle's *A Wrinkle in Time* and Norton Juster's *The Phantom Tollbooth*. Her favorite novels included *Anna Karenina* (Leo Tolstoy), *Dandelion Wine* (Ray Bradbury), *Germinal* (Emile Zola), *The Heart Is a Lonely Hunter* (Carson McCullers), *Lord of the Flies* (William Golding), *A Moveable Feast* (Ernest Hemingway), *1984* (George Orwell), *Slaughterhouse-Five* (Kurt Vonnegut), *We Have Always Lived in the Castle* (Shirley Jackson), *A Tree Grows in Brooklyn* (Betty Smith). In an interview with *Entertainment Weekly*, Collins reports that she was assigned Thomas Hardy's *The Mayor of Casterbridge* while in 10th grade but "just couldn't get into it." She continues: "About seven years later I rediscovered Hardy, and consumed four of his novels in a row. Katniss Everdeen owes her last name to Bathsheba Everdene, the lead character in *Far from the Madding Crowd*. The two are very different, but both struggle with knowing their hearts" (Jordan, 13 August 2010). In an interview posted on the Scholastic website, Collins reports English as being her favorite subject.

After returning to the United States, the family settled in Alabama, where Collins completed high school at the Alabama School of the Fine Arts, graduating with a specialization in the theatre arts in 1980. She went on to college at Indiana University, where she earned Bachelor of the Arts degrees in theater and telecommunications. As a student there, she met Cap Prior, whom she eventually married. After graduating, she worked as a local reporter for National Public Radio, as a country western DJ, and as a data entry programmer for a company that produces yearbooks (Springen 2008).

In 1987 Collins moved to New York City, where she entered graduate school at New York University, eventually earning an M.F.A. in dramatic writing. While in NYC she worked for an Off Broadway theatre company, the Classic Stage Company, and for a film producer for more than a year. She began writing for television in 1991, beginning with *Hi Honey, I'm Home!*, and went on to write for *Clarissa Explains It All* (1993). In 1997–8, she worked as a scriptwriter for *The Mystery Files of Shelby Woo*, and the following year, published a book based on the show, *Fire Proof: Shelby Woo #11*. She also wrote scripts for *Little Bear* and *Oswald*, became head writer for *Generation O!*, and she also co-authored a Rankin/Bass Christmas special, *Santa, Baby!* (2001) with Peter Bakalian, for which she received an award nomination from the Writer's Guild of America. In addition, she worked as the head writer for *Clifford's Puppy Days*.

While working for *Generation O!* in 2000–2001, she was encouraged by James Proimos, the show's creator and the author of the *Johnny Mutton* children's series, to write children's books herself, Proimos going so far as to recommend her to his literary agent, Rosemary Stimola, who took on Collins as a client once she saw a sample from *Gregor the Overlander* (Italie). Stimola comments: "Quite honestly, I knew from the very first paragraph I had a very gifted writer.... It happens like that sometimes. Not often, but when it does it's a thing of beauty. From the very first paragraph she established a character I cared about. She established a story and a mood that touched my heart" (Italie).

According to Collins, her training as a playwright and experience as a scriptwriter greatly influenced the way she structured both *The Underland Chronicles* and the *Hunger Games* trilogy: "My books are basically structured like three-act plays. I'm very conscious of pacing because you get very little downtime in television. You have to be moving the story forward and developing the characters at the same time" (Springen 2008). Collins's experience as a television writer also seems to have helped her learn how to relate a complex story through a series of narratives that are interrelated yet can stand on their own. Collins also attributes the skill with which she uses cliffhangers to her work as a scriptwriter, ending chapters while characters are in peril or when important information is about to be provided. She comments: "That seems like the natural place to break because we do that in television so the viewers will come back after the commercials" (Springen 2008).

Collins credits her father as a major influence upon *Gregor the Overlander* and the four volumes that followed, not only because she consulted with him frequently about military strategies and tactics employed by various characters, but because she learned from him the importance of teaching children to question what makes war necessary — "at what point is it justifiable or unavoidable?" (Margolis 2010). She adds that for him, these were "very personal questions" since he had fought in war himself, as had his father and brother: "He would discuss these things at a level that he thought we could understand and were acceptable for our age. But, really, he thought a lot was acceptable for our age, and I approach my books in the same way" (Margolis 2010). Questions about what makes a war necessary became even more pressing after the September 11th attacks on the World Trade Center and the Pentagon. Like her father, who "strongly opposed" the War in Iraq, Collins does not take going to war lightly, having learned from him about the human cost in both lives and suffering (Springen 2008). With this in mind, it should not be surprising that the protagonist of *The Underland Chronicles* is reluctant to enter into war and, as it proceeds, is increasingly doubtful about the cause for which he is fighting. Although Michael Collins died before the first volume was published, he is very much a presence in it and is included in the dedication along with Collins's mother.

Gregor the Overlander was released in September 2003, just six months after the invasion of Iraq. Although not a runaway bestseller, the book did well commercially and was critically acclaimed, *Kirkus Reviews* describing it as "supremely absorbing" and "wonderful," and *Publishers Weekly* calling it "fantastically engaging." None of the major contemporary reviews acknowledged any link between Collins's book and the wars in Afghanistan or Iraq, however, or seemed to regard it as anything but a children's fantasy-adventure novel that is a little more violent than most, *The Horn Book Magazine*, for example, noting that the book "features vivid battle scenes (complete with gore), dangerous alliances, some frighteningly close calls, and the sobering death of comrades-in-arms."

After completing *Gregor the Overlander*, Collins moved to rural Connecticut with her husband and two children, Charlie and Isabel, and began to devote more of her time to fiction. There she wrote four more volumes of *The Underland Chronicles—Gregor and the Prophecy of Bane* in 2004, followed by *Gregor and the Curse of the Warmbloods* (2005), *Gregor and the Marks of Secret* (2006), and *Gregor and the Code of the Claw* (2007). She also published *When Charlie McButton Lost Power*, illustrated by Mike Lester, in 2005. Despite her success as a children's author, each volume of *The Underland Chronicles* selling well and being critically-acclaimed, she continued writing scripts through 2008, freelancing for *Wow! Wow! Wubbzy!* as she began work on the *Hunger Games* Trilogy. She describes writing for the children's show as "an excellent mental break" because it was "delightful" and because "no one dies in it," adding that "it was almost good therapy" (Springen 2008).

Collin's next major project was *The Hunger Games*, which she realized would develop into a series almost from the start: "Once I'd thought through to the end of the first book, I knew there would be repercussions from the events that take place there" (Hopkinson). She had not worked out all of the details, however, leaving herself "breathing room for the characters to develop emotionally ... which they often do." In an interview with the *New York Times Review of Books*, Collins indicates that the books, which she thinks of as "one story," almost wrote themselves: "When I sat down to write the series, I assumed it was going to be like the previous series I had written, *The Underland Chronicles*, which means it would be written in the third person and in the past tense. And when I began writing, the words just came out, not only in the first person but in the present tense in Katniss's voice. It was almost as if the character was insisting on telling the story herself" ("Book Review Podcast").

In her original book proposal to Scholastic, which outlined the content of all three volumes, she described the project in the following terms: "Although set in the future, *The Hunger Games* explores the disturbing issues of modern warfare such as who fights our wars, how they are orchestrated, and the ever-increasing opportunities to observe them being played out" (Egan 9). Thematically, at least, the *Hunger Games* trilogy was to be very much like *The Underland Chronicles*: whereas her first series was written for intermediate readers, however, her second was intended for young adults and therefore could represent the horrors of war much more directly. Receiving the completed manuscript of *The Hunger Games* in 2007, Scholastic's editorial director David Leviathan described it as "astonishing," and the book was quickly put into production. According to Leviathan, "our editorial consensus pretty much consisted of one word: Wow" (Egan 10).

In 2008, *The Hunger Games* was published, becoming a *New York Times* bestseller and winning a number of awards, ranging from *Kirkus Reviews*' "Book of the Year" for young adults to the Cybil Award for science fiction and fantasy. It was also included on many editors' choice lists as well as the American Library Association's Amelia Bloomer list of recommended feminist fiction. In addition, it was recommended by prominent writers including Stephen King, who wrote in *Entertainment Weekly* that the book was "addictive," and Stephenie Meyer, who reported on her website that she "was so obsessed with the book" that she took it with her when going out to dinner and hid "it under the edge of the table" so she could continue reading it, adding that she has "been recommending it to total strangers at Target." As with *Gregor the Overlander*, none of the major reviewers acknowledged the book's political content in any way or related it to the United States' ongoing wars in Afghanistan and Iraq. Rather, they seemed to regard the novel as offering commentary on the entertainment industry and how it not only desensitizes viewers to real-world violence but promotes unhealthy beauty ideals, much as Scott Westerfield's acclaimed young adult series, *The Uglies*, does.

With the success *of The Hunger Games*, Collins finally gave up writing for television, focusing instead upon completing the trilogy and writing a screenplay of the first volume for Color Force Productions, which purchased the film rights in conjunction with Lions Gate Entertainment in March 2009. Although the producer, Nina Jacobson, initially worried about making a film for children that features violence between them, she decided that the project would work if the film took the same approach Collins did in book, "staying inside of Katniss's character and managing to comment on the violence without ever exploiting it" (Egan 12). According to Jacobson, she was able to acquire rights for Color Force by convincing Collins that she was committed to making "an ethical version of the movie" (Egan 13). For her part, Collins reported, "There were so many great choices, but ultimately I felt that Nina had the greatest connection to the work. I believed her when she said she would do everything she could to protect its integrity" (Egan 13).

Catching Fire was published on September 1, 2008, the release date being moved up at the behest of booksellers so that it would be available to children before their summer vacation ended (Sellers 2009). Though not so highly acclaimed as *The Hunger Games*, the second volume of the trilogy sold well, reaching #1 on the major bestseller lists and receiving generally positive reviews. Although some reactions were critical of the sequel, Jennifer Reese of *Entertainment Weekly*, for example, calling it "decidedly weaker" than *The Hunger Games* and giving it a "C," in her review for the *New York Times*, Gabrielle Zevin wrote that Collins had done "a rare thing," writing "a sequel that improves upon the first book," and *Publishers Weekly* named it one of their books of the year. Whether they liked it or not — and most did like it — reviewers seemed to recognize a certain seriousness to the novel, *Booklist*, for example, observing that it is "brimming with potent themes of morality, obedience, sacrifice, redemption, love, law, and, above all, survival," and *Kirkus Reviews* opining that the book offers "acute social commentary," though it does not specify what it comments upon.

Mockingjay, published in 2010, was an unequivocal success, both popularly and critically, debuting at #1 on the *New York Times* bestseller list after selling almost half a million copies in the first week ("*Mockingjay* Sells ..."). Noting its "sharp social commentary," *Publishers Weekly* described the final volume of the *Trilogy* as "being the best yet, a beautifully orchestrated and intelligent novel that succeeds on every level" ("Children's Review: Mockingjay"). The *Los Angeles Times*, too, recognized the novel's political content, relating it directly to the Iraq war (Carpenter), and the *New York Times* observes that it "channels the political passion of *1984* (Roiphe). Even reviewers who found the book horrifically violent recommended it: the *School Library Journal*, for example comments that Collins is "absolutely ruthless in her depictions of war in all of its cruelty, violence, and loss," and then goes on to compare *Mockingjay* favorably to *Lord of the Flies* and Stephen King's *The Stand*.

Work continued on the screenplay for *The Hunger Games* throughout 2010 as Billy Ray, writer and director of *Shattered Glass* (2003) and *Breach* (2007), helped develop the script Collins had written earlier. Upon joining *The Hunger Games* project as director in November 2010, Gary Ross, the writer and director of *Pleasantville* (1998) and *Seabiscuit* (2003), redrafted Ray's script with help from Collins. According to Ross, he and Collins become "actual collaborators," writing the shooting script as a team (Egan 16). Collins, who was very much concerned about the integrity of her story, ended up being very happy with the final version of the script: even though the need for "compression" forced them to cut Madge Undersee and some of the Career pack from the film, Collins was satisfied that no damage was done to "the emotional arc of the story" (Egan 14).

Collins was included in casting decisions as well, a process that generated a huge buzz for the film as fans reacted vociferously to every decision. Collins herself announced the selection of Jennifer Lawrence as Katniss in a letter to her readers published in *Entertainment Weekly* in March 2011, and other decisions were released one-by-one, generating tremendous publicity for the project. Josh Hutcherson was cast as Peeta Mellark and Liam Hemsworth was cast as Gale Hawthorne. The cast also includes Woody Harrelson as Haymitch Abernathy, Lenny Kravitz as Cinna, Elizabeth Banks as Effie Trinket, Stanley Tucci as Caesar Flickerman, and Donald

Sutherland as President Snow. Filming began later that month in 2011, taking place principally in North Carolina, and continued through mid–September, production costs coming in at just under $100 million. Although Collins visited the set, she was not present for most of the filming.

With the success of the *Hunger Games* trilogy, Collins has become a prominent figure, being named to *Time* magazine's list of 100 people who most affect our world. Although she agreed to participate in a limited book tour following the release of *Mockingjay*, she protects her privacy and avoids publicity as best she can. As Susan Dominus notes, "Collins's read ings and appearances are usually off-limits to television cameras, and she declines almost any interaction that involves capturing her on videotape." According to the Scholastic Books website, she is unavailable for speeches, conferences, school or library appearances, Skype appearances, video conferences, or teleconferences. The website does feature an extended video interview with her, however, in which she discusses things ranging from major influences to her favorite movies, which she lists as *The Thin Man* (1934), *Shadow of a Doubt* (1943), and *A Bridge Over the River Kwai* (1957).

Currently Collins lives in Sandy Hook, Connecticut, a borough of the Newtown township, about 60 miles northeast of New York City.

CHAPTER ONE

Make of It What You Will

The Hunger Games *Trilogy as a Literary Production*

"[T]he worst books are often the most important because they are usually the ones we read earliest in life. It is probable that many people who would consider themselves extremely sophisticated and 'advanced' are actually carrying through life an imaginative background which they acquired in childhood...."
— George Orwell, "Boys' Weeklies" [482].

"There are some themes, some subjects, too large for adult fiction; they can only be dealt with adequately in a children's book."
— Philip Pullman, Carnegie Medal Acceptance Speech

As the above quotations suggest, attitudes towards young adult (YA) fiction have changed significantly over the years. When Orwell made his observation about children's books in 1940, YA fiction as we know it today did not exist: the books most popular with children and adolescents tended to be fantasies such as J.M. Barrie's *Peter Pan* and Lewis Carroll's *Alice's Adventures in Wonderland* or adventure stories such as Robert Louis Stevenson's *Treasure Island* and H. Rider Haggard's *King Solomon's Mines* — books that were not written with a teenage audience in mind (Richards 3). With Baby Boomers coming of age in the 1960s and a concomitant increase in funding for public libraries under President Lyndon Johnson's Great Society initiative, YA fiction began to emerge as a genre in its own right, space literally being made for it in libraries and bookstores across the United States (Aronson 2002, 82). According to Marc Aronson:

At first those young adult sections featured a mix of the adult titles teenagers might like: the trippy weirdness of a Carlos Castaneda, the black rage of an Eldridge Cleaver, the angst and sense of Jungian mystery of Herman Hesse, the fearless honesty of a J.D. Salinger. Side by side with these titles were books for children or adults, such as J.R.R. Tolkien's *Lord of the Rings Trilogy*, as well as science fiction by masters such as Robert Heinlein, Isaac Asimov and Ray Bradbury [82].

Soon, however, writers such as S.E. Hinton, Peter Dickinson, and Ursula Le Guin began writing books specifically for adolescents, and YA fiction came to address themes ranging "from the everyday-realistic to the abstract, theoretical, and conjectural," as Peter Hollindale observes. Hollingdale adds that YA fiction also came to employ "a wide range of modes from parochial urban naturalism to cosmic fantasy," and a variety of narratological approaches, "from simple linear story to complex multi-voiced, multitemporaral, intertextual strategies" (316). Not every YA novel was engaging or sophisticated, of course: as with most genres, there are formulaic, conventional stories; strikingly original ones that push the boundaries of the genre itself; and everything in between. Although young adult fiction was generally not considered to be worth serious attention by reviewers and critics at first, with the appearance of books such as Paul Zindel's *Pigman* and Judy Blume's *Are You There God? It's Me Margaret*, critics gradually came to accept the idea that some YA novels are more literary than others, and that at its best, YA fiction could be quite sophisticated.

Judgments about which texts are literary and which are not involve more than just applying a set of objective criteria to them, despite what critics would have people believe. Rather, as Alan Sinfield argues, "Literature is writing that is acknowledged as such within a powerful publishing, reviewing and educational apparatus" (29). Although the specific reasons as to why a particular text is accorded literary status can be difficult to discern, those that are deemed literary were almost certainly vetted by publishers, critics, librarians, and educators, who consider cultural issues as well as aesthetic ones, promoting only texts that are socially and politically acceptable to the ruling classes and the social institutions that represent their interests (Sinfield 36–7). Sinfield's formulation explains in part why texts such as Herman Melville's *Moby-Dick* and Zora Neale Hurston's *Their Eyes Were Watching God* were rejected by the literary establishment when they were first published. In *Moby-Dick*'s case, many contemporary reviewers found Melville's meaning too obscure, his themes irrelevant or offensive, and his style wanting. Henry Chorley of *Athenaeum*, for example, comments, "This is an ill-compounded mixture of romance and matter-of-fact," adding that "[t]he style of his tale is in places disfigured by mad (rather than bad) English" (quoted in Higgins 356). The literary establishment seemed to be particularly uncomfortable with Melville's irreverence toward religion and other established authorities. The *London John Bull*, for example, observed that for all of its merits, *Moby-Dick* is "defaced ... by occasional thrusts against revealed religion ... and cannot but shock readers accustomed to a reverent treatment of whatever is associated with sacred subjects," and *The Church Review and Ecclesiastical Register* commented that Melville "is at times shockingly irreverent — without any great proof of wit" (quoted in Higgins 358, 410). Seventy-five years later, however, as modernism became the dominant literary movement, Melville's work was re-evaluated and his stylistic innovation lauded by critics more open to experimentation and challenging traditional authority. As Nick Selby demonstrates, *Moby-Dick*'s literary status rose even further with the United States' entry into the Second World War as critics came to regard it as affirming not only American beliefs and values but the idea that the United States is special and has a unique role to play in world affairs (53). Similarly, *Their Eyes Were Watching God* was initially criticized by key elements of the literary establishment when it appeared in 1937. At a time when the support of African-American critics was essential to establishing the literary reputation of black-authored texts, Richard Wright, Alain Locke and other leading critics were sharply critical of Hurston's novel for failing to address racial issues explicitly and, as a result, despite receiving praise from a number of white critics, the book quickly went out of print and was largely forgotten. Thirty-five years later, however, *Their Eyes Were Watching God* was rediscovered by academics as Women's Studies and Black Studies established themselves as legitimate areas of study. Deemed by the academy to be one of the important social and political texts of the twentieth century, it began to be widely taught in colleges and universities and is now well-established as a canonical text (Washington x).

As the examples of Melville's and Hurston's novels suggest, literariness "is less a property of texts than a way of reading and placing texts" (Sinfield 29). Rather than being intrinsically literary, Melville and Hurston's novels *became* literary because the dominant culture decided to classify them as such. Given the many thematic and aesthetic considerations that go into rendering a text literary, there is still some question today as to whether even the most celebrated YA fiction will ever be canonized in the same way works by Jane Austen and Virginia Woolf are, that is, as works that are deserving of serious study because they focus on themes that are recognized as being important and intellectually challenging to adult readers. This is not to suggest that books popular with young adults are never deemed literary: Betty Smith's *A Tree Grows in Brooklyn*, J.D. Salinger's *The Catcher in the Rye*, and Harper Lee's *To Kill a Mockingbird*, for example, are all classified as literature. None of these books were written for children in particular, however, and, in any case, they are generally assigned a lesser status than works read primarily by adults.

In the 1990s, attitudes towards YA fiction finally began to change as adults increasingly began to read and discuss books such as Lois Lowry's *The Giver* and Philip Pullman's *The Golden Compass*. It is with the unprecedented popularity of the *Harry Potter* series that questions about the literariness of young adult fiction gained widespread attention, however, particularly after *Harry Potter and the Prisoner of Azkaban* was nominated for 1999 Whitbread Book of the Year prize along with Seamus Heaney's translation of *Beowulf*. Although *Beowulf* won the prestigious prize, Rowling's novel being given the Children's Book of the Year prize, the very fact that a young adult novel was nominated generated unprecedented controversy (Whited 6). The problem, according to *New York Times* columnist William Safire, was not so much that children were reading the *Harry Potter* series but rather that adults were, too, leading to an "infantilization of adult culture, the loss of a sense of what a classic really is." That *Beowulf* itself may have been written for an audience that included children seems to be entirely lost upon Safire. Although none of the subsequent *Harry Potter* novels won the Whitbread Book of the Year prize either, in 2001 the prize was awarded to the final volume of Philip Pullman's *His Dark Materials* series. Young adult fiction, it seems, could no longer be ignored by the literary establishment.

The *Hunger Games* trilogy cannot be ignored, either, if only because the books have sold millions of copies, received positive reviews in respected venues like the *New York Times*, *Kirkus Reviews*, and become part of the curriculum in middle schools, high schools, and colleges throughout the United States. The question of its literary status remains open, however. While it is certainly considered by most to be more literary than YA titles such as *The Twilight Saga* or the *Sweet Valley High* series, neither of which is likely to be deemed literary in the near future since they present themselves as genre fiction, the fact that the trilogy is written so as to be comprehensible to pre-adolescents may be held against it since, in the wake of modernism, literature is still expected to be difficult in a way that popular fiction is not. Other considerations include the way the trilogy is structured; the ways in which Collins negotiates both literary and popular genres; the narrative mode she employs; and her use of the present tense and other deictic markers to generate immediacy, thereby not only making her narrative more engaging but enabling readers to process events independently of Katniss when circumstances make her unreliable; and her use of various motifs and imagery to guide readers through the text. The remainder of this chapter will focus on issues of form and style that are likely to figure in decisions being made about the *Hunger Games* trilogy's literary merit, leaving discussion of content — that is, the way it addresses various social issues — to other chapters.

The Structure of the Novels

As with each of the volumes of *The Underland Chronicles*, the novels comprising the *Hunger Games* trilogy are each divided into three parts consisting of nine chapters, something Collins attributes to her graduate training in dramatic writing (Springen 2008): to her, the parts are like acts in a play, each serving a different dramatic purpose. As with most conventional three-act plays, the first part is primarily devoted to exposition, the second to crisis, and third to climax and resolution. In *The Hunger Games*, for example, Part I: "The Tributes" introduces us to Katniss, Peeta, and the other primary characters; Part II: "The Games" presents the conflict and builds up the tension; and Part III: "The Victor" provides the climax and dénouement. Whereas in conventional dramas, acts generally end with a certain measure of closure, in the *Hunger Games* trilogy the acts end with the immediate action being unresolved: Part I of *The Hunger Games*, for example, ends with Peeta declaring his love for Katniss on national television and Part II begins moments afterwards with her response. There is virtually no gap between Parts II and III either, as the former concludes with Katniss involuntarily calling out Peeta's name and the latter starts with her clapping her hands over her mouth so she will not be overheard. Breaking up action sequences in such a manner not only generates suspense but enables Collins to shift both mode and tone in a pronounced manner before continuing narration. Peeta's declaration of love at the end of Part I, for example, not only signals the end of the book's dramatic exposition but creates a space for readers to reconsider the significance of everything that has happened between Katniss and Peeta up to this point in the narrative. His words, which represent both a personal revelation and a strategic decision on his part as to how to present himself to the audience during the Games, change the very nature of his relationship with Katniss, and therefore everything is different in Part II even though only a moment has passed.

Although such continuity of action between acts is rare in theatre, it is common in television, characters sometimes going so far as to open a new act by repeating the last line of the previous act. As someone who spent more than two decades writing for television, Collins seems to be very comfortable with continuing action across acts in this manner, using it to maintain her narrative's momentum even as she shifts its focus. In effect, she deploys a convention of children's television that is usually used to help viewers reengage with a story after commercial breaks to help her readers engage with her stories in new ways at the ending of Parts I and II of each volume of the trilogy.

Collins also draws upon her experience as a scriptwriter when it comes to the pacing of her stories, constantly "moving the story forward and developing the characters at the same time" in order to maintain reader interest (Springen 2008). In the first two volumes of the trilogy, at least, Katniss rarely pauses to reflect upon her circumstances, and even in *Mockingjay*, in which Katniss is much more contemplative, her reflections are frequently interrupted by a sudden need to act. This is particularly true in the latter half of the book as she tries to sort out her relationships with Peeta and Gale as she and what remains of the Star Squad attempt to make their way to the President's Mansion to kill Snow: there is simply no time for her to think things through because of the imminent danger of pods, Peacekeepers, and muttations.

The manner in which Collins uses cliffhangers is also characteristic of television writing as she herself acknowledges in an interview with Karen Springen in *Newsweek*. According to her, these cliffhangers typically "involve physical peril, or the moment a character has a revelation" (Springen 2008), for example when, in *Catching Fire*, Peeta is electrocuted by the force field surrounding the arena or when Katniss realizes that the arena is modeled on a clock (279, 325). Because such cliffhangers occur at the end of almost every chapter, the trilogy has a quick rhythm, drawing the reader through the novels rapidly and keeping attention focused on plot rather than characterization, setting, detail or style, at least on the first read.

To the extent that she employs techniques drawn from media such as theatre and television when writing prose, Collins is a *bricoleur*, someone who makes novel use of "the means at hand" to achieve desired effects (Derrida 360). Although some commentators find her technique pedestrian because to them it is reminiscent of supposedly vulgar media like television, Hollywood films, and video games, Collins seems more concerned with communicating her ideas than with being literary and is very open about have been influenced by popular culture, identifying Stanley Kubrick's *Spartacus* (1960) as a primary influence, for example, and indicating in a number of interviews that she came up for the idea *of The Hunger Games* while "channel surfing" (Blasingame; Springen 2008). Indeed, she continues to present herself as a dilettante when it comes to fiction despite having written eight novels, telling Rick Margolis of the *School Library Journal* that she "still feel[s] very new to the book scene and writing prose": "Prose is full of many challenges and unexplored territory for me because I came to it later in my life. Maybe it always feels that way for everybody, even if they started in prose in the beginning. But for me, so much of it has a brand-new or a 'How do I do this?' ... There are just worlds of stuff for me to learn" (Margolis 2010). Certainly one could argue that Collins's lack of pretention not only makes her writing more accessible to many readers but more appealing and more powerful. John Green, for example, notes in his review of *The Hunger Games* for the *New York Times* that rather than "calling attention to itself, the text disappears in the way a good font does" so that "nothing stands between Katniss and the reader, between Panem and America." It is not that Collins's writing lacks style, of course, but that she employs the unadorned style appropriate to her first-person narrator, who is young, relatively uneducated, and very direct. Although in his review of *The Hunger Games* for *Entertainment Weekly*, Stephen King describes Collins as "an efficient no-nonsense prose stylist," he might just as well be describing Katniss, who offers little description or analysis as she relates her experiences in *The Hunger Games* and *Catching Fire*. In *Mockingjay*, the narrator is both more descriptive and reflective as she struggles to come to terms with the various forms of trauma she had undergone, the novel having a different feel to it. As John Booth observes in his review of *Mockingjay* for *Wired* magazine, "The pacing is different from the first two books," Collins balancing "harried action sequences" with "quiet sections" in which a now more contemplative Katniss attempts to figure out who she really is and what she is fighting for. Collins's ability to move back and forth between action and contemplation in the final volume without disrupting the narrative's flow is a good measure of the sophistication of her writing: Katniss remains Katniss, even though she is very different from the person she was when the trilogy opened.

Genre Considerations

Genre is also an important consideration when determining a text's literary status, not only because the ways in which books are classified help determine readers' expectations and how they receive and negotiate the text, but because some genres are considered more literary than others since some have more prestige than others. Collins's work, however, defies easy genre classification: it is young adult fiction that addresses themes usually reserved for adults; a science fiction novel that is largely unconcerned with science and technology; a dystopian fiction that ends hopefully, at least on a societal level; a survivor story in which the survivor never fully recovers; and a *Bildungsroman* in which the protagonist regresses as much as she progresses. Collins's work, it seems, draws from a number of genres without confining itself to any of them. As a result, her work rarely comes across as generic or formulaic.

For some readers, Collins's simultaneous engagement with various genres makes her work more compelling, Bob Minzesheimer of *USA Today*, for example, describing *Mockingjay* as "a blend of sci-fi, mythology, horror and romance" that continually surprises readers by defying convention. Readers expecting strict adherence to genre conventions are likely to be disappointed, however. Kathy Morrison, for example, criticizes *Mockingjay* for being a survivor story that ends in "exhaustion, not joy — or peace," and Cheryl Mahoney complains that the novel fails to "follow the normal conventions of a coming-of-age story, or of a traditional romance." Those expecting a YA romance made similar complaints about both *The Hunger Games* and *Catching Fire*, Rollie Welch of *The Plain Dealer*, for example, noting, "after 150 pages of romantic dithering [in *Catching Fire*], I was tapping my foot to move on." Like a number of genre readers who report in web chats enjoying the novel more upon a second read, Welch ultimately recognizes that there is more to the book than just a "*Twighight*-esque" love triangle, and that the book should be judged accordingly, ultimately giving it a strong recommendation because of its complex characterization and attention to social issues.

The Hunger Games *Trilogy as YA Romance*

Like much young adult fiction, including Stephenie Meyer's *The Twilight Saga*, Carrie Ryan's *The Forest of Hands and Teeth*, and Michelle Rowen's *Demon Princess* series, *The Hunger Games* trilogy is structured around a love triangle, at least initially. As often happens in YA fiction centering on young, female protagonists, Katniss is presented with a choice between two very different love interests who compete for her affection, creating a romantic tension that is drawn out over the course of the entire trilogy. The first, Gale Hawthorne, whom she has hunted with for years in the woods outside of District 12, is literally tall, dark, and handsome; he is also emotionally volatile, barely able to conceal his rage against the Capitol, and sexually aggressive, imposing himself physically upon Katniss at one point, explaining himself afterwards, "I had to do that. At least once" (*Catching Fire* 27). The second, Peeta Mellark, whom Katniss thinks of as "the boy with the bread" because he provided her and her family with food when they were starving, is also strong and handsome, but is much more empathic, sensitive, and socially-oriented than Gale. So far, it would seem, we have the makings of a typical teen romance. As Jennifer Lynn Barnes notes, however, Katniss "is far more than a vertex on some love triangle," and the trilogy itself is anything but conventional. Although attracted to both young men in different ways, she is not interested in either romantically and does not understand why they both press her to make a choice. In her mind, she "can survive just as well without either of them" (*Catching Fire* 330). In the end, the love triangle is not so much resolved as dissolved: any possibility of a relationship between Gale and Katniss disappears when Prim is killed by bombs that Gale may very well have designed. As a result, when Katniss becomes involved with Peeta long after the trilogy's main action has ended, it is not so much by choice as default. As Katie Roiphe comments in her review of *Mockingjay* for the *New York Times*, "the book's dogged and perverse resistance of the normal romantic plot in which the heroine genuinely prefers one of her suitors is one of its more appealing and original features." Refusing to choose either man, she remains independent of both, much to their consternation (*Mockingjay* 329).

The Hunger Games *Trilogy as Science Fiction*

The trilogy also resists easy classification as a science fiction novel, even though it is set in a high-tech future that is presented as being an extension the present world. This is largely because it does not have the feel of a typical science fiction novel, not only because the protagonist is a Robin Hood like figure, complete with bow and arrow, but because the novels never address technological issues in a sustained way: the trilogy is set in the future but might as well be set in the present or even past, the force fields, hoverplanes, and muttations serving primarily as a means of marking of the text as an alternative space for rethinking social institutions and relationships (Ricoeur 16–7). In this sense the *Hunger Games* trilogy is very much in the tradition of George Orwell's *1984*, Margaret Atwood's *The Handmaid's Tale*, and Chuck Palahniuk's *Fight Club*, each of them novels that feature technology that was unavailable at the time the novels were written but never make that technology their subject.

Collins never makes science a primary subject, either. Whereas most science fiction has at least an implicit attitude toward science and its role in society, whether positive or negative, Collins's position is difficult if not impossible to discern. This is not to say that Collins never raises issues pertaining to science. As Cara Lockwood argues in "Not So Weird Science," Collins's depiction of muttations can be related to ongoing developments in biotechnology and their potential use as weapons. They play only a minor role in the story, however — Lockwood herself describing them as making cameo-appearances (114) — and certainly do not seem to be a significant factor in the war with the Capitol. Indeed, as frightening as they are, muttations are not particularly effective in terrorizing people as evidenced by Rue's matter-of-fact attitude towards tracker jackers in *The Hunger Games* (200). The closest Collins comes to making science an issue is when Katniss overhears Beetee lamenting the fact that weapons such as "high-flying planes, military satellites, cell disintegrators, drones, biological weapons with expiration dates" are no longer available because of "the destruction of the atmosphere or lack of resources or moral squeamishness" (*Mockingjay* 130). A discussion of scientific ethics never emerges, however, Katniss making only a quick observation about weapons being "toys" to him. Unlike most science fiction, the *Hunger Games* trilogy represents science as being neither the cause of society's problems nor the solution. Collins's attitude seems to be that if people did not have guns to fight with, they would use sticks, and if they did not have sticks, they would use their hands.

The Hunger Games *Trilogy as Dystopia*

Although the trilogy fits easily into the category of dystopia, being set in a horrific, alternative world so that potentially negative consequences of present-day behaviors can be explored, the novels are markedly different from young adult dystopias such as Robert O'Brien's *Z for Zachariah* and Susan Beth Pfeffer's *Life as We Knew It*, which end hopefully, and adult utopias such as *1984* and Aldous Huxley's *A Brave New World*, which end darkly (Sambell 164). As Todd VanDerWerff observes in his review of *Mockingjay* for the A.V. Club, "[t]he final slog toward doom for Katniss and her friends gets as grim as any book aimed at teens ever written, a death march that leaves Katniss and the readers choking on ashes." Although he goes on to note that the book ends with "two improbable moments of grace," he suggests that as "stunning as they are," they will be "too little" for many young readers, who will find the ending too dark. Ironically, as dark as the ending of the trilogy is, it is much lighter than most adult utopias, which, as Kay Sambell notes, generally end with "the protagonist's final defeat and failure" in order to maintain their "didactic

33

impact" (164–5). Rather than offer either a happy ending or a sad one, Collins leaves the ending open just as Lois Lowry does in her acclaimed YA dystopia, *The Giver*. As Sambell suggests, eschewing narrative closure in such a manner may represent a means "of increasing the scope for the reader's interaction with the fictional world" (173). She continues:

> The text itself becomes a space that sometimes tries to create conditions for young readers to rehearse, actively, almost playfully, a way of reflective thinking that focuses on asking questions, discovering analysis, and hypothetically testing out solutions at their own pace in an imaginative environment that is affirming and supportive but also articulates dark truths. The reader is invited to exercise a degree of choice in the narrative, thus affecting what it will become [173].

Collins leaves the ending of *Mockingjay* open in just such a manner, leaving it for readers to work out what might happen once the narrative closes: Katniss is neither defeated and broken the way Winston Smith is in *1984*, nor hopeful of a better future as Miranda Evans is in the end of *Life as We Knew It*. In this sense, at least, the volumes that comprise the *Hunger Games* trilogy defy the conventions of dystopia as genre, which dictate that narratives resolve themselves one way for children and another for adults. Accordingly, the trilogy may begin like a dystopia but it does not end like one.

The Hunger Games *Trilogy as Survivor Story*

As will be discussed in Chapter Seven, The trilogy is not a typical survivor story either, even though it presents itself as one. According to Shani Orgad, survivor stories as we know them today developed out of efforts by those who lived through Nazi atrocities to narrate their experiences in order to better come to terms with them and to put them on record for the benefit of others, the idea being that we can only prevent future atrocities by confronting them directly. As the genre developed, certain conventions became fixed, including a promise of recovery at the end, survivor stories being expected to serve as sources of inspiration to those who themselves are undergoing trauma. Although the *Hunger Games* trilogy adheres to most of the conventions of the genre — that is, it is a first-person account of how someone regains agency after suffering trauma — Katniss's assertion in the epilogue of *Mockingjay* that her "nightmares ... won't ever really go away" suggests that full recovery is never really possible. Indeed, the trilogy ends with Katniss imagining telling her children how she survives from day-to-day, her use of the present tense indicating that she is still reliving the trauma.

The Hunger Games *Trilogy as Bildungsroman*

Finally, if the *Hunger Games* trilogy can be read as a *Bildungsroman*, that is, a novel about the growth and development of an individual as she or he enters society, then it is of an unusual sort. Like most *Bildungsromans*, the trilogy is a coming-of-age story: Katniss is forced to leave her home in District 12 and integrate herself into the larger world, a long process that ultimately changes who she is. What makes Katniss's story atypical when compared to other stories in the genre, is that she changes the world as much as it changes her. As "the girl who was on fire" and later the Mockingjay, she has a tremendous impact upon society, becoming an emblem of resistance that eventually proves critical to bringing down the Capitol. Although as Peeta notes, Katniss remains ignorant of "the effect" she has upon others for much of the first two volumes and exhibits little interest in social issues (*Hunger Games* 91), at the end of *Mockingjay* she takes positive action in an effort to effect change, assassinating the would-be leader of the new government so that the cycle of violence and revenge that has dominated Panem for so long will finally end.

The trilogy also differs from the conventional *Bildungsroman* in that it concerns itself less with the formation of its protagonist than her deformation. In *The Hunger Games* and most of *Catching Fire*, Katniss is an indomitable, independent young woman who seems capable of mastering any challenge. As the narrative proceeds, however, she becomes increasingly less self-assured and less capable, eventually becoming passive to the point that she no longer eats or cleans herself. Although she recovers somewhat by the very end of the novel, she is no longer the strong, independent person she once was as evidenced by the fact that she marries and has children despite having declared repeatedly in the first two volumes that she would never do either. In effect, rather than "grow up," Katniss "grows down," to use Annis Pratt's term, reversing the trajectory of normal coming-of-age story (14).

Narrative Mode

Collins's success in sustaining the first person over the course of three novels also marks her work as being potentially literary. Although the first-person narrative mode is regarded by some as being unsophisticated, if only because it is often resorted to by beginning writers, maintaining a first-person narrative in a compelling way can be challenging even for the most accomplished writers. This is particularly true when the narrator is the protagonist since, in novels at least, they are generally expected to develop and change, something that often necessitates continually adjusting the narrative voice to match the narrator's current state of development. Even highly-regarded works such as Evelyn Waugh's *Brideshead Revisited* and J.D. Salinger's *Catcher in the Rye* are sometimes criticized for a certain flatness that is attributed to a narrative voice that is too static. Employing the first person can also be difficult because it usually limits the writer when it comes to representing the thoughts of characters other than the narrator since the narrator presumably has no direct access to them: the writer must rely upon atmosphere, dialogue, use of suggestive detail, and the like to represent the interior states of characters, something that can be particularly challenging to writers attempting realism since the obvious use of literary devices can undercut the effects they are trying to generate.

Collins succeeds in sustaining a first-person narrative by making Katniss an extremely dynamic character who changes not just over the course of the trilogy but over the course of each individual volume. For example, in *The Hunger Games* she goes from being a detached, matter-of-fact young woman who allows herself to care only for her younger sister to someone who learns to connect with other people and even become emotionally dependent upon them, the novel closing with Katniss worrying that "the boy with the bread is slipping away..." (374). In *Mockingjay*, the changes she undergoes over the course of the novel are even more apparent since the book both begins and ends in District 12, providing a point of comparison. As she walks through what remains of her still smoldering home district at the beginning of the book, she reports her interior states almost continually, verbalizing not only her thoughts but her emotions, which include guilt, hate, and regret. Although traumatized by her experiences in the Quarter Quell and afterwards, she is still engaged with the world, communicating not only what she sees and hears but how the leather of her father's old hunting jacket feels against her skin and the smell of the white rose President Snow leaves for her on her dresser (14). When she walks through the same place less than a year later, the detached way in which she reports things suggests that she is essentially a different person. She speaks of a mass grave in the Meadow, for example, but does not describe it in any detail or report her thoughts or feelings about it (385). Ironically, Katniss's silence reveals more about her interior state than any description could: because of the various forms of trauma she has undergone, she has lost not only the ability to articulate how she feels but the ability to feel itself.

Despite employing the same first-person narrator through the trilogy, Collins succeeds in conveying the stories of other characters as well, something that is remarkable given the fact that Katniss is emotionally detached if not catatonic throughout much of the narrative. Rather than report in any detail events she does not experience personally, Gale's evacuation of District 12 during the bombing being an important exception (*Mockingjay* 7–8), Katniss provides detail in bits and pieces as she reports brief exchanges between herself and others or as she reflects upon things momentarily. For example, the reader learns about the relationship between Katniss's father and mother over the course of all three novels through references to things such as the depression her mother fell into after the father dies, how Katniss's father won the mother over with his voice, how her mother yelled at him for teaching Katniss "The Hanging Tree," and how she ran to the mines on the day of his fatal accident, not even checking on her children. Through the careful placement of detail, the reader gets a strong sense of not only their relationship but Katniss's home life before the accident, even though little is actually said about it. Collins uses detail in a similar manner to convey a sense of Finnick and Annie Cresta's relationship and in the characterization of Prim, who emerges as an important character even though she rarely is represented directly in the narrative.

Immediacy

Collins's use of deictic markers to generate a sense of immediacy at critical moments in the text also marks the *Hunger Games* trilogy as a sophisticated literary production. Through the strategic use of the present tense, fine-grained detail, proper nouns, articles, and adverbs, Collins is able to make Katniss's world more immediately available to the reader (Chafe 229). As Michelle Ristuccia notes, "...we learn what she [Katniss] learns when she learns it," almost as if we were co-present with her. For example, when in *Catching Fire* President Snow appears in District 12 to inform Katniss that she must continue her showmance with Peeta, she describes "*the* large desk of polished wood" where he sits, adding that it is "where *Prim* does her homework" and other fine-grained detail to enable readers to more fully visualize the setting (20, my italics). The fact that she uses a definite article in reference to the desk also makes the scene more present to readers since it refers to a shared context between writer and reader, as does her use of the name "Prim" instead of a phrase such as "my sister." Collins again employs deictic markers to great effect later in the passage when Katniss sits across from Snow so that "now only *a* desk separates them" (20, my italics): because of her proximity to him, Katniss can see his "overly full lips, the skin stretched too tight" and smell the "roses and blood" on his breath, Collins switching the indefinite article "a" for the definite article "the" before "desk" in order to reinforce the shift in focus from the desk to Snow (20). She even comments on his tone of voice, noting that "the way" he speaks reveals more than his words themselves (20). The use of fine-grained detail that includes specific images, smell, and tone of voice creates a powerful sense of immediacy, particularly when combined with other deictic markers such as the word "now" instead of "then" and the continued use of the present tense and definite articles. In a sense the reader participates in the narrative rather than simply reads it.

In addition to making the text more engaging, Collins use of the present tense and other devices to create a sense of immediacy puts the reader in a position to interpret Katniss's experiences independently of her, at least to an extent. Were she to report events as she remembered them rather than as they happen, then they would already be subject to her interpretation since, as most contemporary researchers agree, memory is "always a reconstruction of the past based on present concerns and purposes" (Lavenne *et al.*). Since Katniss reports her experiences in the present, however, they are not mediated by her memory, and therefore readers have more immediate access to them. This is not to suggest that readers have unfiltered access to Katniss's experiences, of course: Katniss chooses what to report and how to report it. Readers are not limited to her interpretation of those experiences, however, since, in a limited sort of way, they co-experience them. For example, in *The Hunger Games*, when Katniss reports that ants crawl out of her blistered hands, travel up her arms and bore into her eyes, readers may realize what Katniss does not: that she is not literally being eaten by ants, the sensation instead being the result of tracker jacker venom. The ability to interpret events independently of Katniss becomes critical at certain points in the text since Katniss's perceptions are sometimes severely affected by her circumstances, most obviously when she is under the influence of sleep syrup in *Catching Fire* and morphling in *Mockingjay*. Her psychological reactions to the various forms of trauma she undergoes also affect her reliability at times since they make it difficult for her to differentiate between what is real and what is unreal, leaving it to readers to determine for themselves what is happening and what to think about it.

Verbal Patterning

The ways in which Collins creates complex verbal patterns to augment major ideas also mark the trilogy as literary. Even though Collins presents her text primarily as the spontaneous-seeming testimony of an untutored young woman, even a cursory examination reveals a certain literariness. *Catching Fire*, for example, opens with Katniss using the sun's inevitable rising as a conceit for her own lack of agency. Katniss introduces the conceit in the first paragraph as she watches the dawn "lighten the woods" outside of District 12, commenting that she "can't fight the sun," that she can "only watch helplessly" as it "drags" her into a day she has long been dreading, the beginning of the Victory Tour (3). After imagining in detail what the coming day will entail, she returns to her conceit: "The sun persists in rising, so I make myself stand" (4). She thinks of the sun again as she checks the snares she and Gale have set, and then, as she prepares to slip under the fence surrounding the district, notes that "the sun is well up," the last observation suggesting that she fully accepts what the day will bring (6). By having Katniss use the sun as a conceit in such a manner, Collins is able to convey a sense of Katniss's interiority without having Katniss report her reflections in detail, something that would be uncharacteristic of Katniss at this point in the narrative.

Collins also employs motifs such as mockingjays and bread to keep important ideas and themes present in readers' minds as the narrative proceeds. As William Freedman observes, the purpose of the motif is to tell readers "subtly" what incidents tell "bluntly," to communicate something about the story, its characters, its import, or its content (202). In the case of the mockingjay motif, the birds, which are "creature[s] the Capitol never intended to exist," correspond to Katniss who, in the final volume of the trilogy becomes the Mockingjay, a symbol of the rebellion itself (*Catching Fire* 92): as a result, repeated references to mockingjays, sometimes in detail, sometimes in passing, provide Collins with a means of reminding the reader continually that Katniss is something that the Capitol never accounted for and therefore represents a potential agent for change. Bread operates as a motif in a similar manner structurally, continually reminding readers that the Capitol rules the districts through the manipulation of resources such as food.

Collins's repeated references to the use of berries and things related to them throughout the text represent a different type of verbal patterning, one that is similar to the motifs discussed earlier but not identical to them. Rather than stabilize the implied meaning of the text by underlining a set theme, Collins uses berries to develop themes and even introduce new ones, the significance of berries themselves changing as the narrative proceeds. Berries first appear in the *The Hunger Games* as part of a bonding ritual between Katniss and Gale: one of them begins Effie Trinket's famous line — "May the odds be *ever* in your favor!" — and tosses a blackberry in the air, the other catching it in his or her mouth and completing Trinket's phrase (*Hunger Games* 8). As with all rituals, the details are important: since foraging in the woods is illegal, the berries they toss symbolize their willingness to defy the Capitol, and the phrase they utter reflects the sense of ironic detachment they share towards the pageantry of the Games. In the passages that immediately follow, there are many more references to berries, the most significant occurring later that day when, while on the train to the Capitol, Katniss marvels that she was just eating blackberries with Gale earlier that day, the mention of berries serving as a reference point for how drastically things have changed for her since the reaping.

If in the first part of *The Hunger Games*, berries function as an ordinary motif, continually reminding readers of the bond that exists between Katniss and Gale, once she enters the Games, they come to represent various other things as she encounters different sorts of berries in various contexts. Early on, for example, she mistakes potentially dangerous, unknown berries for blueberries, only noticing that their shape is slightly different right before eating them, the lesson seemingly being that little differences can have big consequences. This lesson is reinforced later when berries Peeta gathers turn out to be toxic, killing Foxface, who has stolen some of them. Primarily, though, berries continue to be associated with relationships, albeit relationships of a different sort. Whereas for Katniss and Gale, berries represent the partnership that has developed between them over the course of years based on their mutual needs and interests, for Katniss and Rue, berries represent the intimacy that quickly develops between them once they become allies. Although Katniss is initially apprehensive about the unfamiliar berries Rue has gathered, Katniss decides to eat them, and from then on the two of them share everything, almost as if they are sisters, a deep trust between them having been established.

Katniss connects with Peeta in a similar manner once they decide to ally, the two of them quickly becoming intimate and trusting each other implicitly as evidenced by the fact that Peeta eats the berries Katniss provides him with. Ironically, Katniss uses Peeta's faith in her to trick him into drinking sleep syrup so that he cannot interfere with her efforts to acquire medicine that he needs in order to survive an infected wound. His willingness to eat the mash of berries and mint leaves containing the sleep syrup demonstrates his unconditional trust in her, and even though he initially considers her actions a betrayal of sorts, he quickly forgives her because she does it out of love and selflessness. The nightlock berries she gives him at the very end of the Games in order to convince the Gamemakers that she and Peeta would rather kill themselves than survive without one another represent an even deeper level of trust and intimacy. Realizing that the Games have to have a victor, Katniss decides that the Gamemakers will have to intercede in order to prevent their suicide. The difficulty for her is communicating her plan to Peeta in a way that the Gamemakers will not understand since she knows that her every word and action is being observed. As it turns out, all she has to say is "Trust me," the two of them having become so intimate that those two words convey everything she needs them to (*Hunger Games* 344): Peeta puts the berries in his mouth but does not swallow them, allowing the Gamemakers time to declare that the 74th Hunger Games will have two winners.

Berries remain important in the volumes that follow, not only providing reference points for how Katniss's relationships with Gale and Peeta change but providing a key to understanding Katniss herself. As in *The Hunger Games*, in *Catching Fire*, berries are used to mark how Katniss's and Gale's relationship has changed, the two of them only being able to perform their berry ritual in a perfunctory manner after Gale betrays Katniss's trust by failing to tell her about the Capitol featuring Peeta in a propaganda broadcast. Berries also serve as reference points for understanding how Katniss has developed and changed. Indeed, Katniss herself recognizes this: "The berries. I realize the answer to who I am lies in that handful of poisonous fruit. If I held them out to save Peeta because I knew I would be shunned if I came back without him, then I am despicable. If I held them out because I loved him, I am still self-centered, although forgivable. But if I held them out to defy the Capitol, I am someone of worth" (*Catching Fire* 118). What Katniss eventually comes to realize is that all three things can be true at once: a single action can be motivated by self-interest, love, and ethical considerations. In order to be at peace not only with her actions but with herself, she has to accept the fact that knowing what is right can be even more difficult than doing what is right since every action has many significations, that actions like eating poisonous berries can mean "different things to different people" (*Mockingjay* 75). In the end she learns that she can only do the best she can and not worry so much that people will misinterpret her actions.

YA Fiction as Literature

In his celebrated 1996 Carnegie Medal Acceptance speech, Philip Pullman indicates that there are subjects and themes that are too large for adult fiction because too often authors are so preoccupied with "technique, style, and literary knowingness" that they lose sight of the story they are telling. He goes on to recommend that "adults who truly enjoy story, and plot, and character ... look among the children's books" to find "books in which the events matter and which at the same time are works of literary art...." Delivered just a year before *Harry Potter and the Sorcerer's Stone* was published, Pullman's speech now seems prophetic in the sense that large numbers of adults did indeed begin turning to children's books to find stories worth reading and talking about. Although some critics may still worry that the increasingly broad appeal of young adult fiction means that the culture is being infantilized, many have come to recognize that at its best young adult fiction can be as literary as any other type of fiction (Kirby 138). With this in mind, the question with regards to the *Hunger Games* trilogy is not so much whether young adult fiction can be worthy of artistic acclaim, but whether the trilogy itself deserves such acclaim. With serious discussions of Collins's novels occurring not only on websites but in classrooms, periodicals ranging from the *New York Times* to the *Christian Science Monitor*, and academic conferences all over the United States, it seems possible at least that the literary establishment will finally deem the trilogy to be not only worth reading but worth celebrating and preserving, a judgment that, in the end, determines whether a text is literary or not.

CHAPTER TWO

The Importance of Being Katniss

Identity, Gender and Transgression

"Gender ought not be construed as a stable identity or locus of agency from which various acts follow; rather, gender is an identity tenuously constituted in time, instituted in an exterior space through a *stylized repetition of acts*. The effect of gender is produced through the stylization of the body and, hence, must be understood as the mundane way in which bodily gestures, movements, and styles of various kinds constitute the illusion of an abiding gendered self."
— Judith Butler, *Gender Trouble: Feminism and the Subversion of Identity* [179]

"...transvestism is a space of possibility structuring and confounding culture: the disruptive element that intervenes, not just a category crisis of male and female, but the crisis of category itself."
— Marjorie Garber, *Vested Interests: Cross-Dressing and Cultural Anxiety* [17]

In an interview with the *School Library Journal*, Suzanne Collins identifies her protagonist, Katniss Everdeen — a young woman whose refusal to adhere to society's expectations of her, ultimately transforms society itself— as "a girl who should never have existed." Like the mockingjays that she is associated with throughout the trilogy, she is not "a part of the Capitol's design," existing only "through the will of survival" (Margolis 2010). Rather than accept the situation she finds herself in after her father's death and slowly starve to death along with her mother and sister, Katniss, who is only eleven at the time, adapts, transforming herself from a dependant into a provider. She becomes "the man of the family," so to speak, not only having to hunt for food in her father's stead but engaging in illegal commerce in order to gain other necessities. As the phrase "man of the family" suggests, succeeding as provider involves not only performing duties usually reserved for men but performing masculinity, something she is very much aware of, as evidenced by the fact that she tucks her braid under her cap and wears her father's jacket while out hunting and trading. As adept at adaptation as the mockingjays are in their own world, Katniss learns through her experiences in both Panem and District 13 that both masculinity and femininity are performances and that they can be performed in different ways depending upon one's needs and desires. More than that, she learns to parody gender, to borrow Judith Butler's terms, masquerading in ways that destabilize the binary opposition between male and female that patriarchal control is based upon. Accordingly, she can be regarded as a radical figure, one that challenges the ideological foundation of Panem itself.

The Social Construction of Gender

Since the 1950s social theorists and scientists have come to accept a basic distinction between sex and gender, sex being physical and gender being social. According to Judith Lorber, whereas sex is typically assigned "on the basis of what the genitalia looks like at birth," gender is not just assigned but affirmed through everyday practices, beginning with naming and dress. She continues: "Once a child's gender is evident, others treat those in one gender differently from those in the other, and the children respond to the different treatment by feeling different and behaving differently." This sense of difference continues through puberty and into adulthood, shaping people's experiences and producing "different feelings, consciousness, relationships, skills — ways of being that we call feminine and masculine." According to Lorber and other gender theorists, the opposition of masculine and feminine has significant cultural and political consequences, "creating distinguishable social statuses for the assignment of rights and responsibilities": accordingly, like race and class, gender is a key component of a hierarchal system that allows for the subjugation and control of a large segment of society. Although not fixed in the same sense that sex is, gender identities are nonetheless generally stable since society demands that they be performed in certain sorts of ways: as Candace West and Don Zimmerman indicate, we are constantly "doing gender," that is, participating in "a complex of socially guided perceptual, interactional, and micropolitical activities that cast particular pursuits as expressions of masculine and feminine 'natures'" (126).

It is possible, of course, to defy both gender norms and the system of control they represent. According to Judith Butler because gender has "no ontological status apart from the various acts which constitute its reality," it can be understood as a "performative," that is, as a phenomenon that is entirely defined by the way it is enacted (1990, 136). Understood in this way, it is easy to see how gender identities can be destabilized and subverted when they are performed in ways other than those prescribed by society. Using cross-dressing as an example, Butler argues that gender can be performed so as to play upon the distinction between the "anatomy of the performer and the gender that is being performed," creating dissonance:

> As much as drag creates a unified picture of "woman" ... it also reveals the distinctness of those aspects of gendered experience which are falsely naturalized as a unity through the regulatory fiction of heterosexual coherence. *In imitating gender, drag implicitly reveals the imitative structure of gender itself—as well as its contingency....* In the place of the law of heterosexual coherence, we see sex and gender denaturalized by means of a performance which avows their distinctness and dramatizes the cultural mechanism of their fabricated unity [1990, 137].

To Butler and others who see patriarchy as a critical component of political systems for control, challenging gender identities through actions such cross-dressing and other forms of gender-bending is a radical political act to the extent that they exposes as arbitrary identities that present themselves as natural.

Ruling Through Division: Gender and Power in the Hunger Games *trilogy*

The Capitol rules Panem primarily through division, pitting various individuals and groups against one another so as to make political opposition all but impossible. Districts, for example, are literally divided from one another by electrified fences and, in some cases, guard towers, and communications between districts is limited and constantly monitored.

Indeed, what little people know of other districts comes largely from the Hunger Games, which are televised nationally, and even then the Games are heavily edited, the Gamemakers not wanting "people in different districts to know about one another" (*Hunger Games* 203). By carefully controlling information about people from other districts, the Capitol does more than just keep the districts from coordinating with one another and possibly resisting its rule: it also prevents people from identifying with those from other districts, from sympathizing with their plights and possibly making common cause with them. If the people of Panem are prevented from identifying themselves as a people, any sort of national rebellion becomes all but impossible.

The Capitol also uses social and economic class to create division between the districts. Being the most affluent, Districts 1, 2, and 4 are "[u]niversally, solidly hated" by all but those from their own districts, and District 12, being the "poorest" region, is the "least prestigious" and "most ridiculed" (*Hunger Games* 162, 203). In addition, the Capitol promotes social and economic division within districts through means such as the tesserae, a system which forces children from poor families to increase their odds of having to participate in the Games in order to acquire enough food to survive: as Gale observes, the tesserae are a "way to plant hatred between the starving workers of the Seam and those who can usually count on supper and thereby ensure we will never trust one another," noting "[i]t's to the Capitol's advantage to have us divided among ourselves" (*Hunger Games* 14).

Gender proves to be one of the most effective means the Capitol has of dividing people against each other within districts, proscribing not just different vocations but different behaviors for men and women. In District 12, at least, the norms seems to be for men to work in the mines and women to remain at home, rear children, and perform other domestic duties. It is only when Katniss's and Gale's fathers are killed in a mining accident that the wives are expected to find work outside of the home, something Katniss's mother proves unable to do, bringing her family to the brink of starvation. Hazel Hawthorne has more success, taking in other people's laundry, but even so she would not be able to feed her children if her teenage son Gale did not become a provider, hunting for food in the woods until he is old enough to work in the mines. Although little detail is provided about day-to-day life in districts other than 12, the evidence that exists suggests that aside from agriculture and factory work, unskilled labor that, historically, has long been open to women, women are primarily relegated to the domestic sphere, unless they are teachers, like Twill from District 8. Women, in short, are expected to be wives and mothers first, entering the working world only rarely and then in only a certain set of vocations. Even rich and famous victors like Katniss are limited in what they are allowed to do. Katniss, like all survivors of the Games, is forced to develop a "talent" that she can talk about when interviewed, and the list of talents the Capitol provides for her consists of things like cooking, arranging flowers, playing the flute, and designing clothes, the latter being the one she settles on (*Catching Fire* 39). Men, in contrast, are valued primarily for their ability to provide for their families, as evidenced by Katniss's observation that Gale could easily find a wife because he can both mine and hunt, and her later comment that Haymitch "could have his choice of any woman in the district because he is rich" (*Catching Fire* 46).

To many readers, of course, the ways in which women are differentiated from men in trilogy might seem unremarkable since it reflects the gender norms of the culture in which they live. Indeed, one could argue that gendering only becomes noticeable because Collins subtly destabilizes the male/female opposition from the very start by giving Katniss a gender neutral name and Gale an androgynous one. In effect, Collins makes gender as an issue more visible by refusing to reveal it through the usual markers such as naming, dress, and behaviors: Katniss's name does not give her gender away, and neither does her manner of dress or behavior, numerous readers reporting that they were initially unaware that she is female (Feminist Cupcake). It is only when we learn that Gale calls her "Catnip"—a nickname that suggests that she has an intoxicating allure—and soon afterwards suggests that he may eventually want to have children with her that both Katniss's sex and gender become apparent.

Heteronormativity and Patriarchy

To the extent that they come from patriarchal homophobic cultures themselves, many readers might find Panem's unfailing heteronormativity unremarkable as well, had Collins not made it an issue by highlighting

Katniss's unwillingness to become romantically involved with Gale early on in *The Hunger Games* even though he is represented as the masculine ideal, being "good-looking," "strong enough to handle the work in the mines," and able to "hunt" (10). Moreover, Katniss declares in the very first chapter that she "never want[s] to have kids" (10). Although Katniss is not presented as being homosexual, she is not presented as being heterosexual either, Collins refusing to define her through her sexuality. This is not to suggest that the other characters in the book do not try impose heterosexual norms upon her: the fact that they do is one reason why her feigned romance with Peeta succeeds with the viewers of the Hunger Games in the first two books. Panem's heteronormativity also explains why President Snow refuses to believe that Gale is simply Katniss's "best friend": he is "too handsome, too male" to be anything but her lover (*Catching Fire* 12). Katniss, however, resists her society's expectations and demands by refusing to enter into a genuinely romantic relationship with either Peeta or Gale, a refusal the two men find maddening. Part of their reaction, of course, is based on jealousy and competitiveness, but what they seem to find really offensive is her refusal to choose between them. That she will not choose either — or any man — is inconceivable to them and, they treat her like a tease, Peeta at one point calling her "a piece of work" with coldness and disdain (*Mockingjay* 232). Towards the end of *Mockingjay*, Haymitch conveys a similar idea, accusing Katniss, who has been deeply traumatized by her sister's death, of being preoccupied with "boy trouble" (362). Despite everything she has accomplished both in the arena and for the rebellion, people still assume that finding the correct mate is the most important thing to her. In a patriarchal society like Panem, it is unimaginable that a woman would refuse to subordinate herself to a man and so patriarchy constructs a heteronormative narrative for her.

Gender and the Games

As Carrie Ryan notes in "Panem et Circenses," the Games' primary function is ideological: the Capitol reinforces the idea that it has absolute power over the populace by forcing children from every district to fight to the death (102). A more detailed analysis of the Games reveals that they are constructed so as to reinforce patriarchy as well, not only separating male from female but privileging the former. As readers learn in *Catching Fire* when survivors of previous games are selected for the Quarter Quell, boys have fared much better than girls in previous games, Johanna Mason being the only female survivor from District 7 and Katniss being the only survivor from District 12 (191). Boys, it seems, have an advantage in the Games just because they are boys, leaving girls with only two obvious strategies for winning: they can either emulate boys to the best of their ability or use their so-called feminine wiles against the boys and then strike when they are vulnerable.

The boys' advantage seems to be both physical and cultural: they are larger than the girls, as Katniss notes, and they have been conditioned by society to be aggressive. Moreover, they are more likely to have at least some training in fighting, Katniss observing, for example, that Peeta was taught wrestling in school, and that, therefore, he will have an advantage in "hand-to-hand combat" (*Hunger Games* 90); there is certainly no suggestion that girls receive similar training, at least outside of the Career districts. Although the Gamemakers will sometimes manipulate conditions within the arena to change the odds — killing a particularly "savage" boy in an avalanche (*Hunger Games* 143), for instance, and more than half of the Careers in the second Quarter Quell in a volcanic eruption (*Catching Fire* 199) — all things being equal, a boy who is masculine in the most traditional sense is most likely to prevail. Katniss herself recognizes this, remarking towards the end of her first Games that Cato — the "ruthless killing machine" from District 2 — was "always the one to kill," the "other tributes" being "just minor obstacles" (*Hunger Games* 125, 327).

The strongest, most aggressive boy does not always win, of course, not only because the Gamemakers sometimes intervene directly but because the arenas are constructed so that there are many ways of dying, ranging from extreme heat and cold to poison. Strength and aggression gives players a distinct advantage, however, as evidenced by the fact that when victors for the second Quarter Quell are reaped from victors of previous Games, it is the Career districts that have the largest pool of survivors (*Catching Fire* 191). That it is the girls from Districts 1, 2, and 4 that are most likely to have survived is significant: they have been trained in combat just as the boys have, and although generally less powerful than their male counterparts, they are as strong as most of the boys from other districts and stronger than the other girls. Consequently, they are in relatively good positions to win if the boys do not. In the second Quarter Quell, for example, Haymitch can only defeat the girl from District 1, who is "bigger than he is and just as fast," by outsmarting her, using a force field which is not supposed to be a part of the Games against her (*Catching Fire* 201).

Since the girls from other districts other than 1, 2, and 4 generally have not been trained to fight like men, so to speak, they have to rely upon alternative strategies if they are to have any hope of surviving, including those that involve using their supposed feminine wiles. Some, like Johanna, feign weakness only to prove themselves ruthless when they have the opportunity, and others, like Rue and Foxface and even Katniss, use stealth and cunning to survive, avoiding direct conflict as long as they can. Whatever their strategy, however, it seems that female tributes often play "social games," to borrow a term that is frequently used in contemporary reality television, in order to put themselves in a position to win. In *The Hunger Games*, for example, Clove's strategy seems to involve managing Cato, who is prone to violent emotional outbursts, trying to calm him down, for example, after he kills his ally from District 3 (224) and insisting that she be the one to take on Katniss at the Feast while he hunts Peeta and Thresh (285). Katniss's social game, too, is key to her success. Her ability to connect with Rue leads to an alliance that brings her not only companionship but medication for her tracker jacker wounds, a more diverse food supply, and critical intelligence about the Careers' camp. It also benefits her indirectly since it is her friendship with Rue that induces Thresh to spare her life after he kills Clove. Katniss also masters the "showmance"—that is, the type of romance reality show contestants sometimes enter into while on camera—which brings her support from sponsors and, in the end, forces the Gamemakers to change the rules and allow two winners. Female tributes, it seems, have to employ social skills in order to survive, while male tributes, particularly those that perform traditional masculinity best like Thresh and Finnick, can often go it alone.

It is not just in the Games that performing one's assigned gender improves one's chances of success: it is also essential in pre–Game programming since tributes often depend upon gifts from sponsors to survive once they are in the arena. Physical attractiveness, for example—something which, as Andrea Dworkin, Naomi Wolf, and Sheila Jeffries among others demonstrate, is largely determined by culture—plays a large role in determining the amount of material support tributes receive from viewers. As

Katniss observes, "The Hunger Games aren't a beauty contest, but the best-looking tributes always seem to pull more sponsors" (58). Not surprisingly, perhaps, given that Panem, too, is a patriarchal, homophobic culture, beauty is very different for men than it is for women, as evidenced by the beauty routines Katniss and Peeta have to undergo before appearing publicly. Whereas the girls' beauty routine lasts for hours, the process leaving Katniss feeling like "a plucked bird, ready for roasting," the boys' routine is minimal, being limited to their faces (*Hunger Games* 61; *Catching Fire* 48). When Katniss asks of Effie whether Peeta "needs prepping," Effie replies, "Not the way you do," and her prep team goes so far as to wish Katniss would be surgically altered in order to make her even more attractive (*Catching Fire* 47–8).

Female tributes also seem to benefit from performing traditional forms of femininity while on camera. Accordingly, Effie coaches Katniss for hours before her first interview on skills such as wearing high heels and full-length gowns, uttering banal phrases, and smiling, and Haymitch tries to teach her how to be appealing to potential sponsors by projecting femininity (*Hunger Games* 115–8). Unable to make herself seem charming, mysterious, or sexy, among other things, on camera, Katniss complains to Cinna, "I just can't be one of those people he [Haymitch] wants me to be," and Cinna, in turn, encourages her to project "spiritedness" while costuming her in a way that highlights her physical attractiveness (*Hunger Games* 121). It is not just Katniss who benefits from performing gender in traditional ways. Katniss's account of other tributes' interviews suggest that each is "playing up some angle"—angles that seem to be gender-based. The girl from District 1 is "sexy all the way," for example, and the boy from 2 is "a ruthless killing machine" (125–6). Apparently the tributes' mentors believe that the best strategy is for each tribute to present himself or herself as a type, and the types available seem to be based on gender norms.

The Gendering of Katniss

Not surprisingly, perhaps, given the fact that she has assumed a role traditionally reserved for men as provider for her family, Katniss initially resists being gendered as female as she is prepped for the games and finds the process alienating, as her "plucked bird" comment suggests: up until the day of the reaping, she has never had to think about herself as an object of desire, her relationship with Gale being purely platonic as far as she is concerned. When, prompted by the reaping scheduled for later that day, Gale expresses his desire for Katniss, she becomes confused and uncomfortable: to her, "[t]he conversation feels all wrong" (*Hunger Games* 10). She feels equally uncomfortable when her mother lays out one of "her own lovely dresses" for Katniss to wear from the reaping, a "soft blue thing with matching shoes" (*Hunger Games* 15): seeing herself in the mirror, she "can hardly recognize" herself, and when Prim comments that she looks "beautiful," Katniss adds, "And nothing like myself" (15). To Katniss, it seems, beauty and personal attractiveness have meant little since they do not seem to be significant factors when it comes to providing for her family.

Once she becomes a tribute, however, she quickly learns that performing traditional forms of femininity is essential to her survival, and so she cooperates with Cinna and his team, all of whom work to make her look unforgettably beautiful. Only rarely does she seem to lose her sense of self, however. Indeed, she bristles whenever Haymitch calls her "sweetheart" and she regards Peeta's assertion of her attractiveness as an attempt to "demean" her (*Hunger Games* 93). She seems to have particular difficulty when she realizes that performing femininity entails performing heterosexuality: it is easier for her to play the "silly girl spinning in a sparkling dress" than it is for her to be "heartbreaker" or a "star-crossed lover" who wants but can never have Peeta (*Hunger Games* 13). Accordingly, after Peeta declares his desire for her in his pre–Game interview, she assaults him for turning her "into some kind of fool in front of the entire country," for making her "look weak" (135). Upon seeing a recording of both her interview and Peeta's, Katniss comes to accept that, as Haymitch indicates, "It's all a big show. It's all how you're perceived" (135). The realization that, like gender, sexuality can be performed in different sorts of ways depending upon the desired outcome, serves her well in the arena when she decides that feigning a romance with Peeta will greatly increase her chances of survival. In *Catching Fire*, she takes her performance of heterosexuality even further, becoming engaged to Peeta and even pretending to be pregnant by him in order to win sympathy from viewers. In *Mockingjay*, she goes further still, pretending to have lost the child because she was forced into the arena, and continuing her romance with Peeta while on camera even after he tries to kill her because of the conditioning he received while a prisoner of the Capitol. To reject Peeta publicly is to reject society's expectations of heterosexual woman and thereby risk losing people's support.

Queering the Hunger Games *trilogy*

Although heterosexuality is compulsory in Panem in the sense that alternative sexualities are never publicly acknowledged, much less countenanced, one could argue that Collins constructs a queer subtext in order to challenge the heterosexual norms that underpin patriarchy by subordinating women to men (Wittig 20). Identifying queer markers can be difficult, of course, not only because doing so is subjective but because it involves utilizing and therefore reinforcing gay stereotypes that are often offensive. Katniss's hairdresser, Flavius, for example, wears purple lipstick and has "orange corkscrew locks" (*Hunger Games* 62), leading many readers to assume he is gay, as a quick internet search will confirm, and the casting of Lenny Kravitz as Cinna for *The Hunger Games* film led to heated debates among fans about whether Cinna is gay and whether Kravitz could be "gay enough." Numerous writers of fan fiction also seem to find a queer subtext and build upon it, much of the slash fiction centering on Peeta, most often in combination with Gale, but also with Finnick and others. Other writers of slash fiction imagine a relationship developing between Johanna Mason and Katniss and some read Madge Undersee as having an unrequited love for Katniss. Even Lavinia, the red-headed Avox whom Katniss befriends while in the Capitol is sometimes read as queer, her inability to speak suggesting "the love that dare not speak its name," to use Oscar Wilde's phrase.

As evidenced by the fact that they can be so easily queered, *The Hunger Games* and its sequels tend to defamiliarize gender, to borrow a term used by Veronica Hollinger: that is, they call into question the very practice of identifying people as male and female, masculine and feminine, heterosexual and homosexual. With this in mind, it is easier to see how, in the end Katniss metamorphoses from being a young woman playing a sexy warrior for propaganda purposes into something entirely new and unaccountable, like the mockingjays she is named for when she agrees to become a symbol of the rebellion. Katniss, who, since her father's death, has defied gender norms in order to support her family when just an eleven-year-old girl, has the potential to be someone who transcends categories such as masculine and feminine and become post-gender, as it were. Once she becomes the true Mockingjay and not just a woman in a superhero outfit, she is neither a masculine nor feminine but something else, something that cannot be understood in traditional gender categories: in Judith Butler's terms, she becomes something that "disrupt[s] the categories of the body, sex, gender, and sexuality and occasion[s] their subversive resignification and proliferation beyond the binary frame" (1990, x). In Garber's formulation, she inhabits another "space of possibility"—a "third" one that disrupts traditional male/female binaries (Garber 11).

For Katniss, being the Mockingjay is initially just a performance, a role she plays at the behest of those who would use her for their own purposes—or for the purposes of a cause they serve: she is fully aware of the fact that others will make her over, costume her as the Mockingjay, provide her with scripts, and manage her appearances (*Mockingjay* 10). What her handlers soon discover, however, is that Katniss performs best as the Mockingjay when she forgets that she is in costume and that cameras are on her, for example when she defies orders to hide in a bunker when District 8 comes under attack from the Capitol, takes a vulnerable position on the roof of the building, and shoots down enemy bombers (*Mockingjay* 95): Plutarch and his team find footage of such events much more valuable to their propaganda broadcasts than anything they can devise. Katniss, it seems, is most effective as the Mockingjay when she is just being herself, essentially doing what Cinna recommended to her just before her first interview with Caesar Flickerman (*Hunger Games* 123). As Cinna recognizes early on, it is not Katniss's courage, physical appeal, or apparent romance with Peeta that people respond to so much as her indomitable spirit: to those who hope to end what seems to be an unassailable system of oppression, she represents something that should not be—something that is able to resist when resistance is impossible.

In order to escape the above paradox—the ability to resist authority when resistance is impossible—a new ideological space has to be opened up, one that can accommodate the paradox. As Antonio Gramsci observes in "State and Civil Society," however, "the new cannot be born" until the old has died (276). It is possible for the new to be imagined while the old still exists, something Cinna helps Panem to do by costuming Katniss in a white silk wedding dress that burns off to become a black, feathered mockingjay outfit while she is being interviewed by Caesar Flickerman before the Quarter Quell (*Catching Fire* 252). That it is a wedding dress that burns is, of course, significant since it gestures towards the patriarchal system that must be destroyed before a more equitable system can be created. Although dressing as a mockingjay does not make her one any more than a drag performance changes one's sex, it does challenge hegemonic culture, pointing towards "a new configuration of politics" that could "emerge from the ruins of the old" (Butler 1990, 148).

Collins narrates the birth of a new political configuration in the closing chapters of *Mockingjay*. Following Prim's death, Katniss enters a liminal space, between death and rebirth: "Dead, but not allowed to die. Alive, but as good as dead" (349). It is here that she recognizes that she has not been the Mockingjay at all but a "fire mutt," "Cinna's bird, ignited, flying to escape something inescapable" (348). She only begins to move beyond this space when, after encountering President Snow in his rose garden, she consciously addresses the possibility that Prim and the other children were massacred by the rebels rather than by the Capitol, and that therefore the system of governance she has been fighting for is as inhumane and unjust as the system it replaces. Her fear that the promised new world is just another version of the old is only reinforced when, instead of helping her think through Snow's insistence that the Capitol was not responsible for the killing, Haymitch attributes her agitation to "boy trouble" (362). Hiding herself in a pile of silken clothing "like a caterpillar in a cocoon awaiting metamorphosis," she tries desperately to transform herself "into something of beauty" but is unable to do so, remaining her "hideous" self, a fire mutt (363). She can only become something new and different, it seems, if the world she is living in changes, too, a change she effects soon afterwards by assassinating President Coin, the leader of District 13, who was planning to reinstitute the Hunger Games not only to punish the Capitol but to consolidate her control of the new Panem. It is only in the aftermath of this act that she truly becomes the Mockingjay, a creature that should not exist but nonetheless does, a creature belonging to a different order. As if to underscore this point, Katniss begins to sing, her voice "rough" and "breaking" at first but then becoming "something splendid," something "that would make the mockingjays fall silent and then tumble over themselves to join in" (376). The steadying of Katniss's cracking voice here seems to both parallel and parody the changing of a boy's voice into a man's, suggesting that she is coming into a position of power in the way a boy does when he enters manhood.

Masculinity and Patriarchy

Masculinity is no more fixed than femininity in the *Hunger Games* trilogy, both being matters of performance rather than essential, sex-based traits. In order to convey this idea, Collins sets up Gale and Peeta as counterparts, using their rivalry over to Katniss to explore not only how masculinity is constructed under patriarchy but how gender norms and the oppressive systems they reinforce can be changed. Unlike Gale, who is essentially a static character, remaining a stereotypical "man's man"—that is, fearless, direct, aggressive, and compelling—throughout the trilogy, Peeta is dynamic, developing into a person who is ultimately able to transcend the gender he was assigned and become someone new.

As Sarah Rees Brennan and others suggest, Gale is presented as the traditional masculine ideal, being handsome, strong, and able to provide for his family (7). He is also decidedly masculine in attitude, embodying the sort of machismo that, according Patrick Colm Hogan, can result from forms of social and political domination (21). Agie Markiewicz observes:

> Gale is an impulsive reactionary who is strongly opposed to the politics of Panem. Katniss points out his frequent outbursts and his fiery ideas that spell out a longing for a violent revolution. Gale is, then, an embodiment of macho masculinity that derives from the oppression to the Capitol—in other words, Gale's masculinity is frustrated by the effeminate position Panem put him in. He is neither able to publicly denounce the political scenario playing out nor is he able to protect his family from the state-mandated cruelty of the Games.

As a result, Gale tries to prove his essential masculinity to himself by seeking confrontation and conflict, both on a private level, as when he ridicules Madge's clothing on the day of the reaping, and on a public one, as when he proposes creating a "death trap" to kill the thousands of people inside the Nut (*Mockingjay* 283). For Gale, it seems, being a man involves not only dominating others but controlling their destinies.

Gale also projects a reactionary masculinity through his sexuality, indicating an interest in having children with Katniss in the very first chapter of *The Hunger Games*. His desire for Katniss seems to be not just physical or emotional but proprietary, however, something that he himself indicates when he tells Katniss that his sexual interest in her began when Darius, a District 12 Peacekeeper, expresses his desire for her in front of him (*Mockingjay* 199). Not surprisingly, perhaps, given his claim on Katniss, Gale feels threatened by Katniss's relationship with Peeta even though she assures him there was no romance: desperate to prove his power over her, he surprises Katniss in the woods and kisses her without her consent, pinning her arms against his chest in a way that makes her feel like an animal ensnared in one of his traps (*Catching Fire* 27). He kisses her in a similar manner in *Mockingjay*, again taking her by surprise in the woods. This time, however, rather than remain passive, Katniss discomfits him by kissing him back. Rather than accept her kiss, he pulls away, thinking that she is being responsive only because she has lost Peeta forever and is choosing him by default (*Mockingjay* 198). For him, apparently, a kiss only "counts" if she chooses him over all other males and thereby affirms his masculinity (198).

Whereas Gale represents the sort of masculine ideal one might expect to find in mainstream romantic fiction, Peeta represents something very different, an alternative form of masculinity that does not eschew everything considered female. Indeed, one could argue that Peeta is presented in a manner that challenges traditional ideas of gender, given his willingness to be openly emotional, his interest in baking and frosting cakes, and the fact that he is the one who needs to be rescued and then protected in the 74th Hunger Games and the Quarter Quell as if he were the damsel in distress. His kindness, sensitivity, and willingness to work in teams also defy masculine stereotypes, as does his general lack of aggression.

It would be a mistake to regard Peeta as a feminized man, however. Although hardly an alpha male, Peeta is stereotypically masculine in the way he performs heterosexuality, making Katniss "an object of love" and then devoting himself to protecting her in the hopes of eventually taking her as a mate (*Hunger Games* 134). Like Gale, he also is proprietary towards Katniss, seeming to think that his interest in her amounts to a claim upon her and that at the very least she must choose between him and Gale. This becomes most evident when Peeta confronts Katniss about her kissing both him and Gale in *Mockingjay*. When Katniss tells him that the kisses they exchanged in the Games meant something to her, he is still unsatisfied because he knows she kissed Gale as well. He asks angrily, "And was it okay with both of us? You kissing the other?" to which Katniss replies that she "wasn't asking your permission" (232). Rather than accept Katniss's reprimand, Peeta responds "coldly" and "dismissively," saying, "You're a piece of work, aren't you?" (232). Like Gale, he seems to accept that she has the right to choose which man she will be with, but no right to choose neither or both.

What differentiates Peeta from Gale in the end of the trilogy is the fact that Peeta changes, becoming a very different sort of person than he was at the beginning. If in *The Hunger Games* and *Catching Fire*, Peeta represents an alternative form of masculinity, one that might on the surface seem more enlightened than that exhibited by Gale, the torture and reconditioning he undergoes while a prisoner of the Capitol brings out the latent misogyny that underlies patriarchy and the subordination of women: as his reaction to Katniss kissing both him and Gale suggests, he is not just jealous of her relationship with Gale but hates her for it. To an extent Peeta's malevolence towards Katniss is a result of the Capitol altering his memories through the use of tracker jacker venom and other techniques. The Capitol does not create Peeta's feelings from nothing, however, Peeta himself admitting to Katniss that he was jealous of Gale before the Games even began and that he has behaved cruelly towards her once the Games were over (*Catching Fire* 51). Rather, the Capitol augments Peeta's existing resentment towards Katniss by convincing him, among other things, that the two of them had a sexual relationship during the Victory Tour and that, therefore, he has an exclusive right to her (*Mockingjay* 243). As in *Othello*, where Iago uses the title character's sexual jealousy to manipulate and ultimately destroy him, in *Mockingjay* the Capitol exploits Peeta's belief that he is entitled to Katniss in order to get him to kill her. Significantly, both men use their own hands to strangle the women they believe have betrayed them sexually.

Unlike Desdemona, Katniss survives Peeta's attack and therefore has the opportunity to confront her would-be killer when the two of them are assigned to the same military squad and sent to join the assault on the Capitol. Rather than justify past actions — actions that, to her mind, need no justification — Katniss tries to deprogram Peeta, helping him sort out what is "real" from what is "not real" (*Mockingjay* 272). More importantly, perhaps, she tries to redefine their relationship so that it no longer involves subordination or an adherence to societal expectations. She accomplishes these things by, in effect, telling him what to think as he recovers from his earlier trauma, by defining things for him. For example, when he asks Katniss if she is still trying to protect him — "Real or not real"— she replies, "Real.... Because that's what you and I do. Protect each other" (*Mockingjay* 302). As her words suggest, their relationship is becoming entirely reciprocal, just as it was in the Games, where their efforts to survive force them to do what is necessary rather than what is expected. As if to underscore this point, the two of them repeat verbatim a conversation they had in the first arena, and then remind each other that they saved each other's lives there (*Mockingjay* 321–2).

Another exchange that they repeat is even more telling. In *Catching Fire*, Katniss asks Peeta to stay with her as she slips into unconsciousness after being given sleep syrup because of injuries she has sustained, and does not quite hear his answer (*Catching Fire* 159). Much later, after being shot during the siege of District 2 and put on morphling, Katniss's unconscious finally supplies Peeta's missing response, which is "Always" (*Mockingjay* 218). The exchange surfaces again while Katniss, Peeta, and the other surviving members of the Star Squad regroup in the sewers of the Capitol after being attacked by mutts. Peeta, who has been conditioned to attack Katniss just as the mutts do, tells her he is "losing it" and that she and the others should abandon him (313). Even though she knows that his homicidal rage towards her seems to have a sexual trigger, she risks kissing him, saying, "Stay with me," to which he replies, "Always." What makes this repetition of the exchange significant is that it lacks the romantic overtones of before. Peeta does not promise to stay with her always because he is devoted to her romantically but because their relationship has transcended romance: they are simply two people who have become interdependent, a man and a woman who can be intimate with one another without their relationship being either sexual or romantic. Katniss, of course, was capable of this type of relationship all the time: it is how she would have preferred her relationship with Gale to have remained, and it is how she hoped her relationship with Peeta would be after they returned from their first Games. For Peeta, though, it is something new, a type of relationship that, before his being reconditioned by Katniss, would have been impossible.

An End to Patriarchy and the Beginning of Something Else

To the extent that the trilogy is structured around a love triangle, Collins seems to be deploying the conventions of the young adult novel: as Jennifer Lynn Barnes suggests, it is becoming increasingly common in YA fiction for "romantic conflict" to take "center stage," a story's tension only resolving itself one the protagonist makes the correct choice in mate (14). The outcome of the *Hunger Games* trilogy is anything but conventional, however, in the sense that, in the end, Katniss no longer has to choose between Peeta and Gale. For all intents and purposes, patriarchy ends in Panem with the defeat of first the Capitol and then the oppressive regime that would replace it, and, therefore, Katniss is no longer defined by her choice in mate. Her mate did not have to be Peeta; rather, it happens to be Peeta. Indeed, one could argue that the Peeta she marries is not the person she knew from before, Peeta, like Panem itself, having been transformed by events that have transpired over the course of the trilogy. At the end of *Mockingjay*, it seems, Katniss and Peeta enter into a third "space of possibility," to use again Garber's terminology, a space that by its very existence challenges the legitimacy of the binaries that earlier governed their lives.

As one might expect, given that they themselves live within patriarchy, many readers were discomfited by Collins's refusal to adhere to the conventions of the young adult romance and have the trilogy resolve itself neatly with Katniss's selection of a mate (Mahoney, Morrison): Katniss is supposed to choose the right man and live happily ever after. Other readers recognized that Collins is doing something much more radical, that is, challenging the idea that a woman's happiness and success is ultimately determined by her choice in a mate. In response to a series on the *Hunger Games* trilogy in *Slate*, librarian Jennifer Klumpp, for example, writes, "I think that the less than thrilling resolution of the Gale/Peeta issue, and the fact that in the end she didn't 'choose' either of them was just right for the character and what she had been through.... In fact, it was clear throughout much of *Mockingjay* that Gale and Peeta were both obstacles to her survival." As comments by Klumpp and others, including Katie Roiphe of the *New York Times* and Rollie Welch of *The Plain Dealer*, suggest, although the trilogy initially seems to be structured around the

Katniss-Gale-Peeta love triangle, in the end it is all about Katniss and the ways she comes to define herself and her own destiny. For these readers the trilogy involves much more than being either "Team Peeta" or "Team Gale": it involves rethinking not only the significance of relationships between people but the social order itself.

CHAPTER THREE

Making War, Not Love
Conflict, Representation and Activism

"I don't write about adolescence," she said. "I write about war. For adolescents."
— Suzanne Collins (quoted in Dominus)

As the above quotation suggests, Suzanne Collins readily identifies herself as a war writer, something that should not be surprising given that both *The Underland Chronicles* and the *Hunger Games* trilogy make war a primary subject (Dominus). What is surprising, perhaps, is how uncompromising Collins is when it comes to depicting war, particularly considering that her work is marketed primarily to children and young adults. As Shannon Donnelly observes, in *Mockingjay* in particular, "Collins's narrative is unflinching—not one shred of wartime realism is sacrificed in order to shield younger readers." To some readers, of course, such realism is troubling: reviewers like Meghan Cox Gurdon of *The Wall Street Journal*, for example, condemn books that provide young readers with images "of damage, brutality and losses of the most horrendous kind," arguing that they may damage "a child's happiness, moral development, and tenderness of heart." Even Maria Tatar, who recognizes a certain value in exposing children to "adult reality," finds the *Hunger Games* trilogy too unrelentingly dark in comparison to books like *Peter Pan* and *Alice in Wonderland*, which balance "perils" with "possibilities." Reviewers and commentators like Monica Edinger and Susan Dominus, however, seem to recognize that in order to present war as it is, Collins's work has to be dark: to do otherwise would be to risk glamorizing war rather than calling into question whether it should be ever used to settle conflicts between peoples or states.

War and Ambivalence in The Underland Chronicles

One could argue that in *The Underland Chronicles* at least, a five-part series published between 2003 and 2007, Collins not only glorifies war but presents it as a legitimate means of resolving otherwise intractable issues between nations. Written primarily for pre-adolescents, the books focus on an eleven-year-old boy named Gregor who unwittingly enters into a fantastical world beneath New York City — a world occupied by oversized rats, bats, mice, moles, and cockroaches that both speak and act like humans do. The hero quickly learns that his father, who has been missing for two years, is a prisoner of the rats, who are on the verge of making war against the humans who began colonizing the underworld hundreds of years earlier. Gregor, whom Underlanders believe to be a great warrior spoken about in prophecies, becomes increasingly involved in underworld affairs, undertaking what Collins describes in an interview as "essentially a series of military missions," usually accompanied by his baby sister, Boots ("Q and A"). Initially concerned only with rescuing his father, Gregor gradually accepts that he is indeed "the Warrior" and that he has no choice but to help the humans in their efforts to become the dominant power in the Underland. As the *Chronicles* unfold, the war begins and Collins's young readers are introduced to many of the more unpleasant aspects of military conflict, including the deaths of combatants and civilians alike, genocide, trauma, and gore. Although the books sometimes call into question certain actions humans and their allies take against the rats, such as the use of germ warfare, humans are generally presented sympathetically: certain humans do terrible things out of cruelty or avarice, but for the most part they try to help those weaker than them — namely the mice — and generally make an effort to do what is right. The rats, in contrast, are depicted as being wicked and bloodthirsty, the final two volumes of the *Chronicles* focusing on their efforts to exterminate the mice, who are entirely unable to defend themselves. By paralleling the rats to the Nazis in the final two volumes — not only by making them genocidal but by having them follow a Hitler-like leader named Bane — Collins leaves her readers no doubt as to whom they should be sympathizing with.

Given the fact that the series appeared at a time when the United States was engaged in war in both Afghanistan and Iraq, it is difficult not to read the *Chronicles* as commentary on the conflicts, commentary that questions both the justification for the wars and the way they are being conducted. Indeed, one could argue that they reflect Collins's own ambivalence, since in an interview Collins remarks that she resembles Gregor in the sense that they "both want to do the right thing but sometimes have trouble figuring out what it is" ("Q and A"). Through Gregor, Collins demonstrates to her readers just how ethically complicated waging war can be, even when one believes one's cause is just. For example, having been told all of his life that killing is morally wrong, Gregor wonders why it is considered acceptable — even celebrated — during times of war (*Gregor and the Code of the Claw* 405). He also has to come to terms with the morality of participating in something that brings about the death of many noncombatants, including children, whether they are targeted directly or not. Finally, he addresses a question many Americans considered following the attacks on the World Trade Center and the Pentagon: to what extent might the people he aligns himself with be responsible for the war even if they were not the first to attack? Despite his doubts about the costs of war and the righteousness of his cause, Gregor, like many Americans, ultimately decides that the war was unavoidable since his side came under attack and that it would be wrong to stand by and not participate in it.

To present a war as being unavoidable if not just is not necessarily to glamorize it. On the contrary, Collins exposes her readers to many of war's horrors, not only by offering realistic representations of people who have been injured, orphaned, or traumatized by violence but by conveying a sense of loss by killing off characters that young readers might care for or even identify with, such as Hamnet, the heroic and loving father of six-year-old Hazard, and a playful young bat named Thalia. As Collins concedes, however, the emotional impact of such horrors is lessened by the fact that they are presented through fantasy, that they play out through "a combination of humans and rats and bats" (Springen 2008). The *Chronicles'* seemingly anti-war message is also undercut by the fact that the war against the rats ends with the establishment of a new and more just social order, one that balances the interests of the warring parties. As a result, readers might reasonably conclude that even though the war is horrific, involving cruelty, injustice, and suffering, it can result in positive change and therefore is justifiable, at least in some cases.

In addition to legitimizing war as a means of resolving conflicts, the

Chronicles also tend to glamorize fighting by presenting readers with a protagonist who not only proves himself worthy of love and admiration through his actions as a warrior but also provides readers with a means of participating in violence vicariously. Gregor is the archetypal reluctant warrior, being called upon to fight, and doing so effectively, but never making it his vocation. Like the ancient Roman leader, Cincinnatus, who assumed power only when it was pressed upon him during national emergencies and relinquished as soon as the crisis was resolved, Gregor has no interest in power for its own sake and even seems repelled by many of the things he is called upon to do (Despain 208). Although, given her propensity to model characters and situations on classical sources, Collins may well have had Cincinnatus in mind while writing about Gregor's recognition that he must sometimes do things he finds distasteful or wrong for the sake of the greater good, her representation of him as a reluctant warrior is also consistent with lead characters in contemporary popular narratives ranging from J.R.R. Tolkien's *The Lord of the Rings* to Rick Riordan's *Percy Jackson & the Olympians*. Though pacific by nature, Gregor is willing to kill when necessary and, when pressed, accomplishes tremendous feats of arms, feats that Collins presents in graphic detail, describing for her young readers, for example, how killing with a sword is "a lot harder than it looked": "The blade had to pierce the hide, then the muscle, and then sometimes ran into bone before it could reach the vital organs inside" (*Gregor and the Code of the Claw* 61). Although Gregor resists fighting as much as he can, once it begins he enters in a battle rage that he finds both empowering and intoxicating. For example, a battle in which Gregor and Ares, the bat he partners with, fight to prevent mice from being slaughtered by rats is described in the following terms:

> Soon Gregor was covered in blood, and Ares's fur had become damp and sticky with the stuff, but neither of them had more than scratches. He didn't have to think about how to wield his sword; it moved instinctively from target to target. And every time it connected, Gregor became more confident, more powerful [*Gregor and the Code of the Claw* 62].

As the above passage suggests, Gregor is more than just a skilled warrior: like Percy Jackson, Harry Potter, and many other popular children's heroes, Gregor has special abilities that, once controlled, make him almost invulnerable. In his climactic battle with Bane, a 12-foot-tall rat who fights with uncontrolled rage, he is finally able to fully master his own "rager" instincts: rather than be "overcome" by them, he is able to "control his actions with a deadly accuracy ...," giving him a decisive advantage (*Gregor and the Code of the Claw* 354).

Like most protagonists of children's stories, Gregor is constructed so that readers can learn through him: he not only models certain traits and behaviors but provides readers with a means of experiencing them, at least to the extent that they are able to identify with him and his situation. Part of what they may experience is the thrill of battle: as readers, they can participate vicariously in Gregor's actions and even become "heady with power" just as Gregor does (354). Although Gregor often reflects on the immorality of killing and expresses regrets at times for some of his actions, it is rats that he kills rather than people, and so, as suggested earlier, the emotional impact is mitigated, at least partially. Indeed, the experience of reading *The Chronicles* might be likened to playing first person shooter games such as *Halo* or *Bioshock* or even strategy games such as *Warcraft* and *Command & Conquer* that are set in non-existent worlds since they, too, allow players to engage in violence that has no immediate real-world consequences. Violence, it seems, can be fun, particularly when it can be both justified and no one really gets hurt.

The Underland Chronicles also risk promoting violence and warfare by rewarding characters who excel at it. Gregor is certainly damaged by his wartime experiences both physically and mentally, but his heroism is rewarded in the very same sorts of ways that it is in stories like *Star Wars* and *Harry Potter*. In particular, he becomes a legendary figure and wins the approbation and respect of the people he most cares about, including that of the girl he loves, Luxa, the Queen of Regalia. He also discovers that his fighting prowess will serve him well in the real world, that, as his friend and ally Ripred tells him, "There won't be anyone you can't take," meaning that he will never have to worry about being bullied or pushed around (397). In short, despite what is arguably an anti-war message, the *Chronicles* nonetheless represents being a warrior as a difficult but potentially rewarding vocation.

Given the fact that her father, a career Air Force officer and military historian, served in Vietnam when she was six and, upon returning to the United States, continued having nightmares about his experiences there for years, sometimes waking up screaming (Dominus), Collins's ambivalence towards war should not be too surprising: even though she grew up in a military family and was raised to respect the soldiers for the sacrifices they make, she knows firsthand that war is traumatizing for combatants and non-combatants alike. Her personal knowledge of the cost of war is augmented by the history her father taught her as the family moved from base to base in the United States and Europe. She comments: "It was very important to him that we understood about certain aspects of life. So, it wasn't enough to visit a battlefield, we needed to know why the battle occurred, how it played out, and the consequences" (Margolis 2008). In *The Underland Chronicles*, Collins presents battles in the same sort of comprehensive manner, detailing the build-up to them, the fighting itself, the immediate casualties, the collateral damage, the indirect casualties due to shortages and damaged infrastructure, and even the disposal of the dead. Like her father, she also concerns herself with "the question of what makes a necessary war — at what point is it justifiable or unavoidable?" (Margolis 2010): In the *Chronicles*, the first book of which was written in consultation with her father, who strongly opposed the War in Iraq, Gregor continually reflects upon not only his own role in the war but whether the war itself is morally justifiable, as do other characters such as Vikus and Hamnet (Springen 2008). Overall, the books seem to suggest that war may be justified, even necessary, but it is never moral: one cannot fight a good war because fighting involves doing bad things.

War in the Hunger Games *trilogy*

If *The Underland Chronicles* expresses a certain ambivalence towards war, the *Hunger Games* trilogy does not, at least when read in its entirety since it is difficult to regard the final volume, *Mockingjay*, as being anything but an anti-war novel. Before *Mockingjay* was released, however, many people apparently felt that the concluding book of the trilogy would represent the war of rebellion against the Capitol as being both necessary and just. John Granger, a prominent web commentator on young adult fiction, seemed to miss the anti-war sentiment of the first two volumes entirely, even though the frequently mentioned Dark Days that followed the previous war only leads to increased suffering. In response to a statement made by Collins just before the release of *Mockingjay* that "the ethical ambiguities of war are introduced too late to children," Granger writes, "The books do not show war in an unsympathetic light, do they? You have to be a pretty cold fish and appeaser not to want the Districts to rise up against the Capitol." He adds that the first two books seem to say to "young people" that "wars are often unavoidable and necessary; there are goods worth dying for and evils we are obliged to resist at the risk of our lives." Travis Prinzi, another frequent commentator on young adult fiction, has a similar if more measured response to the first two books, concluding that Collins knows that war "must happen at times," if only because some people do "evil," "forc[ing] the hand of those who must fight."

It is possible, of course, that Granger, Prinzi, and others gauged the militaristic tone of *The Hunger Games* and *Catching Fire* correctly and that the story arc changed in *Mockingjay*. Indeed, Collins seems to allow for this possibility herself, noting that she "briefly plotted out all three books," but found "that you learn so much about the story and the characters yourself as you go along that it's not good to overplot towards the end because, hopefully, you'll discover even better things along the way" ("Book Review Podcast"). Collins has given no indication that she rethought her attitude towards war while writing the trilogy, however, and in an interview with *Entertainment Weekly*, she states that she was very much concerned with keeping her story unified as she worked simultaneously on *Mockingjay* and the screenplay for *The Hunger Games* (Valby). Certainly the first two volumes do not glamorize fighting or suggest that war is an acceptable means of resolving social or political issues. On the contrary, those who enjoy fighting, namely the Careers, are depicted negatively, and the only two wars that are mentioned in the narrative — the "brutal" one that followed the environmental collapse and the rebellion that resulted in the destruction of District 13 and the creation of the Hunger Games — only made already horrific situations worse (*Hunger Games* 18). With this in mind, it seems more likely that the anti-war themes that becomes manifest in *Mockingjay* develop out of ideas that were introduced in the preceding volumes rather than depart from them. *The Hunger Games* and *Catching Fire* may seem to be less anti-war than *Mockingjay* because it is only in the final volume of the trilogy that Collins makes war her primary subject.

War as Subject in Mockingjay

That *Mockingjay* makes war its subject is clear from the very beginning, the novel opening in a "killing field" as Monica Edinger notes.

Through Katniss, who returns to District 12 for the first time since it was firebombed by the Capitol, Collins provides readers with a panoramic view of a holocaust: as Katniss moves from the remains of the home she grew up in to the "sea of gray" that covers most of the district, we see along with her how an entire community has been destroyed (3). Collins does not allow her readers to remain detached from the destruction, however, having Katniss describe how "piles of ash ... shift here and there" in response to her "footsteps," and how a skull that she initially mistook for a rock makes her wonder how her own skull would look (5). Katniss even considers her own culpability in the massacre since it appears to have been triggered by her escape from the Quarter Quell arena: as she passes bodies in "various states of decomposition," she thinks, "*I killed you ... And you. And you*" (5). By opening the novel in such a manner, Collins suggests that the human costs of war are almost beyond comprehension: Katniss can think about the war and contemplate its consequences, but the horror can never be reduced to words or thoughts. Accordingly, just contemplating what has happened in District 12 induces a somatic response in Katniss: it is not the billowing ash that makes her choke as she runs through the town so much as the thought of "who" she is breathing in (9).

Collins also presents the ethical complexities of war as being almost beyond comprehension through Katniss. Unlike Gale, who wants only to avenge the destruction of his home, telling Katniss that if he could, he would "hit a button and kill every living soul working for the Capitol," Katniss reflects on the significance of what has happened and wants no part of killing for the sake of revenge (31). This is not to suggest that she does not feel bitterness or anger towards the Capitol or that a desire for retribution plays no part in her decision to become active in the rebellion: when she thinks about Rue's death, Gale being whipped, and the destruction of her home district, her "blood turns hot" (30). Ultimately, her decision to become the Mockingjay is rational rather than emotional, however: she only resolves to do so after she realizes that she cannot allow things to "go back" to the way they were — that the Capitol can no longer be allow to control populations through terror, starve them into submission, or engage is mass killings. Ironically, upon joining the rebellion, Katniss becomes party to all of these things since the rebellion's tactics mirror those of the Capitol, as becomes evident during the sieges of District 2 and the Capitol. Collins's point here seems to be that no matter what the cause, war cannot be prosecuted in an ethical manner.

Katniss does not join the conflict blindly, of course; having seen the ruins of District 12, she knows full well what war entails. To her, the ends justify the means, however, at least in the early part of the novel: she joins the rebellion knowing that as the Mockingjay every public action on her part is likely to bring about "suffering and loss of life" (12). More than that, her statement to the Capitol — "...if we burn, you burn with us" — indicates that she accepts the position put forth by Gale that, since its cause is just, the rebellion has the right to use any tactic the Capitol does, including those that result in civilian casualties (100). She even seems to approve of weapons that target non-combatants, including things like the booby-trapping of water supplies and what appear to be safe havens, apparently drawing the line only at weapons that exploit people's more humane impulses like bombs designed to kill "people who rush to the aid of the wounded" (186). Having witnessed cruelty and suffering for her entire life, Katniss is not at all squeamish about death and is perfectly willing to kill, at least when she considers it necessary. Having said that, it is significant that she takes no particular pleasure in killing and later feels tremendous guilt for her role in bringing about the deaths of others (*Mockingjay* 382).

Katniss is not a static character, and although she continues to accept in principle the idea that killing is necessary in war, her judgment about when it can be justified changes. In other words, she begins to think that the ends may justify certain means but not any means. This becomes clear when Gale proposes neutralizing the Capitol's primary military base, the Nut, which is contained in a mountain, by blocking its exits and suffocating those within. Although initially inclined to support the plan, her hatred of the Capitol being so strong because of what they did to District 12 making her want to see "everyone in the mountain dead," she remembers that she is "a girl from District 12" and not someone like President Snow who will do absolutely anything in order to achieve his ends (204): as someone who lost her own father in a mine accident, she cannot justify condemning others to a similar fate. Ultimately she acquiesces, however, donning her Mockingjay outfit so that she will be ready to play her part when an "opportunity for a propo arises."

Once Gale's plan is executed and thousands of people die, Katniss realizes that she is morally culpable even though she initially objected to

71

the attack since her contributions to the war effort helped put the rebellion in a position to bring the Capitol's main base under siege. Imagining "the hell inside the mountain" that must have followed the attack leads to her to remember in detail the day her own father died buried within a mountain. Reflecting upon what has transpired, Katniss asks herself reprovingly, "*What did we just do?*" (208). As her use of the word "we" suggests, she takes responsibility for the killing of those within the mountain even though she publicly challenged the decision to trap the people within it: to be part of a war effort is to share in the responsibility for everything that happens during the war, even things of which one might not personally approve.

From this point onward, Katniss is no longer able to commit herself to the war, either intellectually or emotionally, continuing in her role as the Mockingjay only because doing so will put her in a better position to kill President Snow. Although she hates the Capitol as much as she ever has, she is no longer willing to wage war against it by killing people from other districts. Told by Haymitch to make a speech encouraging supporters of the Capitol to surrender after the Nut has been neutralized, Katniss breaks from the script when two trainloads of armed survivors from the Nut appear before her in front of the Justice Building. Rather than continue her speech, she runs towards them, yelling to the rebels on the rooftops to hold their fire (214). When one of the survivors points a gun to her head and demands that she give him a reason for not shooting her, she can only reply that there is none, adding, "That's the problem, isn't it? ... We blew up your mine. You burned my district to the ground. We've got every reason to kill each other" (215). Disarming herself, she continues to speak, observing that the killing "goes around and around" and nobody wins, except for the Capitol, and then asserting that she is "tired of being a piece in their Games" (215). Although she does not yet say it, her refusal to simply repeat the speech Haymitch provides her with suggests that she is no longer willing to be a piece in District 13's Games either. Having seen that in pursuing their interests the rebels can be as brutal and inhumane as the Capitol, she decides to act independently of them, pursuing her "own personal vendetta" rather than the rebel cause (234). Upon returning to District 13, Katniss discovers that the rebels have little use for her now that, as the Mockingjay, she has succeeded in uniting the districts against the Capitol. She nonetheless insists upon having a role in the siege of the

Capitol, however, hoping for a chance to kill Snow, and is assigned to a Star Squad along with Gale, Finnick, and eventually Peeta, so that the rebellion can continue to create propaganda featuring Hunger Games victors and other celebrities. When her commander, Boggs, is killed, Katniss takes the opportunity to break completely with the rebellion, lying to her squad about having direct orders from President Coin to kill Snow. Finally a free agent, she pursues her own agenda, committing what amounts to an act of treason against the very cause she joined voluntarily earlier.

Although no longer a District 13 soldier, Katniss is nonetheless in a position to witness the ongoing war firsthand as she continues moving towards the City Center to find Snow. As before when surveying the ruins of District 12, Katniss relates the horrors of war directly, the key difference being that in this case she not only reports upon events but participates in them. Emerging from Tigress's shop just blocks from the City Center, she and Gale insinuate themselves within a group of refugees heading towards Snow's mansion. Almost immediately, the streets become a battlefield as "[g]unfire rips through the crowd" and some of the people near her "slump to the ground" (339). After taking cover, Katniss looks around and sees a "little girl in a lemon yellow coat" who "kneels besides a motionless woman, screeching and trying to rouse her." As she watches, "Another wave of bullets slices across the chest of her yellow coat, staining it red, knocking the girl onto her back." Looking at the girl's "tiny crumpled form," Katniss is overcome by horror, unable to speak. Her horror deepens as she realizes that it is the rebels who have been shooting into the crowd, killing Peacekeepers and refugees alike. As the battle continues, she becomes a killer of innocents herself. Moving on to the next block, Katniss and Gale are caught in the crossfire between rebels and Peacekeepers, along with a large number of refugees, many of whom are wounded (347). Rather than retreat, take cover, or help others as best she can, she begins to kill indiscriminately: "Peacekeeper, rebel, citizen, who knows? Everything that moves is a target. People shoot reflexively, and I'm no exception. Heart pounding, adrenalin burning through me, everyone is my enemy.... There's nothing to do but move forward, killing whoever comes in our path" (341). By presenting it in such terms, Collins denies Katniss any glory: she is a murderer more than a hero, killing others — whether friend or enemy, adult or child — not only to save herself but to pursue a personal vendetta. She has, in short, become exactly the sort of person she herself despises, a person like Snow or Coin who will do whatever she has to to achieve her ends.

As a dynamic character whose attitude develops and changes over the course of the *Hunger Games* trilogy, Katniss provides readers with a means of thinking through the costs of war, not only to society but to the individual. In the opening volumes of the trilogy, Katniss is a heroic character in the sense that she not only defies powers that are greater than herself but also risks everything in order to help others. Once she joins the military, however, she becomes a different person, not only because of what she sees but because of what she does. To fight in war is to murder innocent people, something that, as Peeta notes, "costs everything you are" (*Mockingjay* 23). Fighting may seem exciting, Collins suggests, even glamorous, but in the end it is just murder, something Katniss learns only when it is too late.

War and Propaganda

In addition to witnessing how terrible war is, Katniss sees how those who promote war use the media in order to "manufacture consent" for it, to borrow Walter Lippman's phrase (248). According to Lippman, "The real environment is altogether too big, too complex, and too fleeting for direct acquaintance," and therefore people construct individualized models of reality—what Lippman terms "pseudo-environments" (16). Although essentially fictions based on an individual's subjective and necessarily limited understanding of the real, these pseudo-environments provide a basis for an individual's actions. Consequently, Lippman argues, controlling a person's pseudo-environment serves as a means of controlling one's behaviors. One obvious way of accomplishing this is through the control of information, something the Capitol does by isolating the districts from one another and monopolizing mass communications. As a result, it can limit what people know about other places and make organized resistance impossible, at least on a national level. The Capitol also uses misinformation to shape people's pseudo-environments, reporting that District 13 has been destroyed, for example, and attributing shortages caused by the rebellion to things like storms. The Capitol even succeeds in controlling personal communications to a large extent by making people fear speaking freely to one another. Indeed, they are so successful in this that Katniss is afraid to be critical of the Capitol in her own home even before she has become a victor with reason to believe that the she may be a specific target of government surveillance. The Capitol generates this fear in part by punishing people severely for even the most minor offenses and instilling in them a sense that they may be under observation at any time. Like the totalitarian governments of Fascist Italy or contemporary North Korea, the government of Panem makes organized resistance almost impossible through the careful control of information on both public and private levels. By controlling people's pseudo-environments, the state makes challenging its authority all but unimaginable, a process George Orwell famously dramatized in *1984*.

To Katniss, District 13 initially seems very different from Panem since its leader, Alma Coin, rules with the consent of the governed, the district being, at least nominally, a democracy. Katniss quickly learns, however, that the government of District 13 controls information just as carefully as the Capitol does, albeit more subtly. Whereas in Panem people are unable to freely criticize the government, in District 13 they can do so without fear of retribution. For example, Dalton, a former resident of District 10 who has lived in District 13 for several years tells Katniss without any apparent fear of retribution that 13 regards new citizens as "breeding stock" (*Mockingjay* 8), and people express their dissent openly when President Coin announces that her government will not prosecute Peeta and other former tributes once the war is over (57). The fact that people can be critical of the government does not make District 13 a free society, however: even though it has to allow a certain level of dissent so that it can present itself as an alternative to the repressive Capitol, Coin and her government are just as controlling in their own way as the Capitol is. Like the Capitol, District 13 has a monopoly on mass communications and it uses television programming to shape people's pseudo-environments and thereby control their beliefs and actions, something Katniss learns firsthand as the Mockingjay.

Being the Mockingjay, it turns out, is not so different than being "the girl who was on fire": in both cases her words, actions, and appearance are managed by others so as to achieve certain effects. The effect District 13 hopes to achieve is to make the girl who not only survived two Hunger Games but openly defied the Capitol and its power into a "symbol of the revolution" (*Mockingjay* 10). In effect, the district's propagandists use her to alter people's pseudo-environments to make resistance to the Capitol conceivable, thereby increasing the likelihood that they will join the rebellion. As it turns out, the propaganda broadcasts featuring Katniss as the Mockingjay are extremely effective, helping the rebels to take Districts 3 and 11 and make significant advances in several other districts (119). The propos are also based on a fundamental lie, however, one that Katniss is aware of from the start: she is no rebel leader, even though she plays one for the cameras, Coin reserving all real power for herself. The question Katniss is forced to consider is whether such a lie is justified: is it acceptable for her to manipulate people by playing the Mockingjay when doing so is likely to lead to the deaths of thousands? When she initially agrees to be the Mockingjay, she does so despite her reservations because she has decided that the Capitol must be defeated at all costs. As she comes to realize that in many ways District 13 is just as bad as the Capitol, however, her opinion begins to change, and eventually she leaves the rebellion to pursue her own agenda and kill Snow.

Life During Wartime

Another element of war Collins explores in detail in the *Hunger Games* trilogy is the way in which it transforms civil society. Early on in *Mockingjay*, Katniss learns that District 13 has essentially been at war since the end of the last rebellion seventy-five years earlier, even though there has been little if any actual combat in that time. Consequently its citizens have been on war footing, production being geared towards armaments rather than consumer goods, food being strictly rationed, and the ownership of private property being severely limited. Citizens are not even allowed to share food when they eat in a commissary together and guards are posted at the exits to prevent people from leaving with food. Violating regulations is punished severely, Katniss's prep team being shackled to a wall for stealing bread, for example.

Civil liberties have also been severely restricted as well, the "president" seemingly having special wartime powers that make her a *de facto* dictator and basic freedoms being limited for the duration of the crisis. The writ of *habeas corpus* has been suspended, for example, and President Coin has set up a war tribunal to render extraordinary judgments. Citizens of District 13 have also come to accept compulsory military service and even regulation of their daily routines, schedules being stamped on their arms in washable ink. What is most striking about the way that people have come to live during the ongoing war with the Capitol, however, is that there is no visible resistance to the ways in which their lives are regulated: people seem to accept without question that the war makes certain measures necessary, apparently believing, as Plutarch does, that, once the war is over, a representative democracy will be re-established and such measures will end (83).

Mockingjay *as Social Commentary*

As with Collins's descriptions of combat and its consequences, it is easy to relate life during wartime in District 13 to life in the United States in the period immediately following the September 11th attacks, particularly with regard to the erosion of civil liberties. People were called upon to make sacrifices during the so-called War on Terror that was declared by a president who assumed extraordinary powers during a time of crisis. In addition to being required to fund a war that might very well be perpetual, Americans were expected to accept additional restrictions in their everyday lives for the sake of security. Police forces were expanded, people were increasingly subjected to random searches, particularly in transportation hubs and other public venues, and military personnel were deployed in major cities. Moreover, with the passage of the Patriot Act, the power of the government to monitor both communications and financial transactions was expanded, and soon afterwards extrajudicial proceedings were authorized by the Bush administration, including those that violated *habeas corpus* and involved torture.

The ways in which President Coin manipulates events in order to maintain a political advantage — for example, by putting Katniss, whom she regards as a political threat, in danger by sending her into combat with Peeta, who has been conditioned by the Capitol to kill her — also seems to provide indirect commentary on events that occurred during the Bush administration such as when Valerie Plame's identity as a CIA operative was revealed to the press after her husband challenged the administration's claim that Saddam Hussein had been trying to obtain uranium from Niger. Like Coin, the Bush administration seemed willing to do almost anything in order to retain power, pressuring Secretary of Homeland Security Tom Ridge to raise the department's risk assessment level from "elevated" to "high" during 2004, an election year, and authorizing the release of Osama bin Laden's threats against the United States days before the elections themselves as an "October Surprise," to give two more examples (Knox).

The Hunger Games *Trilogy and Activism*

If, as Jane Henriksen Baird writes in her review of *Mockingjay* for the *School Library Journal*, "Collins is absolutely ruthless in her depictions of war in all its cruelty, violence, and loss," she is ruthless for a reason: she believes that war, with all of its "ethical ambiguities" is "introduced too late to children," and that they need to learn how to make ethical decisions earlier (Neary). More importantly, perhaps, they need to question the world around them, "decide whether it's right or not and if it isn't," decide what part they will take in going about changing it (Neary). The *Hunger Games* trilogy does more than introduce young readers to the horror of war, however: as Robin Kirk notes, "The books also take readers inside the mechanisms of propaganda and manipulation, and how resistance can subvert these powerful tools of control." Through Katniss's experiences as a media figure in both the Capitol and District 13, readers see how television can be used to control people's thoughts and behaviors. They also learn through her that individual action can make a difference, and that one does not have to accept things as they are. Even the little acts of resistance, like covering Rue's body with flowers, have great significance if only because it shows that resistance is possible, and Katniss's later actions, like refusing to be the sole survivor of her first Hunger Games or destroying the force field that surrounds the Quarter Quell arena, lead to open resistance to the Capitol in some districts and even uprisings. Katniss's final act as the Mockingjay makes the biggest difference of all, of course, since shooting Coin rather than Snow in front of all Panem changes everything forever. Making Katniss's action even more remarkable is the fact that she takes responsibility for it: she knows full well that killing the president will most likely lead to public execution, but to her the public good has become more important than the private. In effect, she sacrifices herself for peace in a way that parallels how so many others in Panem and District 13 sacrifice themselves for war. War will only end, Collins seems to suggest, when people are willing to do anything for peace.

CHAPTER FOUR

Isn't It Pragmatic?

Intelligent Practice, Ethics and Law

"In point of fact, the *use* of most of our thinking is to help us to *change* the world. We must for this know definitely *what* we have to change; and thus theoretic truth must at all times come before practical application. But the pragmatist writers have shown that what we here call theoretic truths is itself full of human contradictions. It will be as irrelevant unless it fits the momentary purpose in hand, as our ideas will be irrelevant when they do not fit the reality — the two factors must fit each other."
— William James, "An Interview: Pragmatism — What It Is" (Bjorkman)

"Whatever the truth is, it won't help me get food on the table."
— Katniss Everdeen, *The Hunger Games*

Toward the beginning of *The Hunger Games*, Katniss recounts how, upon being driven away from the trash bins near the bakery when seeking food for her starving family by Peeta's mother, she gives in to despair, losing the power to act. Provided with a burnt loaf of bread by Peeta, however, she regains the strength to continue, and the next day, upon seeing the first dandelion of the season, she realizes that she can save herself and her family by employing knowledge she has acquired from her father while hunting in the woods with him and building upon it. On one level, seeing the dandelion helps Katniss find a course of action, one that is essential to her physical survival. On another level, however, seeing the dandelion initiates a new way of being for Katniss: she realizes that she must be active rather than passive in order to survive, that doing something is better than doing nothing since at the very least action provides a means of acquiring new knowledge that might prove critical. In effect, she becomes a pragmatist, utilizing the information at hand to act even though that information may be incomplete or unreliable so as to put herself in a position to acquire better information and, as a result, attain more satisfactory outcomes. As the trilogy proceeds, she becomes increasingly adept at making informed decisions and is ultimately able to act in ways that not only improve her situation but that of society at large. In particular, having learned through experience that acting out of revenge only continues the cycle of violence, Katniss sets aside her emotions and acts intelligently, killing President Coin rather than Snow towards the end of *Mockingjay*. Ultimately, her pragmatism ends the conflict and division that has long dominated Panem, thus making a new beginning possible.

Pragmatism and the Intelligent Practice

According to C.S. Peirce, the nineteenth-century philosopher often credited with founding the American school of pragmatism, one can only apprehend something clearly by observing its real-world effects. Since determining real-world effects, or consequences, involves considering an object or event in a variety of situations and contexts, acquiring knowledge is a recursive process, one that involves hypothesizing, observing, and rehypothesizing based upon the new information that has been obtained. Unlike rationalism, which is essentially deductive, or empiricism, which is essentially inductive, pragmatism as introduced by Peirce and developed by others, including William James and Chauncey Wright, incorporates both types of reasoning into a dynamic process that begins with abduction, that is, the creation of an initial hypothesis that can be tested through observation. In this sense, at least, pragmatism very much resembles the scientific method, wherein abduction is used to generate hypotheses, deduction is used to formulate means of testing conjectures, and induction is used in explaining what the observations mean. Whereas the scientific method is generally used to investigate physical and social phenomena, however, pragmatism concerns itself with epistemology, particularly with the ways in which theory and practice are can be used in conjunction with one another to produce knowledge. As William James observes, "the theoretic truth upon which men base their practices is itself resultant of previous human practice to-day, based in turn upon still more previous truth, and so on in indefinite regress, so that we may think of all truth whatever

81

as containing so much human practice" (quoted in Bjorkman). To James and other pragmatists, theory and practice are inextricably linked in a way that makes it possible to discover truth through action; in other words, one can discover truth by doing.

As its name suggests, pragmatism is very much concerned with the practical, that is, with everyday efforts to determine the best course of action and put it into practice. Rather than proceed according to dogma, pragmatism calls for what John Dewey and others call "intelligent practice," that is, the eschewing of "guess and opinion" in favor of "belief authorized by inquiry" so as to take "a hand in the making of knowledge" (Dewey 75). Because it involves continually gathering new intelligence and acting upon it, intelligent practice is necessarily dynamic: in addition to requiring forethought, it requires putting provisional hypotheses into practice so that initial outcomes can be evaluated and the original hypotheses can be modified in light of newly-acquired information before again being put into practice. "Uninformed practice," in contrast, is essentially static in the sense that it does not involve going back and forth between theory and practice. Accordingly, uninformed practice includes not just impetuous action but considered action that is subjected to reconsideration as new information is acquired.

Katniss in Action: Intelligent Practice

Although moving from passive to active proves essential to Katniss's survival after her father dies, she quickly learns that action is not enough in itself: she must learn to act intelligently, putting theory into practice and using outcomes to refine her original plan. Having hunted and gathered food with her father, she knows that the woods contain the basic resources that she and her family need to survive but she does not have the knowledge or skills to procure them, being only eleven. She manages to procure the necessary skills systematically, however, venturing further into the woods each day and discovering new food sources, including game, eggs, and, fish (*Hunger Games* 51). Among her greatest strengths is her awareness of her own ignorance, something that is made evident by the way she harvests plants. When she is unsure of something, she researches it to the best of her ability, repeatedly consulting a book with detailed pictures of edible plants so as to minimize risk. She does not rely entirely upon received knowledge, however: rather, she challenges herself, continually learning and even developing "new tricks" when it comes to trading and trapping (*Hunger Games* 52).

Once Katniss enters the arena, it becomes clear that, there at least, the general ability to master new skills is the most valuable skill of all since she can easily adapt to new situations (Rees 48). As a pragmatist, she addresses problems by identifying a promising approach, implementing it, analyzing the results, and then reconsidering her original hypothesis. For example, when looking for water towards the start of the Games, she decides that since water runs downhill, she should follow the downward slopes rather than rises even though she is more comfortable at higher altitudes, valleys making her "feel trapped" (152). Although the strategy yields no immediate results, she reasons that if she were heading in the wrong direction, then Haymitch would have had her sponsors provide her with enough water to survive: in other words, she treats the fact that she is not receiving water as a piece of valuable information and acts accordingly, continuing in the same direction rather than reacting emotionally and turning back, the latter being a course of action that almost certainly would have led to her death.

Katniss's penchant for acting upon a hypothesis, assessing the results, and then rehypothesizing serves her again and again while she is in the arena, helping her to work out a plan to escape the Career pack after they have trapped her in a tree; to locate Peeta, who has hidden himself in some mud; and to gain support from sponsors by feigning a romance with Peeta. Her pragmatism even helps her come up with the scheme that forces the Gamemakers to change the rules and allow both her and Peeta to be victors. Based on a lifetime of viewing the Games, Katniss hypothesizes that the Gamemakers will do almost anything to ensure that the Games provide compelling entertainment for those living in the Capitol. This conjecture is confirmed by the things she observes in the Games, for example when the Gamemakers use fire to drive tributes into confrontations with one another in order to prevent the audience from "getting bored" and when they announce a rule change that potentially would allow both her and Peeta to be victors so that she will take risks in order to rescue him (173, 244). Since her initial conjecture about the Gamemakers' need to keep the Games interesting appears to be valid, she continues playing to the audience, feigning a romance with Peeta to keep viewers entertained, thereby buying time for her and Peeta to recover from their wounds. When the Gamemakers change the rules again after all of the tributes from other districts have been killed, announcing that only she or Peeta can be victor, Katniss continues to act intelligently in the pragmatist sense of the term: knowing that the Games will be a failure if there is no victor, she convinces the Gamemakers that she and Peeta would rather kill themselves than let there be a sole survivor, going so far as to put poisonous berries in their mouths. Rather than risk letting the apparent suicide pact succeed, the Gamemakers change the rules yet again before the berries can be swallowed, indicating that, indeed, two victors will be allowed. Through intelligent practice, it seems, Katniss has figured out how the Games work and gone on to become their master.

In *Catching Fire* Katniss again demonstrates how intelligent practice can lead to better outcomes in the way she develops alliances with other tributes in the Quarter Quell, particularly Finnick Odair. At first she is repelled by Finnick, not only because he seems decadent but because he is overly familiar with her (208): a brief conversation with him before the opening ceremonies leaves her "skin ... crawling" and in a later dream she associates him with Snow. As a result, she refuses to consider allying with Finnick, even though Haymitch insists that she at least consider the possibility (223). Her attitude towards him begins to change, however, as she acquires new information: after seeing how carefully he looks out for Mags, an elderly woman who volunteered to participate in the Quell so that Annie Cresta, another victor, will not have to, Katniss realizes she cannot hate him, and the conversations she has with him during their training have a similar effect. As a result, once she finds herself face-to-face with him at the bloodbath, she enters into an alliance with him, if only on a provisional basis, ready to turn on him should it prove to her advantage to do so. Throughout their first day together, Katniss continually assesses Finnick's actions and eventually decides that killing him "would be a little premature" since he has "been helpful so far" (278). Once Finnick resuscitates Peeta after he is electrocuted by a force field, however, she assesses her alliance with him again and decides that she will never turn on him, though she continues to doubt whether continuing the alliance with him indefinitely will best serve her interests. Her attitude changes again after he sacrifices Mags's life to save Peeta, carrying the latter to safety when they are threatened by a deadly chemical fog. Accordingly, rather than abandon Finnick when he becomes incapacitated by the fog and thus dispose of him without bloodying her hands, she treats his poisoning, even though doing so puts her and Peeta at risk of an attack from the Careers: apparently she has finally decided that having a longer-term alliance with Finnick would help her achieve her own goal, which at this point is protecting Peeta. Her assessment proves correct as he battles monkey-like mutations side-by-side with her and Peeta and so she decides to trust Finnick even more, reflecting that just a day earlier he was on her "kill list" and now she is willing to sleep while he is on guard (314). Following an exchange with him the next day in which he demonstrated a willingness to laugh at himself, Katniss decides that he is "not as vain or self-important" as she had once thought and that they could even be friends (317). As it turns out, Katniss's ability to move beyond her initial dislike of Finnick by continually reassessing him on the basis of new information proves to be key to her survival, not only in the Quarter Quell arena but later in the Capitol when he sacrifices his life so that Katniss can escape the mutts that are pursuing her and continue on her mission to kill Snow.

Katniss also moves between conjecture, action, and observation to escape the Quarter Quell arena by bringing down the force field that surrounds it. Having learned from a recording of a previous Hunger Games that arenas are enclosed in force fields and that they can be used as weapons since they forcefully repel objects, she familiarizes herself with them, not only by questioning Beetee and Wiress about their weak points, which can sometimes be located by sight (229), but by experimenting with the one that surrounds the Training Center (245). After Peeta walks into the force field surrounding the Quarter Quell arena and is electrocuted, she surmises that the fields must be comprised of energy, something that is confirmed when nuts she throws against the force field are burned. Eventually she benefits from what she has learned about force fields: finding the unconscious Beetee near the force field with a knife wired to an electrically conductive tree that is about to be hit by lightning, she deduces that Beetee intended to throw the knife through a weak spot in the force field and short it out electrically. At this point she makes a critical decision, deciding to use her bow to short out the force field rather than kill Enobaria, thus enabling agents from District 13 to effect a rescue.

Uninformed Practice

Whereas in *The Hunger Games* and *Catching Fire* Katniss demonstrates not only initiative but also the ability to adapt her understanding as new information emerges, in the beginning of *Mockingjay*, Katniss has seemingly lost all capacity for action, wondering if there is "any point in doing anything at all" (8). That Katniss is essentially paralyzed should not be surprising, of course, given the trauma she experiences in the Quarter Quell and afterwards: she has killed one person and witnessed the death of several others; she has been knocked unconscious by Johanna Mason, who also removed a tracking device from her arm with a knife, severely injuring her; her friend and ally Peeta has been captured by the Capitol; her home district has been destroyed and most of the people she has known are dead; she has been relocated to District 13, where she has been classified as "mentally disoriented"; and she has been put on morphling, a powerful medication that makes her hallucinate (*Mockingjay* 19). No longer able "to sort out what is true and what is false" because of the horrors she has endured, she recites to herself the short list of things she can be certain of such as her name and age, working towards more complicated things, rebuilding her world from little to big in an almost Cartesian manner: she has only limited success in this, however, being unable come to terms with her uncertainty about Peeta's status after he is captured by the Capitol.

Although Katniss's mind begins to clear in some ways as time passes, she remains incapable of intelligent practice throughout much of *Mockingjay*, behaving impulsively rather than thinking through how to best achieve her desired outcome and adjusting her strategies and tactics as her information changes. Despite her impetuousness, her actions often seem to have positive outcomes, for example when she breaks from her bodyguards during a bombing raid in District 8, scales a building, and shoots down a number of the attacking aircraft with her bow — actions that are captured on video and incorporated in powerful propaganda pieces. Uninformed actions like these sometimes have unforeseen negative consequences, however, as evidenced by the fact that her heroics on top of the building lead to Peeta being tortured in the Capitol. Once Katniss realizes that her performances as the Mockingjay only cause further suffering on Peeta's part, she again becomes paralyzed, seemingly incapable of formulating a new strategy for assisting the rebels without hurting Peeta.

Even after Peeta is rescued by District 13 operatives, Katniss remains reactive, unable to think things through completely or adapt her behaviors when new information becomes available because she is preoccupied by Peeta's poor mental condition. Rather than assess her goals and work out possible ways of achieving them as she does in *The Hunger Games* and *Catching Fire*, she throws herself into dangerous situations, almost being killed in District 2 while single-handedly confronting the armed survivors of the Capitol's main base there, for example. Before fully recovering from her severe injuries caused by being shot in the abdomen, she behaves impulsively again, insisting that she be included in the assault upon the Capitol only because it may give her an opportunity to revenge herself upon Snow. Rather than being given an opportunity to hunt Snow, however, she is assigned to a squad that is supposed to create footage for propaganda films rather than fight.

Pragmatist Ethics

The *Hunger Games* trilogy is also a pragmatist text in the sense that it suggests that morality is neither absolute nor relative but instead contingent upon outcomes and how they are achieved. Rather than define morality in terms of "ends" justifying "means," Collins suggests that "ends" are ethically irrelevant since they are merely professed aims and have no concrete status. If "ends" are too abstract and unstable to provide a legitimate basis for action, "means" can only be evaluated in relation to reasonably expected outcomes and judged accordingly.

The issue of whether any means can be justified by reasonably expected outcomes first comes into focus during the siege of the Nut. When Gale proposes using bombs to create avalanches that will trap soldiers and workers within the Capitol's primary base, Katniss objects, arguing that the death those trapped in the mountain will face is too horrifying and that casualties will include not only people who have been coerced into serving the Capitol but some who have actively supported the rebellion. In response, Gale makes a classic ends-justify-the-means argument, insisting that war always involves collateral damage, the sacrifice of innocents, and inflicting tremendous suffering upon others, and that, in any case, the rebels have every right to employ the sorts of tactics the Capitol has been using against them. Ultimately, the rebels try to balance military needs with humanitarian concerns by maintaining a potential means of egress for any survivors, and although Katniss remains unsatisfied with the ethics of the decision since it will still result in the deaths of many non-combatants, the operation succeeds, not only in sparing the lives of the rebel soldiers who would have been lost in a direct assault but also in shortening the war, an outcome that presumably saves lives on both sides. From a pragmatic point of view, at least, the assault upon the Nut appears to be justified to the extent that one could reasonably expect it to result in a net saving of lives and an overall reduction in human suffering.

The personal dilemmas Katniss faces as she pursues Snow can also be better understood in terms of pragmatics than in terms of either absolute morality or relativism. If, as suggested earlier, Katniss's vendetta against Snow leads her to involve others in a mission that cannot possibly succeed since it entails both her and Peeta, two of the most recognizable people in Panem, passing unnoticed through crowds that have been warned of their presence, then her actions are neither intelligent in the pragmatic sense nor ethically justifiable. Not every action she takes while pursuing Coin is uninformed or ethically insupportable, however. Her decision to not only tolerate Peeta's presence in her squad but also become proactive in helping him to recover seems to be both intelligent and ethically sound since she can reasonably hope for a positive outcome given the fact that his condition has been steadily improving, and because it is she herself who is most at risk. Other actions she takes are more questionable, however, such as her shooting an unarmed woman in her own home when she sees that the woman recognizes her and is about to call for help. Given that the woman is alone in her apartment and poses no threat, Katniss's killing of her is hard to justify. The indiscriminate killing she engages in while advancing towards the president's mansion is even more problematic. Although one could argue that she is in a kill-or-be-killed situation and therefore has little choice, Katniss puts herself in this situation because of her obsession with killing Snow: from a pragmatic point-of-view, Katniss's shooting of "[e]very-thing that moves" is unethical since she cannot reasonably expect to succeed in her mission.

The Ethics of Inaction

In addition to considering the ethical implications of various types of action, Collins explores the ethics of inaction, suggesting that refusing to act can be just as significant as acting. Like William James, who in "The Will to Believe" argues that "[m]oral questions immediately present themselves as questions whose solution cannot wait for sensible proof," Collins suggests that there are times when one must choose to act even though the information available may be incomplete, so long as one is willing to change one's course of action as better information is acquired (341). In general Katniss does just that: although she sometimes behaves impetuously, such as when she takes Prim's place in the Hunger Games or faces the armed survivors of the Nut by herself, she usually considers numerous possibilities and is willing to change course if necessary. For example, although reluctant to be the Mockingjay because she knows that joining the rebellion will put people at risk, including those she loves the most, she agrees to take on the role when she realizes that the Capitol must be defeated no matter what the cost. The decision is provisional, however, and upon recognizing that District 13 is in some ways as bad as the Capitol, she effectively deserts the rebel army and begins acting independently again.

On occasion, however, she finds herself unable to act, for example when she sees a boy and girl running for their lives through the woods outside of District 12 and becomes "immobilized" (*Hunger Games* 82). Rather than try to help, Katniss and Gale only watch as the girl is captured and the boy is killed. Reflecting upon this later, Katniss wonders if she and Gale "could have helped them escape" if they had "moved quickly" enough (82). Eventually she takes moral responsibility for her inaction and apologizes to the girl, who she later learns is named Lavinia, telling her that she should have tried to save her (118). Collins's representation of Katniss's misgivings about failing to have acted raises important ethical questions about the circumstances under which one is obliged to take risks on behalf of others. Although Lavinia signals to Katniss that any attempt to save her most likely would have resulted in Katniss's own capture or death, Katniss continues to feel guilty about her inaction, counting Lavinia as one of the many who has died because of her (*Mockingjay* 274). The blame Katniss places upon herself seems to be undeserved, however, at least from a pragmatic perspective, since it is unlikely that any action she or Gale might have taken would have succeeded in saving the boy and girl. The same seems to hold true when Finnick is killed before her eyes by the lizard-like mutts that are coming for her. Although Katniss feels as if she has "abandoned" Finnick and other members of her squad, leaving them to suffer horrible deaths, there is nothing she could have done to save them, and therefore her failure to take action cannot be considered unethical (312). Indeed, Katniss comes to recognize this on some level, shining a light in Finnick's direction just in time to see him decapitated and then forcing herself to move on, telling herself that there will be time for "human feelings" later (313).

Katniss's decision to kill Coin rather than Snow can also be better understood in terms of pragmatist ethics than in terms of absolute morality or moral relativity. Upon returning to the Capitol after Prim's death, Katniss has no intention of assassinating Coin: she blames Snow for the death of her sister and has every intention of executing him herself, Coin having "saved him" for her (350). At this point her insistence upon being the one to kill Snow seems to be motivated primarily by a desire to revenge the death of her sister. Even though such a desire may be understandable given the horrors Snow has visited not only upon Katniss and her family but upon all of Panem, executing Snow would only be justifiable from a pragmatic point of view if the action could be reasonably expected to significantly benefit either Katniss or others. Rather than bringing her any long-term psychological relief, however, it seems likely that revenging herself upon Snow, who is no longer in power and therefore can no longer harm others, would only make her psychological situation worse since his name would just be added to the long list of the dead that has haunted her since the opening pages of *Mockingjay*. As Katniss herself suggests, once Snow is dead, "nothing will be left" but for her to die herself (351).

Executing Snow is unlikely to benefit Panem either because in doing so, Katniss would only again be serving as "a piece" in President Coin's "game," helping her in her efforts to become the unchallenged ruler of all Panem (*Mockingjay* 59). To Coin, Katniss is a political obstacle since Katniss, who "may have more influence than any other single person," neither likes her nor approves of her (266). By arranging for Katniss to execute Snow publicly while dressed in her Mockingjay outfit, Coin hopes to symbolically put an end to not only the Capitol's rule of Panem but also of Katniss's career as a public figure. Once the Mockingjay kills Snow, the revolution is complete and the new regime, led by Coin, can take over.

Although Katniss has long recognized that Coin is just as much of a tyrant as Snow — that the "republic" that the rebels have been fighting for will never come to be as long as Coin has political supremacy — she has been too damaged by the things that have transpired to offer any sort of public challenge to her when she assumes control of post-war Panem (*Mockingjay* 83). When Coin demands that the surviving tributes vote on whether to reinstitute the Hunger Games, however, Katniss realizes that she must take action, that she has a moral responsibility to do whatever she can to end the cycle of violence and destruction that has been going on in Panem for more than 75 years. Realizing that arguing against reinstituting the Hunger Games in Coin's presence will only make Coin more wary of her, she "think[s] everything through" and votes for a final Games, hoping that her compliance will lead Coin to let her guard down and make action against her possible (370). Katniss's strategy works: no longer feeling threatened by Katniss, Coin makes a public appearance at what is supposed to be Snow's execution and ends up being killed herself. No longer a piece of anyone else's games, Katniss takes definitive action because to do any less would be unethical.

Katniss, Pragmatism and Law

One of the things that makes Katniss unusual is her willingness to operate outside of the law on a regular basis, particularly because she lives in a totalitarian society where even the smallest of transgressions is severely punished. For her, law has no moral component, instead being a matter of what the hated government requires and what it forbids, and therefore her compliance with it or lack thereof is a practical matter rather than an ethical one. Even though she engages in criminal behavior every time she leaves District 12 to hunt in the woods, she does not regard herself as a criminal; on the contrary, for her it would be criminal to let her family starve when she could save them by procuring food for them on her own. In this sense she is very much a pragmatist, defining for herself what is right and wrong and then endeavoring to be true to herself, even as she recognizes that her own sense of right and wrong is subject to change and that she may have to modify her actions accordingly.

Katniss is not alone in denying the law any moral authority over her: virtually everyone in her district breaks laws in order to survive (17). What differentiates her from everyone else is the fact that she does so in such a flagrant manner, not only poaching in the woods on a regular basis — something punishable by death — but selling illegally acquired goods directly to local Peacekeepers and even the mayor. Although her illicit activities are initially motivated by the need to provide for her family, she soon becomes accustomed to living outside of the law, continuing to hunt and violate other laws even after she has no need to do so because as a victor she receives enough money from the government to meet the material needs of herself and her family. Indeed, at times she seems to take pleasure in flouting the law, if only because it gives her a sense of empowerment.

That Katniss and the other citizens of District 12 regularly disregard the law and even show hostility towards it reveals just how significant the disconnect between the public and the government is: the laws the Capitol imposes are not only contrary to the desires of the public but also inconsistent with its needs, many of the people having no legal means of providing for themselves adequately. As a result, the laws become impossible to enforce on a consistent basis, as evidenced not only by Katniss's illegal activities but also by the existence of a permanent black market in an abandoned warehouse that is not only tolerated by Peacekeepers but frequented by them. The government even lacks moral authority over things like prostitution since its policies with regards to food have made it the only alternative to starvation for some. Katniss herself reflects that if she had been a little older when her father died, she might have joined those who are "forced to feed their families by selling their bodies" (115). "Instead," she adds, she "learned to hunt."

For all of their disregard for the laws imposed upon them by the Capitol, the people of District 12 are not a lawless people, having developed an informal code of conduct that governs many of their interactions with one another and helps them to maintain a civil society despite the suffering and privation. Although people are expected to be self-sufficient, providing for themselves and their families, they support one another when they can, helping to feed Greasy Sae's developmentally disabled grandchild and coming together to assist Gale after he is almost beaten to death for poaching. They tend not to ask things of other people and dislike being in other people's debt, as do the people from District 11. They also shun Peacekeepers, racketeers, and others who would dominate or exploit them to the extent that they can do so safely and do not inform upon others when they break the law even though doing so presumably might bring them some material benefit. They even have a gesture for signaling collective approval, saluting Katniss when she volunteers to replace Prim in the Hunger Games, and have developed an informal marriage ceremony to sanction partnerships that means more to them than the official ceremonies that take place in the Justice Building.

Katniss is not lawless, either: although she does not hold herself accountable to the Capitol's laws, she adheres to the District's code of conduct very closely, assisting others when she can, shunning those who hurt others out of greed or maliciousness, refusing to inform upon others, and, most notably perhaps, avoiding being in debt to other people to the extent that she can. Even when in the arena she is very much aware of society's expectations of her and she conducts herself accordingly so as not to shame herself, her family, or her District. For example, when during her first Hunger Games she learns that rules have been changed so that both tributes from a single district can be victors, she realizes that she has no choice but to ally herself with Peeta: "Whatever doubts I've had about him dissipate because if either of us took the other's life now we'd be pariahs when we returned to District 12. In fact, I know if I were watching I'd loathe any tribute who didn't immediately ally with their district partner" (*Hunger Games* 247). As a member of the District 12 community, Katniss feels bound by its rules, even if they are unspoken, gauging the community's expectations of her according to what hers would have been if she were at home watching the Games. Her resolve to abide by District 12's rules is soon put to the test when she has to decide whether to let Peeta bleed to death or violate the unwritten rules of the Games by entering into what appears to be a suicide pact with another tribute and forcing the Gamemakers to allow two victors. To her there is no doubt as to what she should do: as someone who has become comfortable living outside of the law, she does not hesitate to do her duty to herself, Peeta, and her community.

Katniss's willingness to operate outside of the law is a critical factor again when she assassinates Coin. Again she puts her sense of social responsibility ahead of the law, doing what seems right to her rather than what is legal. Ironically, she knows that since she will have no opportunity to escape after killing Coin, she will ultimately have to submit to the law and will very likely be executed by the new government of Panem. Recognizing that Coin is as malevolent as the now innocuous Snow — the other side of the coin, as it were — she makes a pragmatic choice, weighing the costs against the benefits, and then acts decisively.

Pragmatics and Social Responsibility

The seventeen-year-old who assassinates President Coin is very much the same person as the eleven-year-old who begins to hunt illegally in order to save herself and her family from starvation, the most significant difference being that she develops a sense of social responsibility. Rather than remain passive and accept things as they are, Katniss considers her options, takes action, observes their effects, and then rethinks her position before taking action again. She does so because she continually seeks to improve outcomes, whether she is trying to protect Prim in *The Hunger Games* or all of Panem from a cruel dictatorship in *Mockingjay*. In short, she is a pragmatist, engaging in intelligent practice so as to achieve her aims. She also seems to be a pragmatist when it comes to epistemology and ethics, rejecting absolute truth and morality in favor of situated beliefs and values. To reject absolute truth and morality is not necessarily to be a relativist, however: rather than accept the idea that she can never know anything for certain and therefore be deterred from taking action, Katniss engages in intelligent practice and works towards right action. Not surprisingly, perhaps, this is just what Collins hopes her readers will do: think about whatever situation they find themselves in, "decide whether it's right or wrong," and, if it's wrong, decide "what part they are going to play" in changing it (Neary). Through Katniss she tries to teach her readers that pragmatism involves not only knowing what is right but doing right.

CHAPTER FIVE

"Real or Not Real?"

Reality Television and the Hunger Games *Trilogy*

> "The Hunger Games is a reality television program. An Extreme one, but that's what it is."
> — Suzanne Collins, "Q & A with Hunger Games Author Suzanne Collins" (Hudson)

According to Suzanne Collins, *The Hunger Games* trilogy began with the recognition of a connection between reality programming and real-world events such as war:

> One night, I was lying in bed, and I was channel surfing between reality TV programs and actual war coverage. On one channel, there's a group of young people competing for I don't even know; and on the next, there's a group of young people fighting in an actual war. I was really tired, and the lines between these stories started to blur in a very unsettling way. That's the moment when Katniss's story came to me [Margolis 2008].

The unsettledness Collins felt seems to result from a number of factors, most obviously a concern with the ways in which popular programming desensitizes people to violence and conflict. She finds reality television particularly "disturbing" since it often involves "people being humiliated, or brought to tears, or suffering physically" (Hudson). The problem with this, she indicates, is that when audiences "see real tragedy playing out on, say, the news, it doesn't have the impact it should."

One could, of course, argue that the *Hunger Games* trilogy is so compelling for the very reasons that reality television itself is — because it offers a "voyeuristic thrill" similar to that of programs such as *Survivor*, *The Bachelor*, and *The Real World* (Hudson). Collins does more than simply depict a particularly horrific reality television program from the future, however. By presenting the Games from the perspective of someone who has both watched them and played them, Collins provides an inside look at the reality genre, one that exposes its social and ideological functions. In particular, she uses Katniss Everdeen's first-hand account of her experiences to suggest that, in addition to providing entertainment, reality programs act as "socializing agents," to borrow April Roth's terms, playing an essential role in maintaining "the dominant ideology" (35). Though largely unscripted, such programs are constructed, edited, and in some cases digitally altered so as to provide compelling narratives that both affirm prevailing beliefs and naturalize them by embedding them in contexts that represent themselves as real. As Christopher Wright observes, it is the latter that makes these programs such effective ideological agents: reality shows are fictions that present themselves as fact (3).

The Structure and Ideology of the Games

Before addressing the politics of the *Hunger Games* trilogy, it is important to examine the Games themselves in detail, identifying both their structure and their ideological implications. In the first book of the trilogy, Collins indicates the Capitol devised the Hunger Games following a rebellion involving all thirteen of Panem's districts. Every year, the twelve districts that survived the war are forced to send two tributes to the Games — a boy and a girl, each between the ages of twelve and eighteen. These children, who are selected by lottery, are transported to the Capitol, offered minimal training in survival skills and weaponry, and then sent into an elaborate, outdoor arena where they must fend for themselves. They are told nothing about the nature of arena in advance — whether it will be wet or dry, forested or frozen, large or small — though they can generally expect to find weapons and possibly other supplies in a giant, golden Cornucopia near the arena's center. Once the Games begin, the tributes are subjected to hunger, thirst, and various dangers such as predators, floods, fires, and earthquakes. The greatest danger generally proves to be the other tributes, however, who kill each other off quickly. Alliances are permitted, though they are generally short-lived since only one tribute can survive in the end. Deaths are signaled by cannons and bodies removed quickly; in the evening images of those killed are projected in the sky so that tributes can know specifically who remains. Some tributes receive food, medicine, or other supplies from sponsors, the gifts being delivered by parachute at the discretion of a mentor from their home district. Otherwise the rules allow for no outside involvement, though the Gamemakers reserve the right to intervene themselves to force confrontations between tributes or prevent certain actions such as cannibalism. The last person alive is declared the victor of the Games and is promised a life of relative ease, though he or she is required to mentor future tributes and participate in other game-related events.

In terms of structure of the game itself, the Hunger Games very much resemble *Survivor*, arguably the most successful of contemporary reality programs, which also pits players against one another in an outdoor arena. Although *Survivor* contestants do not engage in hand-to-hand combat and are not placed in deadly situations, they are subjected to various forms of privation and required to participate in physical competitions that sometimes involve violence, such as when contestants must knock each other off of platforms or wrestle over objects. Both games also are at once social and individual since winning typically involves forming alliances that can only be temporary since only one contestant can win. Most importantly, perhaps, both *Survivor* and the Hunger Games are structured so as to reinforce a particular set of beliefs and values. In the case of *Survivor*, according to Graham St. John, the game is a "powerful pedagogical vehicle for transmitting the rules and appropriate conduct for market capitalism (ruthless individualism, corporatism, and acquisitive materialism) to both players and home viewers," something it accomplishes by presenting a spectacle that seems to reward certain types of behaviors and punish others (21). The basic lessons of the game are reinforced by the way the game is concluded: the victor is selected from a group of finalists by the losing contestants, the losers being expected to accept that they have been outplayed and that the betrayals they experienced were justifiable because money was at stake. Losers like the first season's Susan Hawk who do not accept that those who defeated them are ultimately deserving are regarded as "sore losers" by other players and treated with disdain ("Season Finale"). *Survivor* host Jeff Probst goes so far as to refer to such people as "bitter bitches" on his official blog for the program. The Hunger Games have a similar dénouement, their outcomes ultimately being affirmed by a ritual that involves those who have lost publicly accepting their defeat, though in the case of the Hunger Games it is not the players who do this but the Districts from which they come, the districts being forced to publicly celebrate the victory even though it entailed the death of its own children.

Whereas *Survivor*'s primary ideological function is to affirm capitalism, celebrating the profit motive, the Hunger Games' function is to affirm the Capitol's absolute dominance over the districts through its control of resources. As its very name suggests, the Hunger Games center on scarcity, every resource in the arena being carefully managed by the Gamemakers, who represent the Capitol itself. Rather than simply set up certain rules and parameters and let the Games play themselves out, the Gamemakers manage everything from food and water to temperature on an ongoing basis, demonstrating that their power is absolute. In the first book of the trilogy, for example, the Gamemakers use medicine desperately needed by Peeta to induce Katniss into a confrontation with the other players and later cut off water supplies to force the tributes to the lake. The Gamemakers' absolute control over resources in the arena is presumably meant to mirror the Capitol's control over the resources of Panem, the Games thereby reinforcing the existing social order by reproducing it symbolically in the arena. By demonstrating that their control of resources gives them control over people's lives, the Capitol is able to convey the idea that a widespread rebellion could not possibly be sustained, and that uprisings would result in further suffering rather than social change.

The Capitol also uses the Games to reinforce the idea that it cannot by resisted physically, occasionally killing tributes "just to remind players they can" (*Hunger Games* 175). Even "Careers"—that is, tributes from Districts 1, 2, and 4 who trained almost from birth to fight in the arena—have no chance of surviving if the Gamemakers decide to kill them. In the second Quarter Quell, for example, the Gamemakers transform a picturesque mountain into a volcano in order to demonstrate the Capitol's power, killing more than half of the Career Pack. The importance the Capitol places in being able to arbitrarily kill tributes at any time within the arena becomes clear in the beginning of *Catching Fire* when President Snow discusses with Katniss the significance of the poison berries she and Peeta take at the end of the 74th Hunger Games in their apparent suicide attempt. Whereas Katniss believes that the taking of the berries presented the Gamemakers with two choices—either letting the two of them commit suicide or letting the two of them live—Snow reveals that the Gamemakers had a third choice, one he believes they should have opted for: "If the Head Gamemaker, Seneca Crane, had any brains, he'd have blown you to dust right there" (*Catching Fire* 20). As Snow's words indicate, the Capitol cannot tolerate any form of resistance, even suicide, if the games are going to have the desired ideological effect: it must always exercise power in absolute terms.

There is, of course, a critical difference in the ways that the Hunger Games convey their ideological message and the way contemporary reality programs such as *Survivor* do: whereas the ideological content of contemporary reality television in the United States is largely determined by market forces, the ideological content of the Hunger Games is determined by a centralized government, and therefore the Games serve as a form of state propaganda. Indeed, the Capitol highlights the ideological significance of the Games before they begin by having the mayors of each district read an official history of Panem, which includes an account of an earlier rebellion against the Capitol and explains that the Games exist as a reminder of the Capitol's power. As Katniss observes, "Whatever words they use, the real message is clear: 'Look how we take your children and sacrifice them and there's nothing you can do. If you lift a finger, we will destroy every last one of you'" (*Hunger Games* 16). The Capitol is even more explicit about the ideological content of the Games when it comes to the Quarter Quells. These special games, which are held every 25 years, are designed to convey a particular message to the districts. For example, in the first Quarter Quell, each district was "made to hold an election and vote on the tributes who would represent it" in order to remind people that the districts' children were dying because of the decision the districts made "to initiate violence" (*Catching Fire* 171). Significantly, the third Quarter Quell, which coincides with a period in which a number of districts are rebelling, draws tributes from those who have survived previous Games in order to remind "the rebels that even the strongest among them cannot overcome the power of the Capitol," according to Snow (*Catching Fire* 172). As Katniss observes, however, even though the means of selecting tributes for the Quells were supposedly determined when the games were instituted 75 years earlier, the message of the third Quell seems to be "too perfect an answer for the troubles that face the Capitol" at the time, suggesting that the Capitol has rewritten the rules for its own purposes (*Catching Fire* 175).

Fashion-Themed Reality Shows and the Objectification Process

The ways in which Collins represents fashion-themed reality programming in the *Hunger Games* trilogy is also worth considering in detail since Collins addresses the fashion industry in all three novels, ultimately suggesting that it has a powerful influence on the way people think and act. Indeed, the pre-game programming that documents Katniss's transformation into a sexual object can itself be regarded as commentary on the ideological implications of programs such as *Extreme Makeover*, *Project Runway*, and *America's Top Model*. By exploring the objectification process through the consciousness of Katniss as she is prepared for the Games by Cinna and his associates, Collins illustrates the challenge women face in retaining a sense of self while they are being constructed as sexual objects by society at large. Although for a time Katniss herself gets caught up in the excitement of her transformation, she eventually recognizes that being sexualized is ultimately oppressive rather than empowering since it reinforces a system that reserves agency for men.

The transformation process is presented as being initially shocking to Katniss, both physically and psychologically. Upon arriving in the Capitol as a tribute, she is sent to the Remake Center, where she is washed down and entirely depilated, leaving her feeling like a "plucked bird" (*Hunger Games* 61). Unlike most contestants on programs like *Extreme Makeover*, however, Katniss feels alienated by rather than appreciative of her transformation, highlighting the sense of vulnerability she feels and describing her team as "total idiots" (*Hunger Games* 63). Although she responds much more positively to her stylist, Cinna, since he does not seem to regard her "as a piece of meat to be prepared for a platter," she is still suspicious of him, fearing that despite his respectful, calm demeanor he may be "a complete madman" (*Hunger Games* 64).

Gradually Katniss comes to accept her transformation and even appreciate the fact that being an object of desire affords certain benefits, commenting, "The Hunger Games aren't supposed to be a beauty contest, but the best-looking tributes always seem to pull more sponsors" (58). She manages to retain her sense of self despite her objectification, however, at least until she sees her own reflection just before her interview with Caesar Flickerman: "The creature standing before me in the full-length mirror

100

has come from another world. Where skin shimmers and eyes flash and apparently they make their clothes from jewels. Because my dress, oh, my dress is entirely covered in reflective precious gems ... I am not pretty. I am not beautiful. I am as radiant as the sun" (*Hunger Games* 119–20). As the shift in subject from the "creature" to "I" suggests, Katniss internalizes her objectification, regarding herself as a "creature." Events that immediately follow confirm this: once onstage, the previously self-assured, independent young woman becomes a "silly girl spinning in a sparkling dress" (*Hunger Games* 136). Upon leaving the stage, however, Katniss quickly regains her perspective, apparently realizing that in allowing herself to be objectified she has compromised herself and her values. By the time she returns to the Training Center, her giddiness has become anger, and she assaults Peeta for publicly declaring his desire for her in his interview: in her view, by making her an "object of love," he has made her seem foolish and weak (*Hunger Games* 136). Even though Haymitch eventually convinces Katniss that presenting herself as a "heartbreaker" gives her the best chance of winning sponsors, going forward she no longer gets caught up in such performances, realizing that it is a just a means to an end and not part of who she really is (*Hunger Games* 135). The same is true in the novels that follow: whether playing a child bride-to-be in *Catching Fire* or a superhero-like leader of the rebellion in *Mockingjay*, she no longer confuses performance with identity. Like an outstanding contestant in a reality show, she has a double consciousness of sorts, existing at once within the Games and beyond them, never fully losing her sense of self. Her experiences in the pre-game ceremonies, processions, and interviews teach her that gender is just another performance, one that does not necessarily define her entire identity (Butler 1990, 137).

The Showmance

The challenges involved in maintaining the double-consciousness necessary to succeed in the Games become most evident in Katniss's relationship with Peeta, a relationship that begins as a "showmance," that is, as a romantic relationship that develops within a reality program (Ryan 2011, 105). In the case of Katniss and Peeta, the showmance is initially strategic: although Peeta has real feelings for Katniss, he declares his love for her in an interview that is broadcast just before the Games begin in the hopes that it will increase sponsor interest, leading to more gifts while in the arena. Katniss, who has no advance knowledge of the scheme, agrees to play along with it once Haymitch convinces her that perceptions are more important than reality in the Games since, in the end, they are just "a big show" (*Hunger Games* 133). Once they are in the arena, there is initially little opportunity for the two of them to develop their showmance further: indeed, Peeta seems to betray Katniss by allying himself with the Careers and helping them to hunt her down. Even then, though, Katniss tries to maintain the appearance of a romance, giving the cameras a "knowing smile" as if Peeta's apparent betrayal is part of their plan (164). It is only after the rules of the Games are officially changed to allow for two victors that the showmance becomes central again as Katniss plays up the romance in order to obtain gifts from their sponsors. As her relationship with Peeta develops, however, Katniss has increasing difficulty in separating her performance from her real feelings. After nearly dying in an effort to get medicine desperately needed by Peeta, she begins to realize how attached she has become to him, how her need to be with him is no longer "about the sponsors" but about "him" (*Hunger Games* 292).

Katniss recovers her sense of purpose when she and Peeta begin to starve while waiting out a storm. Knowing that the showmance is much more important than any real romance, at least in the context of the Games, she begins playing to the cameras again, "ramp[ing] up the romance" in the hopes of receiving food from sponsors (*Hunger Games* 295). The performance succeeds and the couple is rewarded with a feast so generous that the leftovers last them for days.

Eventually Katniss's recognition that her showmance with Peeta has emerged as the Games' primary narrative allows her to manipulate not only sponsors but the Gamemakers themselves (Vizzini 103). When, towards the end of the Games it is announced that the earlier rule change has been revoked and that there can only be one survivor — that either Katniss or Peeta will have to die — Katniss is able to convince the Gamemakers that she and Peeta would both rather die than survive alone. As Katniss realizes, a double suicide would subvert the ideological purpose of the Games, which is to dramatize the government's absolute power over its citizens: in killing themselves, Katniss and Peeta would be demonstrating agency, albeit in a very limited way, something that is entirely unacceptable to the Capitol. Moreover, a double suicide would deny the Capitol a victor to parade through the districts as a living reminder of their power over life and death. Consequently, the Gamemakers capitulate and both Katniss and Peeta are declared winners, Katniss in effect defeating the Capitol at its own game.

Interactivity and the Subversion of the Games

One distinguishing characteristic of both contemporary reality programming and the Hunger Games is the extent to which they allow for viewer participation. In *Big Brother*, for example, viewers participate in decisions that affect conditions within the household, and in *American Idol* viewers help decide which contestants are eliminated. Even *Survivor* has an interactive element, with viewers voting on a $100,000 Player of the Season award in some of the later seasons. By incorporating viewer input into the program, producers give their games another dimension, one that theoretically, at least, increases the viewers' level of engagement by making them part of the show (Simon 195). Audience participation also increases engagement by establishing relationships between viewers and contestants, at least to the extent that contestants such as *Survivor*'s Boston Rob play to the camera in order to win additional prizes or gain some advantage within the game. The Hunger Games allow for viewer participation in a similar manner: tributes who find ways to connect with viewers are often sponsored by them. Indeed, one of the reasons Katniss succeeds in her first Hunger Games is because she is able to play to the cameras when necessary, knowing that gifts from sponsors depend upon how she is perceived by them. Even before the Games begin, Katniss plays to the camera, her appearance and deportment in pre-game ceremonies and in her interview with Caesar Flickerman giving her an advantage over less appealing tributes. Certainly Haymitch recognizes the importance of making a good impression upon viewers in pre-game ceremonies, insisting that both Katniss and Peeta do exactly as their prep teams and stylists advise.

In theory, at least, the Games' interactive elements should increase their ideological power since the more viewers participate in the Games themselves, the more likely the Games' lessons are to be impressed upon them. As Tarleton Gillepsie suggests, however, the fact that producers have the power to determine the "ideological qualities" of a program does not mean that they can control its "ideological effects," if only because producers cannot control how programs are perceived, interpreted, and enacted: like all forms of mass media, reality programs resist "discursive closure" and allow for "alternative readings," including subversive ones. Katniss's emergence as "the Mockingjay" is a case in point. To Katniss, the gold pin of a "bird in flight" that her friend Madge Undersee gives her to wear in the Hunger Games means little at first — she does not even recognize the bird as a mockingjay — and the Capitol, for its part, regards it only as an innocuous "district token" (*Hunger Games* 38, 143). To viewers, however, the mockingjay becomes a symbol of the resistance, largely because they associate it with Katniss's defiance of the Capitol while she is in the arena. That it is viewers who ultimately determine the Games meanings should not be surprising: as Gillepsie suggests ideological content cannot be fixed by producers, however much they try. What is surprising, perhaps, is the way that viewers are able to utilize the Games themselves to promote rebellion. In effect, viewers are able to use the Games' interactivity to subvert the producer's ideological intent: sponsoring Katniss while she is in the arena becomes a means of defying the Capitol's power since to them Katniss has come to represent resistance. District 11 does just this, sending Katniss bread even though she is from another district. As Katniss recognizes, such a gift is unprecedented, an act of defiance in itself since it undercuts the efforts of the Capitol to keep the districts divided.

In *Catching Fire* Katniss finally learns that she has become a symbol of resistance as a result of the Hunger Games when two refugees from District 8 she encounters in the woods outside present her with a piece of bread with the mockingjay symbol baked into it in order to show that they are part of the Rebellion. When Katniss fails to recognize the symbol's meaning, the refugees are "genuinely surprised" (140) and go on to express how amazed they are to have met the "girl who was on fire" (23), one of them saying, "I can't believe we actually got to meet you. You're practically all anyone's talked about since —" (149). The woman is so overwhelmed by being in Katniss's presence that Katniss has to complete the sentence for her: "I know. I know. Since I pulled out those berries" (149). It is only at this point that Katniss begins to realize what she has come to mean to those who would defy the government — that she has become a larger-than-life figure who has the power to influence others. In *Mockingjay*, Katniss discovers that her actions during the Quarter Quell have made her an even more important public figure — the living incarnation of the Mockingjay. Although Katniss initially has difficulty in accepting the new identity viewers have assigned her, she comes to appreciate how important she has become to the rebel cause when she visits a hospital in District 8 and sees how her presence brings those who are suffering not only comfort but inspiration. She also realizes that she had no choice in the matter, commenting, "I was their Mockingjay long before I accepted the role" (90).

The Games and the Capitol

So far we have discussed the Hunger Games significance primarily in relation to the districts, the Games providing the government with a means of reinforcing the idea that they have absolute power over the populace (Ryan 2011, 102). The Games seem to have an additional function in the Capitol itself, where the decadent population has come to expect the government to provide them with entertainment, just as the citizens of ancient Rome did, according to Juvenal (89). Indeed, Collins indicates herself in an interview with her publisher that she had ancient Rome in mind:

> In keeping with the classical roots, I send my tributes into an updated version of the Roman gladiator games, which entails a ruthless government forcing people to fight to the death as popular entertainment. The world of Panem, particularly the Capitol, is loaded with Roman references. Panem itself comes from the expression "Panem et Circenses" which translates into "Bread and Circuses."

To those living in the Capitol, it seems, the Games serve as a form of distraction: citizens are so caught up in the artificial drama that plays out on television that they pay little attention to the fact that their "president" is, in fact, a dictator who attained power by murdering his rivals or that their affluence comes at the cost of great privation elsewhere.

The Hunger Games do more than just distract its viewers in the Capitol, however; they also affirm the existing political structure by validating the idea that those on top are there because they have proven themselves most worthy, and the idea that ruthlessness is not only acceptable as a means of acquiring power but even necessary. These ideas seem to pertain not only to the government in relation to the people but, more broadly, to Capitol in relation to the rest of Panem: the Games reinforce the idea that those living in the Capitol are deserving of the privileges they enjoy, privileges denied to those living in the districts, and that their government's ruthlessness in maintaining these privileges is justified.

Although Collins draws from the past in order to create a story set in a dystopian future, the *Hunger Games* trilogy is really about the present, as all such fiction is. In particular, Collins seems to be commenting upon present-day America as she sees it, a nation that allows itself to be not only distracted by reality television and celebrity drama but manipulated by it (Ryan 2011, 110–1). Like those living in the Capitol, Americans by-and-large are more likely interested in who wins *American Idol* or how Whitney Houston died than they are about the consequences a U.S.–led embargo on Iran will have upon civilians in Iran or how the presence of U.S. troops in Haiti are likely to affect governance in that nation. Artificial drama, it seems, has become more important than real-life suffering, and so suffering continues, unacknowledged and unchecked by the very people who benefit from it. More than that, though, Collins suggests that programs such as *Cops*, *Survivor*, *Extreme Makeover*, and *The Biggest Loser* have a powerful ideological effect, affirming Americans' sense that they are worthy of the privileges they enjoy and that almost any sort of action can be justified in maintaining them. Like the Hunger Games, these programs accomplish this by dehumanizing people: they stage conflicts, elicit negative behaviors, and then construct narratives around those behaviors that present them as authentic, ultimately suggesting that people get what they deserve.

The Hunger Games *trilogy as Media Criticism*

As Darren Franich suggests, *The Hunger Games* offers "incisive satire of reality television shows," targeting tropes such the makeover and the showmance. The *Hunger Games* trilogy does more than just parody shows such as *Survivor*, *Extreme Makeover*, and *Project Runway*, however: it also offers indirect commentary on the ways in which such programming influences people's beliefs and behaviors through its representation of the Hunger Games as an ideological agent. More than that, though, the trilogy serves as a form of media criticism, one of Collins's primary concerns being how to make her readers, particularly children, more conscious of the way media informs their thinking. In particular, she hopes to help them differentiate between "what is real and what is not real" by exposing reality television's political and ideological functions in her work (Hudson). By presenting a detailed account of the ways in which reality programming affects the ways in which her protagonist thinks and acts, Collins demonstrates how accepting what one sees on television at face value makes one vulnerable to manipulation and control. Ultimately Collins suggests that only way to protect oneself is by approaching things critically, by recognizing that even unscripted, reality-based programming are constructions, and that as such, they reflect the beliefs and values of their producers.

CHAPTER SIX

Dystopia with a Difference

The Lessons of Panem and District 13

> "I think it's crucial that young readers are considering scenarios about humanity's future because those challenges are about to land in their laps. In the *Hunger Games*, I hope they question elements like global warming and the mistreatment of the environment but also questions like: How do you feel about the fact that some people take their next meal for granted and so many other people are starving in the world? What do you think about the choices your government, past and present, or other governments around the world make? What's your relationship to reality television vs. your relationship with the news, for instance? Was there anything in the books that disturbed you because they reflected aspects of your own life, and if there was, what can you do about it, because, you know what, even if they're not of your own making, these issues and how to deal with them will become your responsibility."
>
> — Suzanne Collins, "Book Review Podcast: Suzanne Collins," *New York Times Review of Books*

Dystopian fictions are essentially political, exploring particular social issues by setting up a horrific alternative world in which those issues figure largely. Many of these fictions present themselves as cautionary tales, that is, as warnings about the consequences of continuing certain policies or behaviors. As Fredric Jameson suggests, such dystopias often read as "sermons," because of their overt didacticism and impassioned delivery (7): they can be provocative, even striking, but are rarely engaging on an emotional level, being driven more by plot than characterization. The *Hunger Games* trilogy represents a different type of dystopia, however, one that is literary rather than polemic. Instead of foregrounding political content, Collins embeds it in a compelling first-person narrative that makes Panem its setting rather than its subject. In this sense, The *Hunger Games* trilogy resembles Anthony Burgess's *A Clockwork Orange* or Margaret Atwood's *Oryx and Crake* more than Aldous Huxley's *Brave New World* or George Orwell's *1984*, the latter two novels being overtly pedantic and pointed in message (Jameson 7). The trilogy also differs from more polemical dystopian novels by presenting its fictive world through the consciousness of a character who develops and changes as the story proceeds, making both her and the world she inhabits seem more dynamic and real. The first-person perspective also affords readers an opportunity to experience Panem just as Katniss does, enhancing its ideological impact by appealing to emotions as well as the intellect. In effect, we learn exactly what it is like to live in Katniss's dystopian world.

Experiencing Dystopia Through Katniss

The Hunger Games begins *en media res* as Katniss wakes up on the morning of the reaping, that is, the public ceremony every district holds to select tributes for the Games. Rather than immediately explain the significance of the day or otherwise provide background about the society in which she is living, Katniss instead discusses her sister, her mother, and even the cat, Buttercup. She mentions living in District 12 only after leaving the house and Panem only after realizing that something she mutters about her dissatisfaction with the government could get her in trouble. Not until the end of the first chapter do we learn anything about Panem's history and the reasons behind the Games, and even then we are provided with almost no detail, the narrative focus remaining on Katniss and her particular situation. We learn much about Panem indirectly, however, as she gradually relates details about her own life. Katniss, we discover, is an adolescent girl, who, having lost her father in a mining accident, has been providing for her family for years by illegally hunting in the woods outside the District. Although she resents the Capitol, which keeps her and the other residents of the District on the verge of starvation in order to better control them, she is more concerned with survival than rebellion, commenting at one point, "Whatever the truth is, it won't help me get food on the table" (*Hunger Games* 42). Like Robin Hood, who also initially violates the law out of necessity, she becomes part of an outlaw community, connecting with others who engage in illicit activities in order to survive. She is particularly close with Gale Hawthorne, a young man who has also turned to poaching after losing his father in the same mining accident that killed Katniss's father. Having hunted together for years, the two have become friends and potential romantic partners, though Katniss insists that she will never marry or have children. To her, life in Panem is so miserable that bringing more children into the world is unthinkable, an attitude she maintains until Panem has fallen and the prospect of a better life has materialized.

Through Katniss's relationship with Gale, Collins is able to powerfully convey a sense of how horrifying Panem is since, presumably, many of her young adult readers are particularly attuned to romance. At the beginning of *The Hunger Games*, Gale is presented as an ideal mate, at least by conventional standards: in addition to being literally tall, dark, and handsome, he is two years older than Katniss and a proven provider. More importantly, perhaps, the two share a certain level of intimacy, their connection being symbolized by a ritual they have developed in which one of them throws a berry in the air and the other catches it in his or her mouth. Their love can never be, however, or so it seems, not just because of conditions in District 12 but because at the end of the first chapter, Katniss is selected to be a participant in the Hunger Games, which is tantamount to a death sentence, no tribute from District 12 having survived the Games in more than twenty years. Not surprisingly, perhaps, Collins plays up the melodrama when the two part, Gale's declaration of love for Katniss being interrupted by two Peacekeepers who "yank" them "apart and slam the door" between them (*Hunger Games* 40).

It is not just young adult readers who are likely to be affected by a story of star-crossed lovers, of course: such stories are a staple of romances ranging from *Romeo and Juliet* to *Twilight*. What makes *The Hunger Games* unusual is the way that it uses melodrama to give the novel's implicit social criticism emotional force, a tactic Collins employs throughout the trilogy. In *Catching Fire* and *Mockingjay*, she uses sentimentality to make her readers suffer in the way her characters do, using Prim's death, for example, to highlight the loss and suffering that war brings. As Jane Tompkins demonstrates in *Sensational Designs: The Cultural Work of American Fiction, 1790–1860*, even though works that employ pathos are generally dismissed by critics as non-literary, it is that very pathos that gives them the potential to shape social reality. The same is true of contemporary works such as P.D. James's *Children of Men* (1992), a novel whose story line very much resembles that of Harriet Beecher Stowe's *Uncle Tom's Cabin*, and Cormac McCarthy's *The Road* (2006), an emotional novel that centers on a dying man's efforts to save his son in a world that has been made nearly uninhabitable due to environmental degradation. As George Monbiot observes, McCarthy's book is "widely seen as both a parable and the logical extension of the earth's physical degeneration," adding, "It could be the most important environmental book ever." What makes McCarthy's narrative powerful, however, is not so much its environmental message as the way it is conveyed through a parent-child relationship. As a survey of online reader reactions to the novel will quickly confirm, many have a powerful emotional response to this relationship, either identifying the man in the story with one of their own parents or identifying with the man themselves. Shawn Oetzel, for example, writes:

> The night I finished reading *The Road* I was unable to sleep. I could not stop thinking about the imagery and absolute bleak existence of the Man and Boy. As a father myself, I was touched and even frightened on a personal level by the choices the Man had to make regarding his son's continued survival. Even now, when I find myself with a few minutes alone I am still compelled to try and find an answer as to what I would have done in the same situation as the Man along with the other questions the novel challenged me with. That is just some of the power Mr. McCarthy has instilled in this novel.

As Oetzel's response suggests, works that evoke an emotional response, if not a somatic one, have a heightened effect upon readers. Affect theorists describe this process in terms of amplification: bodily responses including emotional ones — or what is termed "affect" — amplify that which seizes the reader's attention, rendering it more powerful (Gibbs 255). Readers of the *Hunger Games* trilogy report a similar sort of response, relating their somatic responses to the text to its power. Indeed, one popular blog on Tumblr — "the hunger games things" — is devoted almost entirely to affect, describing itself as follows: "for every little (or big) thing in the hunger games that made you laugh, made you cry, or just stuck with you." Its creator, Courtney, who solicits suggestions from visitors, has so far identified more than 200 moments in the trilogy that meet her criteria.

The Lessons of Panem: Environmentalism and Climate Change

Like *The Road*, one of the *Hunger Games* trilogy's primary messages involves the environment, which has been severely damaged by pollution and war. Rather than present readers with a history of the future, that is, with a detailed account of how the Earth came to be a "broken planet," Collins instead only hints at what has happened in North America over the course of hundreds of years, never being specific (*Mockingjay* 84). Although we eventually learn that civilization as we know it has ended because environmental damage has resulted in droughts, floods, fires, the destruction of the upper atmosphere, and rising sea levels, we are never provided with specific detail or even told what happens to other parts of the world. Providing such information would change the very nature of the trilogy, of course, since the narrator herself knows almost nothing about Panem's past or the present state of the world, the government controlling knowledge as carefully as it controls resources such as food and energy. We learn about the world in which Katniss lives only as she does, sharing her consciousness, as it were, as she sees every district of Panem for the first time through a train window.

By presenting Katniss's dystopia on a personal level rather than a political one, Collins is able to help readers imagine what living in a radically degraded environment might be like. To Katniss, who lives hundreds of years in the future, the consequences of global warming are a part of her everyday life: she and others suffer in the future because of decisions we are making now. To the extent that readers identify with her and her situation, they feel what she feels and, in a sense, experience what she does. As a result, the trilogy rarely seems preachy or pedantic: it shows us what may happen in the future rather than tells us. Only once does Collins comment directly on the causes of the environmental damage through Katniss, having her observe that the people responsible for the damage clearly "didn't care about what would happen to the people who came after them" (*Mockingjay* 84). The fact that Collins is so rarely didactic makes her commentary that much more powerful when it does occur.

Mass Media and Social Control

Collins also presents a critique of mass media on a personal level, demonstrating through Katniss how it can be used to control people's beliefs and behaviors as well as how it can be resisted and even appropriated and used for other purposes. In *The Hunger Games* and *Catching Fire*, the focus is on reality television, Collins suggesting that the genre is not so "real" as it appears. To Katniss, the Hunger Games are a part of her everyday life, the Games being required viewing for everyone in Panem. Although she recognizes that the Games are used by the government both to affirm their political power over the districts and keep the people divided against one another, she only develops a true critical perspective on the Games when she becomes a participant in them, seeing them for what they really are: elaborate fictions that present themselves as fact. With this realization she is able to master the Games themselves, taking control of the narrative and rewriting it, as it were, so that both she and Peeta can survive. In effect, she goes from passive to active, refusing to be interpellated into the Gamemakers' narrative. She goes even further in *Catching Fire*, ending the Games themselves by destroying the force field that surrounds the arena and escaping to District 13. In *Mockingjay*, Katniss is able to apply the lessons she learned in the Hunger Games to real life by refusing to play a passive role in the complex narrative Alma Coin, Plutarch Heavensbee, and others create for her. Although she initially agrees to be the Mockingjay, Katniss eventually realizes that doing so involves sacrificing what little agency she has, and so she abandons the role, deserting the star squad and pursuing President Snow on her own. After the fall of the Capitol, she returns to District 13 and briefly becomes the Mockingjay again. This time, however, she refuses to follow the script others provide her with, assassinating Coin on live television rather than executing Snow as she is supposed to, thereby changing the course of history: the final Hunger Games that Coin had planned for the children of the Capitol's most powerful people are cancelled and the cycle of vengeance can end (369).

In addition to addressing the ways in which mass media influences people's beliefs and behaviors and how that influence might be countered, Collins offers implicit commentary on what is happening in U.S. media today. Taken as a whole, the government's programming seems to parallel that of Fox Entertainment, the parent company of both Fox Broadcasting and Fox News Channel, a company that mixes — and sometimes merges — news and entertainment programming, and possibly other media conglomerates such as NBCUniversal Media, Clear Channel Communications, and Viacom. Rather than make any effort to be objective or, alternatively, to represent diverse points of view, the Capitol uses various types of programming to reinforce its own power. State-controlled news programs, for example, convey misinformation by manipulating footage and having reporters present stories that serve the government's interests, and clips from the Hunger Games are re-broadcasted in order to remind people continually of the state's overwhelming power. Once the rebellion begins, war footage is added, accompanied by stories designed to reassure loyalists while demoralizing rebels, and Peeta is forced to undermine the rebels in scripted interviews with Caesar Flickerman that present themselves at least in part as the sort of tell-all programming that follows shows like *Survivor* or *The Bachelor*. It is not just Fox Broadcasting that tends to blur news and entertainment as it promotes a particular point of view, of course, and Collins has said nothing in interviews to suggest that she has this particular corporation in mind. Given the overt manner in which Fox mixes news, politics, and entertainment (Gillepsie), however, it seems reasonable to surmise that Fox was at least one of Collins's models.

The trilogy is as concerned with the ways in which the blurring of fact and fiction desensitizes viewers to real suffering as it is with ideological bias, Collins noting that when viewers "see real tragedy playing out on, say, the news, it doesn't have the impact it should" ("A Conversation..."). In particular, she worries that the lines are being blurred not only between different types of media but between media and reality, resulting in passivity on the part of viewers. Asked what she hopes her audience will come away with after reading her books, she replies, "Questions about how elements of the book might be relevant in their own lives. And, if they're disturbing, what they might do about them" ("A Conversation..."). Collins suggests that the problem with our lives being permeated with media, it seems, is that we lose agency, becoming viewers rather than actors, a point Katniss makes by comparing her own inaction when Lavinia and her companion are being pursued by Peacekeepers in the woods outside of District 12 to "watching the Games" and again after workers from District 2 turn on their former allies from the Capitol following the siege of the Nut and slaughtering them (*Hunger Games* 85; *Mockingjay* 222).

By constructing a highly elaborate fictional world that readers access through a first person narrator who provides events in the present tense, Collins makes it possible for her readers to experience things along with Katniss, to participate in the action, as it were. As Kay Sambell observes, this sort of approach has become increasingly common in dystopias directed primarily at younger people, the text itself becoming "a space that sometimes tries to create conditions for young readers to rehearse, actively, almost playfully, a way of reflective thinking that focuses on asking questions, discovering analyses, and hypothetically testing out solutions at their own pace in an imaginative environment that is affirming and supportive, but which also articulates dark truths" (173). According to Steven Johnson, this is just the sort of thing that happens in video games, the programs being constructed so that players engage with them actively rather than passively (25–27).

The Politics of Scarcity

The trilogy also uses dystopia to demonstrate how those in power can use scarcity to control the population. Indeed, the nation's very name — Panem — underscores this, "panem" meaning "bread" in Latin. Controlling food supplies can be a particularly effective means of social control during times of unrest. When there is any hint of an uprising, the government can cut off the food supply as it does in District 12 in *Catching Fire* when miners begin to organize: the mines are shut down, food deliveries are cancelled or ruined by vermin, and, as a result, "the people cower in their homes" (168). What makes the state's use of scarcity as a means of control seem particularly nefarious is the fact that the scarcity seems to be artificial, at least to an extent: as Adrienne Kress observes, as the trilogy proceeds we learn that the novels are not about "a world where there are no commodities, but rather a world where most exist in terrible conditions in order to support those who have great luxury and food aplenty" (184). Children may starve to death in the districts, but there is no shortage in the Capitol, where the rich use emetics at parties so that they can eat even more (*Catching Fire* 80).

The government also uses scarcity to divide people against themselves, making it easier to control them. In Panem there are literally "haves" and "have-nots," the former being comprised almost entirely of those living in the Capitol and the latter being just about everyone else. The districts, it seems, are devoid of luxury, there being no middle class at all. The merchants hold themselves above the poor even though they also suffer from privation. Peeta's family, for example, lives on old stale bread, being unable to afford the cakes their own bakery sells to government officials and Peacekeepers. Rather than sympathize with those who are even poorer, however, the merchants are antagonistic towards them as evidenced by Peeta's mother, who drives the starving Katniss away from her garbage can, screaming "how sick she is of having those brats from the Seam pawing through her trash" (*Hunger Games* 29). The poor, in turn, "resent those who don't have to sign up for tesserae" and therefore increase their chances of being selected for the games in order to have enough grain and oil for the year (*Hunger Games* 13).

As one might expect, given that the Hunger Games are the state's primary ideological tool for controlling people's thoughts and behaviors, scarcity figures largely in the Games as well. By making the Hunger Games a part of people's everyday lives, the government is able to constantly remind people that they have absolute power over them. In a sense, the Games — which the people of Panem are forced to watch — are a spectacle of power, since the state controls everything in the arena, including food, water, and even the weather. The Gamemakers also orchestrate events within the Games in order to force confrontations between tributes. "Feasts," for example, are sometimes announced so that players will congregate in a particular area and fight, even though, as Katniss notes, the feast itself will only be "a loaf of stale bread." By forcing tributes to literally fight over scraps, the state is able to dramatize its primary means of control over the population: the tributes provide living lessons about the power of scarcity. In effect, the Games teach viewers that when it comes to survival, it is everyone for themselves.

The Games are also used by the state to pit the districts against one another and prevent feelings of solidarity from developing. In the pregame ceremonies, tributes are costumed in ways consistent with their district's principal industry, and they are often identified by district number rather than name so as to highlight the fact that it is district against district (*Hunger Games* 66). This idea is further reinforced by a rule that makes long-term alliances between people of different districts impossible: there can only be one winner of the Games, and therefore, one cannot have real allies, even from one's own district. The fact that districts are represented by children is also important, viewers presumably engaging with the Games on an emotional level as they watch children from their district battle children from other districts. It is not just children who are dehumanized by the Games: the government dehumanizes viewers as well to the extent that they induce them to cheer for the slaughter of children from other districts.

Although Collins is careful not to talk about politics in her interviews and personal appearances, it seems evident that in her depiction of class division she is responding at least in part to the erosion of the middle class first noticed during the Reagan administration and which has continued into the twenty-first century (Koepp). In particular she seems to be reacting to the idea that as the rich get richer, the poor are left to fight amongst themselves for the limited resources made available to them, something that is becoming more evident today as retirement plans and other social safety nets are being dismantled with the consent of many of those people who are most likely to need them, namely the working class. In the *Hunger Games* trilogy, fighting for scraps has become a part of everyday life to the point that selflessness and generosity become revolutionary acts — for example when District 11 sends bread to Katniss in *The Hunger Games* and when Peeta pledges to provide the families of the District 11 tributes with a share of his winnings in *Catching Fire*. With this in mind, it should not be surprising that rebels identify themselves to one another by passing pieces of bread with the Mockingjay symbol baked into it (*Catching Fire* 139). Sharing resources such as food is one of the few ways to resist a government that uses scarcity to control the population.

The Lessons of the Capitol

Although the people living in the Capitol do not suffer anywhere near the same sort of privation those in the districts do, it becomes increasingly clear as the story proceeds that the Capitol is a dystopia in its own right. Despite the city's relative affluence, physical beauty, and technological advancement, as Katniss discovers, the people there are nearly as oppressed as those in the districts, the primary difference being those in the Capitol are either disinterested or unaware of their condition. Although they presumably have more day-to-day freedom that those in the districts — being allowed by the government to visit the sites of past Hunger Games, for example — they have no more say in their political leadership than those living in the districts do, Snow being the undisputed ruler of everyone. As Plutarch observes in *Mockingjay*, the government manages the Capitol's population by providing them with "Bread and Circuses," offering "full bellies and entertainment" in exchange for power (223). Collins alludes to more than just ancient Rome here: as Sarah Darer Littman observes in "The Politics of *Mockingjay*," she is also making a pointed reference to post-9/11 Americans, who, according to her, "preferred to lose themselves in 'reality TV' than pay attention to the erosion of civil liberties during the War on Terror" (175). Collins also seems to be alluding to the fact that, like those in the Capitol, most Americans "never hav[e] missed a meal" and therefore have no sense of what hunger really is (*Hunger Games* 59).

Collins also uses the Capitol to offer indirect commentary upon American materialism, which, in her view, has resulted in debilitating decadence. As Adrienne Kress argues in "The Inevitable Decline of Decadence," one of the problems with decadence is that "it leads to dependency" (181). If the denizens of the Capitol have plenty of food, material goods, and luxury items, it is only because the people in the districts have very little. That plentitude has made them weak becomes evident when the Capitol is under siege: being entirely dependent upon the workers in the districts for food and material goods and Peacekeepers for security, the citizens of the Capitol have no means of protecting themselves or their way of life and can only retreat into the town center and hope to be taken care of by the government. Having lived lives of ease, they are nearly as vulnerable to the attacking workers as the Eloi are to the Morlocks in H.G. Wells's *The Time Machine*.

Another problem that Collins identifies with the decadent lifestyle of those in the Capitol is that it comes at the expense of others: in order for some to live in luxury, others have to suffer (Kress 182–3). If the denizens of the Capitol have plenty of food, material goods, and luxury items, it is only because the people in the districts have very little (Green). For the most part denizens of the Capitol are no more concerned about conditions in the districts than Americans are about working conditions in overseas apparel factories. Effie Trinket, for example, resents the people of District 12 for making her job as an escort difficult, comparing the previous year's tributes to "savages," complaining about Haymitch's poor presentation on camera, and becoming frustrated with Katniss's inability to walk in high heels or wear a gown properly (*Hunger Games* 44). Though more sympathetic than Trinket, addressing Katniss as "you poor darling" in a patronizing way, Octavia is also incapable of empathizing with Katniss and others from the districts, as are Flavius and Venia. When, for example, seafood becomes unavailable — because of bad weather in District 4, according to the government, but really because an uprising has halted production — Octavia show no concern about the workers there who must surely be starving, instead complaining about being unable to get "shrimp for a party" (*Catching Fire* 165); similarly, Flavius and Venia regard difficulty in getting crabmeat, music chips, and ribbons as "hardships," never considering the true difficulties that others might be facing (*Catching Fire* 165). Only Cinna seems capable of empathizing with those who are impoverished, realizing just how "despicable" the people in the Capitol who have food "at the press of a button" must seem to Katniss (*Hunger Games* 65).

Indeed, one could even argue that citizens in the Capitol derive both pleasure and affirmation from the suffering of others. As in Franz Kafka's story, "A Hunger Artist," privation becomes a spectacle for those unused to want, Kafka's character capturing "the attention of the entire city." The Hunger Games captures the Capitol's attention in the same sort of way, reminding citizens that they are indeed privileged. More than that, though, the Games reinforce citizens of the Capitol's sense of their own superiority over those living in the districts by dehumanizing tributes in the arena. In this the Hunger Games resemble contemporary reality television. As psychologist Jim Taylor observes, "Most of the joy of reality TV is not in seeing contestants succeed, but rather in seeing them not only fail, but fail in the most humiliating ways." To Collins, who indicates in interviews that she was inspired to write the *Hunger Games* trilogy after seeing war footage juxtaposed with a reality show, programs like *Big Brother*, *Survivor*, and *Extreme Makeover* are anything but innocuous: like the Hunger Games, they reinforce what is worst in people not only personally but politically, encouraging them to hold themselves above those who are suffering rather than empathize with them and try to help them.

The Lessons of District 13

The districts and the Capitol are not the only nightmarish societies featured in the *Hunger Games* trilogy, for in *Mockingjay*, District 13 emerges as a third, and in some ways even more frightening dystopia than Panem. What makes District 13 so chilling is the fact that it seems to be modeled on what has been happening in the United States following the September 11th attacks as the executive branch under George W. Bush suspended the right of *habeas corpus* for some, allowed extraordinary rendition and torture to be utilized, authorized bombings sure to kill civilians, and manipulated events for political reasons. As J. Maureen Henderson observes, "today's teens know what dystopia looks like because there's ample evidence of its elements in their daily lives": whereas Panem serves primarily as a warning about what might happen in the future because of environmental degradation, the political use of mass media, and a government that rules through division and fear, the story of District 13 mirrors the world we are living in now.

Ironically, District 13 first seems to be more of a utopia than a dystopia in the sense that people have a shared sense of purpose and have their basic needs taken care of during a time of crisis by a government that has broad popular support (Despain 206). Although things may be difficult in the short term because of the ongoing war with the Capitol, the people make sacrifices in the present for the hope of a better future. Indeed, they seem to believe that democracy will resume once the war is over, an attitude reflected by Plutarch, who declares, "We're going to form a republic where the people of each district and the Capitol can elect their own representatives in a centralized government" (*Mockingjay* 83–4). Although Katniss remains skeptical about the possibility of District 13 ever becoming a free society, she concedes that it has little choice but to closely regulate resources and behaviors by rationing food, assigning personal quarters, and even tattooing daily schedules on people's forearms: "Maybe they are militaristic, overly programmed, and somewhat lacking in sense of humor. They're here. And willing to take on the Capitol" (29).

Certainly Katniss has good reason for sympathizing with the difficulties District 13 faces. Because of its near obliteration in its war with the Capitol, District 13 has been in perpetual crisis for 75 years, surviving only through the "strict sharing of resources, strenuous discipline, and constant vigilance against any further attack from the Capitol" (17). As Katniss quickly learns, though, even though the district's leader, Alma Coin, styles herself "president," she is in fact a dictator, reserving final say for herself in everything from military strategies to Finnick Odair's wedding. To an extent, Coin seems to be modeled on wartime leaders like Abraham Lincoln, Franklin Delano Roosevelt, and Winston Churchill, leaders of democratic nations who assumed near-dictatorial powers during wartime. The parallel between Coin and Churchill seems to be particularly close, given Churchill's willingness to use his wartime powers against political enemies and his desire to remain in control after hostilities ceased (Addison 343). Moreover, District 13 itself seems to be modeled at least in part on London while under German bombardment in 1940, a period Collins most certainly learned about from her father, a military historian, who, according to Collins, "did his best to pass his understanding of history, politics, and world events on to his children" (Blasingame 726).

As she indicates in interviews, however, the *Hunger Games* trilogy is as much a response to the present as it is to the past, Collins having conceived of the books after watching a combination of war footage and reality television (Blasingame 726–7). In a very real sense, the trilogy is about the so-called War on Terror and the way it impacted American society and government. As suggested earlier, many of the things that happen in District 13 as a result of their ongoing crisis reflect things that were happening in the United States after the September 11th attacks, namely extra-judicial arrests and detainments, cruel and unusual punishment, indifference to civilian deaths, and the manipulation of events for political reasons. *Mockingjay* in particular addresses larger, ethical questions, such as whether the killing of non-combatants is justified while pursuing a military objective and whether the enemy's depravities can be used to justify depravities of one's own. District 13's willingness to kill combatants and non-combatants alike during the siege of the Nut in District 2 and its implementation of terror weapons like the exploding gifts that ultimately kill Prim are cases in point: in many ways District 13 has come to resemble the very enemy it denounces as evil, employing similar tactics and strategies. As if to confirm this, Collins not only names the president of District 13 "Coin" (as in "two sides of the same coin") but relating her to President Snow through a pun, describing her eyes being "[t]he color of slush that you wish would melt away" (10).

Dystopia and Social Change

The Hunger Games trilogy offers more than just a highly-engaging cautionary tale about global warming, mass media, and political oppression. In addition to identifying problems, the trilogy considers solutions, the latter two volumes in particular helping readers to imagine how social change might be effected. As noted earlier, in *The Hunger Games*, Katniss has little political consciousness and, indeed, seems to have little patience for Gale's analysis of the Games' ideological function, describing it as ranting (*Hunger Games* 14). It is only after meeting with President Snow in *Catching Fire* that Katniss begins to realize fully how the Games function as a means of ideological control and how such control might be resisted (21). Although many of her earlier actions have political implications, notably decorating Rue's body with flowers and using poisonous berries to alter her first Hunger Games' outcome, they are not done for political reasons. In *Catching Fire* her political consciousness develops quickly as she sees more of Panem and sees how various districts and their populations interact with one another and the Capitol. Her first conscious political act occurs during her private session with the Gamemakers in preparation for the Quarter Quell when she labels a target dummy with the name of the Head Gamemaker, Seneca Crane, who had been executed, bloodies it with dye, and hangs it by the neck. As she explains to Peeta afterwards, her actions had a specific purpose—to show the Gamemakers she is "more than just a piece in their Games" (242).

Katniss soon learns that it is not just the Gamemakers and the Capitol that want to use her. At the end of *Catching Fire* she learns that she was but "a piece" in the rebels' "elaborate plan" to begin a civil war by disrupting the Quarter Quell (385), and towards the beginning of *Mockingjay* she becomes cognizant of the fact that she is being used by President Coin to enhance her own power (59). Her realization Coin is again using her when she coerces her and the other surviving victors to vote on whether to hold another Hunger Games ultimately leads her to take action, to assert that she is a subject rather than an object and do what is right rather than what she is told to do. Rather than shoot Snow as she is expected to, she shoots Coin, ending the cycle of violence and retribution that has dominated Panem for at least 75 years. Collins's hope here appears to be that her readers, too, will begin "to look at the government and situations throughout the world and wonder if they are moral or not" (Neary). More than that, though, she hopes they will take action: "You have to have that. You have to at some time in your life begin to question the environment, the political situation around you and decide whether it's right or not and if it isn't, what part you are going to play in that."

Happy Endings

In a 2011 article in *The New Yorker*, Laura Miller argues that the works of dystopian fiction that have become so popular with young adult readers are not as dark or pessimistic as classic dystopias such as *Brave New World* and *1984*, and that, therefore, their social messages do not have the same urgency or power. Indeed, she goes so far to suggest that in books like *The Hunger Games* "social criticism" is not the "real point": "'The Hunger Games' is not an argument. It operates like a fable or a myth, a story in which outlandish and extravagant figures and events serve as conduits for universal experiences. Dystopian fiction may be the only genre written for children that's routinely *less* didactic than its adult counterpart. It's not about persuading the reader to stop something terrible from happening— it's about what's happening, right this minute, in the stormy psyche of the adolescent reader." While Miller is certainly correct in thinking that books like the *Hunger Games* trilogy appeal to young adult readers because they can identify with the characters and situations such books feature, she seems to overlook the fact that many young adult readers are socially and politically engaged and therefore very much interested in issues such as war and oppression. Indeed, one could argue that concern about social and political issues contributes to the "the stormy psyche of the adolescent reader" that Miller finds so significant — that is, that young adults are frustrated and angry not only with their own lives but with the world at large.

In "Dark Materials in Young Adult Fiction," Robin Kirk responds directly to Miller's argument, suggesting that dystopias written for young adults not only help acclimate readers to a world that seems increasingly dark and pessimistic but teach them to consider how it might be changed:

> At the core of dystopias is a very human question: how people really behave. Especially as teenagers, children are beginning to see that the world is not all that has been promised. The best dystopias ask the essential questions: Why

is this so? Does it need to be so? And who says this must be so? Through dystopias, children can begin to experience what it means to be human in the twenty-first century, with all the despair — and hope — that this implies.

Young adult readers, Kirk suggests, need to balance despair with hope so that they can move forward and enact change, just as Katniss does. If, as Kathy Morrison, observes, "the emotion in the final pages [of *Mockingjay*] is exhaustion, not joy — or peace," it is because ending the novel any other way would undercut the trilogy's message about the need take action now to prevent places like Panem from coming into being in the future. As dark as the ending of the *Hunger Games* trilogy is — with Katniss still having to remind herself "of every act of kindness" she has ever witnessed in order to "survive" — the world has nonetheless become a better place because of her actions, a place in which she is willing to have children herself (*Mockingjay* 388). In ending the trilogy this way, Collins adheres to fellow author Monica Hughes's dictum, "You may lead a child into darkness, but you must never turn out the light" (156).

CHAPTER SEVEN

Survivor Stories
Trauma, Recovery and Narrative

"One of the strongest themes in the literature of trauma is the urge to bear witness, to carry the tale of horror back to the halls of 'normalcy' and to testify to the people the truth of their experience."
— Kalí Tal, *Worlds of Hurt* [120]

"I drag myself out of nightmares each morning and find there's no relief in waking"
— Finnick Odair, *Mockingjay* [156]

The *Hunger Games* trilogy is very much a survivor's story, that is, an attempt by someone who has escaped ongoing trauma to narrate her experiences so as to better come to terms with them on a personal level as well as to put them on record for society's benefit. As Shani Orgad observes in "The Survivor in Contemporary Culture and Public Discourse: A Genealogy," survivor stories are more than just escape narratives: they provide those who have been traumatized with a means of establishing identities for themselves that are active rather than passive. Accordingly, not every survivor's story is a *survivor story*, according to Orgad: in order to qualify as such, the narrator must adopt the subject position of a survivor and adhere to the conventions of the genre. To the extent that they are part of a "regularized and sanctioned practice," survivor stories can be understood as "performatives" in Judith Butler's sense of the term since their primary function is "to produce that which it declares" (1993, 107): to tell a survival story is to become a survivor, the utterance doubling as an action. This is just what happens in Katniss's case: telling her story affords her an opportunity to remake it a way that gives her agency, making it easier for her to move beyond her traumatic episodes.

Survival stories — at least those that are published — have social functions as well. Whether autobiographical, like Harriet Jacob's *Incidents in the Life of a Slave Girl* and Joe Simpson's *Touching the Void*, or fictional, like Daniel Defoe's *Robinson Crusoe* and Margaret Atwood's *The Handmaid's Tale*, survivor stories tend to be compelling narratives since they often center upon a series of harrowing experiences and escapes. In addition to providing entertainment, survivor stories have a didactic function, conveying both general information about survival strategies such as the importance of thinking things through and persevering, and specific information that might help certain people in certain situations. They may also prove inspirational, leading people who are in difficult situations to take action themselves to change things. CancerGuide, for example, a website created by cancer survivor Steve Dunn in order to provide resources to help others with cancer, includes not only a page of "Inspirational Patient Stories" but links to wilderness survival stories that Dunn finds "inspiring and relevant," including *Touching the Void* and Alfred Lansing's *Endurance: Shackleton's Incredible Voyage to the Antarctic*.

Finally, survivor stories have ideological functions to the extent that they provide social commentary. In some cases, the social commentary is largely implicit, as in Zora Neale Hurston's *Their Eyes Were Watching God*, a novel about an independent-minded black woman who survives not only the great Lake Okeecobee Hurricane of 1928 but a series of abusive relationships, finally shooting her partner before he can kill her. When it was published in 1937, few commentators recognized the novel as "serious fiction" (Wright 22), and many reviewers, including Richard Wright, Ralph Ellison, and Alain Locke, sharply criticized Hurston for her failure to address social issues explicitly. It was only 35 years after its original publication that Hurston's novel came to be widely regarded as an important social and political text, one that addresses how people can free themselves from both personal and political oppression through strength, courage, and perseverance (Washington x). In other cases, the social commentary is overt: In *July's People*, for example, South African writer Nadine Gordimer uses the story of a white family's efforts to survive a black uprising by moving to the village of one of their servants to interrogate social relations under Apartheid and imagine how they might change once white rule ends (Erritouni 68).

Dystopian fiction in particular frequently employs conventions of the survivor story to offer an ideological critique as evidenced by Jack London's

The Iron Heel, Doris Lessing's *The Memoirs of a Survivor,* and Chuck Palahniuk's *Fight Club.* As Kay Sambell notes, however, dystopian fictions often end with the most "morally appealing characters" failing "unequivocally" in their efforts to either escape their dystopian societies or change them, and therefore, one could argue they are not survivor stories at all (164). Certainly the most celebrated dystopian novels such as *A Brave New World, 1984,* and *A Clockwork Orange* offer neither happy endings nor any suggestion as to how positive social change might be effected (164). The same is not necessarily true of dystopian fiction written for young adults, however. In *Z for Zachariah,* for example, a post apocalyptic YA novel in which the sixteen-year-old female narrator survives a nuclear war only to have to escape exploitation from the only other survivor of whom she knows, ends hopefully as the protagonist leaves the man and everything he represents behind in order to search for other survivors. Similarly, Adam Rapp's *Copper Elephant,* a novel set in a world that has become all but uninhabitable because of acid rain ends hopefully as the first-person female narrator escapes her horrific life under an oppressive, patriarchic Syndicate to join a free community of women.

The *Hunger Games* trilogy has both social and ideological functions as well. In addition to entertaining readers with a fast-paced, first-person account of Katniss's traumatic experiences, the trilogy presents Katniss as a survivor, that is, as someone who regains control over her life following a series of traumas, thus providing readers with potential inspiration to take the initiative and improve their own situations: although readers are unlikely to undergo the sorts of trauma Katniss does, they nonetheless may benefit from her example as she struggles to not only save herself and her loved ones but make her world a better place for others. Finally, like *Z for Zachariah, Copper Elephant,* and other young adult survivor stories set in dystopian worlds, the trilogy offers social commentary, not only critiquing the social practices that have resulted in the horrific world in which she lives but offering suggestions about how change might be effected.

Loss, Emotional Trauma and Recovery

The *Hunger Games* trilogy makes trauma one of its primary subjects, leading one commentator to term it "The Trauma Games" (Nel). Indeed,

Katniss's life seem to be defined by trauma, Katniss having lost her father, to whom she was very close, in a mining accident. Katniss, who was just eleven at the time, is unable to grieve for her father properly, being pressed into providing for her family by herself because of "the crushing depression" that her mother fell into following the father's death (*Catching Fire* 31). Although the mother has largely recovered in the five years since the accident, Katniss remains resentful of what she perceives as her mother's weakness, not trusting her to take care of her Prim, after she herself volunteers to participate in the Hunger Games in Prim's stead. Katniss's mother, it seems, has been suffering from post-traumatic stress disorder (PTSD), as evidenced by her "immobilizing sadness" (*Hunger Games* 36): it is only after she has suffered similar symptoms herself following Prim's death in *Mockingjay* that Katniss can understand that her "mother was locked in some dark world of sadness," that she has a "sickness" and is not just being weak (*Hunger Games* 27, 36).

Katniss, too, seems to suffer from PTSD following her father's death, the malady presenting itself in a very different way than it does in her mother. Rather than "clock out" entirely as her mother does, Katniss suffers from bad dreams, is continually anxious, and has difficulty forming relationships with other people (*Hunger Games* 35). It takes her years to regard Gale as anything more than a hunting partner, for example, and she refuses to accept Madge as a friend even though they eat lunch and attend assemblies together at school and partner up for physical activities (*Hunger Games* 12). Indeed, she seems surprised that Madge visits her before she leaves for the Capitol as a tribute for the Hunger Games, only conceding that Madge is a friend after Madge gives her a mockingjay pin and a kiss on the cheek (*Hunger Games* 38). Her difficulties in forming close relationships continue in the Training Center, where she keeps Peeta at a distance even though he is consistently friendly and supportive, and in the arena she is only able to connect with Rue because she reminds her of Prim.

For the most part Katniss attributes her emotional detachment from others to her circumstances at the time: she tells herself that she cannot afford to enter into relationships with other people because it is all she can do to provide for her family and, after she becomes a tribute, to keep herself alive. On some level, though, she seems to recognize that there is a psychological cause as well, noting, for example, that she has "put up a wall" to "protect" herself from needing her mother (*Hunger Games* 53).

Only gradually does she realize that she must let herself depend upon other people physically and emotionally as she once did with her father, and even then she keeps Peeta, Madge, and later, Finnick, at a distance, accepting their friendship only reluctantly. Like many people suffering from PTSD, Katniss cannot begin to recover from trauma until she addresses it (Woolston 161).

Katniss finally begins to do this in the woods outside of District 12 while filming propaganda for the rebels. During a lunch break, she "intentionally sit[s] at the far end of the group, next to Pollux," an Avox, so she will not "have to talk" (*Mockingjay* 121). Seeing a mockingjay, she points it out to Pollux and then whistles to it to show him how mockingjays take up tunes. To her surprise, her usually silent companion whistles to the mockingjay, too, and is delighted at its response, entering into a conversation of sorts with it and the other mockingjays that soon gather. Afterwards he writes the word "sing" in the dirt, hoping that Katniss will sing to the birds so that he can hear what it sounds like when mockingjays take up words. Katniss is initially reluctant to do so: a mental Avox herself, to borrow a term Dr. Aurelius later uses for her, she is uncommunicative, particularly about personal things. Because she sympathizes with Pollux, and perhaps even identifies with him because of the way he has been silenced by the Capitol, she sings the four notes Rue taught her while in the arena, the same notes the mockingjays sing when Rue was killed. Horrified to hear again the "background music to her murder," Katniss quickly offers to sing "a real song" instead so as stop the mockingjays from forcing her to confront the trauma of her first Hunger Games (*Mockingjay* 123). Almost in a panic, she begins to sing "The Hanging Tree," a song her father taught her when she was very young, performing it "softly, sweetly," as he did (123). As she sings all four verses of the song, the birds fall silent for her just as they did for her father long ago, triggering a flashback from her childhood, one involving her father, mother, and sister. This memory of her entire family being together — the first such memory in the trilogy — proves therapeutic, enabling Katniss to finally begin coming to terms with all that she lost when her father died.

Katniss is able to further process her father's death after imagining what it must be like in the Nut after the rebels seal the Capitol forces within it to die, "the hell inside the mountain" triggering a memory of the day her father died in the mines (207). Rather than re-experiencing the event as if it were happening again, the way someone suffering from PTSD might do (Woolston 148), she is able to maintain distance from it, as evidenced by the fact that she reports the events in the past rather than the present tense. Moreover, she is able to maintain perspective on what has happened, reinterpreting her original experiences according to what she now knows about how people respond to disasters (208). That she is now able to regard the trauma of her father's death with some detachment suggests that she has finally made significant progress in her recovery. Soon afterwards Haymitch informs her that upon seeing a recording of her singing "The Hanging Tree," Peeta recalled her father singing it once years ago when he had come into the bakery to trade. In response Katniss muses: "My father. He seems to be everywhere today. Dying in the mine. Singing his way into Peeta's muddled consciousness ... I miss him so badly it hurts" (211). Finally, it seems, Katniss is able to confront the loss of her father and begin to mourn, enabling her to begin to recover. As her return to the present tense here indicates, she is now able to address her father's death directly rather than repress it, as she has been doing.

From Victim to Survivor

The loss of a loved one is not the only form of trauma Katniss faces in the trilogy, of course. In the 74th Hunger Games, she also undergoes physical trauma repeatedly, being burned badly by a fireball, stung by tracker jackers, and nearly killed by a knife thrown by Clove. In the Quarter Quell she fares little better, being seriously injured once when Johanna knocks her unconscious with a heavy coil of wire and then removes a tracking device from her forearm by cutting it out. She is critically injured in *Mockingjay* as well, being shot in the abdomen by a refugee from District 2 and later being severely burned in the bomb blasts that end up killing Prim. She also experiences various forms of emotional trauma, witnessing the horrific deaths not only of people she has come to care about but those of people she herself has killed such as Glimmer and Cato. She is also traumatized by the suffering of others, including her mother, Peeta, Gale, Finnick, and even Haymitch. Finally, she has witnessed horrific events such as the bombing of a hospital, the burying alive of the people within the Nut and the slaughter of children and medical workers outside of President Snow's mansion, Prim being among those killed. As one commentator succinctly puts it, "Katniss starts off the series scarred and ends the series severely traumatized. She has PTSD like nobody's business, and if she didn't, it would be incredibly unrealistic" (LadyG). With this in mind it should not be surprising then that she is emotionally numb, suffers from nightmares, has difficulty entering into relationships with others, and self-medicates. What is surprising, perhaps, is that she generally refuses to see herself as victim or accept her situation passively. Rather, she is a survivor, and as such, serves as an inspiration to others, eventually helping the people of Panem to regain their own agency and rebel against the Capitol.

As Shani Orgad observes, the concept of "the survivor" is a relatively recent construction, emerging from post–World War II discourse regarding those who lived through the Holocaust. According to Orgad, the word "victims" was initially used to denote those who were passive and silent, accepting their situation, "survivors" denoting those who actively resisted their own destruction (137–8). By the 1960s, however, psychotherapists increasingly came to define reactions to other forms of trauma in terms of the victim/survivor opposition, including military combat, sexual abuse, physical and psychological injury, and chronic illness. More than that, though, they began to "encourage" patients to stop being victims — "to engage with their experience; to talk, and to transform their personal suffering into a validated recognized experience; to fight against the invisibility and silencing; to remember, but at the same time move on and look to the future — to become survivors" (Orgad 142). As Orgad points out, other discourse communities, both within the medical community and without, also began employing the victim/survivor opposition, and the concepts eventually entered the popular culture, as evidenced by everything from daytime talk shows like *Oprah* that feature people taking control of their lives and refusing to be victims anymore to songs like Destiny's Child's "I Am a Survivor" (134, 141).

Katniss is identified as a survivor even before she is sent to her first Hunger Games, Peeta's mother observing, "She's a survivor, that one" (*Hunger Games* 90). Like the mockingjays she is later identified with, once her father dies Katniss is essentially "abandoned to die off" by the Capitol, which takes little interest in the welfare of children, often letting them starve when their families cannot provide for them (*Hunger Games* 43). The mockingjays "didn't die off," however, and neither does Katniss (43): when she and her family face starvation, she learns to hunt, and when she herself is hunted in the arena, she learns to kill others. Katniss, in short, refuses to be a victim, something that is remarkable, considering the fact that the Hunger Games themselves are part of an elaborate ideological apparatus designed to convince people that they must passively accept any situation the state assigns them. As Collins herself indicates, Katniss "is a girl who should never have existed" (Margolis 2010): she comes into being only because the Capitol has been "lax" in District 12, regarding it as too "small and poor" to be a concern (Margolis 2010).

It is not Katniss's prowess as a hunter that makes her dangerous to the Capitol so much as her attitude, something President Snow makes clear when he indicates that her refusal to kill Peeta in her first Hunger Games has been interpreted as an "act of defiance" against the Capitol by some and inspired people in some of the districts to rise up against the government (*Catching Fire* 21). Fully recognizing that Katniss has provided "a spark that, left unattended," could "grow into an inferno" that brings down the government, Snow forces her to continue her showmance with Peeta so that her defiance in the arena will be attributed to her love for Peeta and not a desire to resist authority (*Catching Fire* 23). Once Katniss escapes to District 13 and starts making powerful anti-government propaganda as the Mockingjay, Snow goes to considerable lengths in an effort to break Katniss personally, to turn her into a victim and therefore once again demonstrate the Capitol's power. Initially he does this by trying to trigger a disabling reaction to her earlier trauma by placing bloody-smelling roses in her home back in District 12, and later on the ground near a blast crater in District 13 — roses whose scent is designed to remind Katniss of Snow's own distinctive odor (Woolston 148). When this fails, he has his scientists create mutts that are specially designed to terrorize her, mutts that not only smell of blood and roses as he does but also hiss her name as they pursue her. He seems to believe that if he makes Katniss a victim, people will no longer be inspired by her. Survivors, however — that is, people who take action in order to save themselves — are potentially dangerous to the Capitol since others might follow their lead.

Emotional Trauma and Recovery

Although Snow never succeeds in making Katniss a victim, at least in Orgad's sense of the term, the trauma he inflicts upon her has both severe short-term and long-term consequences. In addition to a recurrence of the sorts of symptoms she experienced after the loss of her father — nightmares, intrusive memories, anxiety, emotional withdrawal, and difficulty in forming relationships — she develops a chemical dependency, physically removes herself from the company of others, and suffers tremendous guilt. Despite her mental health issues, Katniss continues to meet her responsibilities as best she can in the first part of *Mockingjay*, sometimes using her duties as the Mockingjay to distract her from her pain, finding it easier to fight in District 2 than to face Peeta after he attempts to kill her, for example. She also finds a certain amount of relief through occupational therapy, tying and untying knots as Finnick does, and, after being injured in District 2, resorting to morphling, a powerful narcotic (156). In addition, her interactions with others suffering from PTSD help her, as does advice she receives from Johanna Mason about accepting that trauma changes people permanently, and so it is best just to "get on with things" (239).

None of the above strategies are adequate once her sister dies, however. Severely burned by the same blasts that killed Prim, Katniss loses both her sense of self and her ability to differentiate between the real and the unreal. Whereas earlier in the novel she is able to employ a technique she learned from a psychiatrist to reorient herself, listing the "simplest things" she knows "to be true and work[ing] toward the more complicated" (4), now it is all she can do to continue moment to moment, apparently unable to separate who she really is from the various roles she has been assigned by others: Katniss Everdeen, the "survivor" who took on adult responsibilities at age eleven and later becomes a Hunger Games victor; the "girl who was on fire," a media persona carefully constructed by Cinna to project both innocence and danger (*Hunger Games* 67); a "love-crazed" schoolgirl who would rather kill herself than lose Peeta (*Catching Fire* 21); a superhero-like Mockingjay created by Plutarch and others to represent the "symbol of revolution" (*Mockingjay* 10); or a renegade soldier who violates her orders in order to pursue a personal vendetta against President Snow. In short, she loses her sense of self.

Following Prim's death, Katniss expresses her confusion about her own identity by referring to herself as a "fire mutt," the word "mutt" suggesting a mix of things that do not cohere into anything of value. Unable to separate dreams from reality, she describes herself as "Cinna's bird, ignited, flying frantically to escape something inescapable," which turns out to be her own wings, the "feathers of flame that grow out of her own body" (348). Still in a dream state, she discovers that beating her wings to put out the flames "only fans the blaze" and so she consumes herself, "but to no end," the flames somehow sustaining themselves (348). As Katniss's "fire mutt" metaphor suggests, she not only cannot maintain the various identities she has been assigned but has lost her sense of self. The fact that she loses her ability to speak seems to affirm this, Dr. Aurelius attributing her "silence" as having been "brought on by emotional trauma" (350). Completely overwrought, the only thing keeping her going is Coin's promise that she will be allowed to execute Snow, and even that, Katniss realizes, will bring her no peace (351).

Ironically, Katniss only begins to emerge from her overwhelming depression after speaking with Snow, who insists that he is not the one responsible for the bombing that killed Prim. Although Katniss does not necessarily believe his assertion, she feels compelled to learn "the truth," so she makes an effort to "hang on" to her sanity as best she can, using physical pain to help herself maintain focus just as Peeta does after being released from the District 13 hospital and joining the Star Squad (359). Realizing that everyone she likes and trusts is either dead or presently unavailable, she decides to consult with Haymitch about Snow's assertion, only to be mocked by him, an action that drives her back into her depression. Looking for a "dim and quiet" hidden space where she can "curl up," make herself "smaller," and "try to disappear entirely," she goes into a forgotten wardrobe and buries herself under a pile of silken clothing (351, 363). Feeling "like a caterpillar in a cocoon awaiting metamorphosis," she tries to make herself into something new but "remain[s] a hideous creature," quickly slipping back into her "old repertoire of nightmares" (363). She is able to rouse herself the next morning, however, when called upon to perform a final duty as the Mockingjay and execute Snow, officially ending the war. As before, performing as the Mockingjay proves therapeutic, if only because playing a role enables her to distance herself from her trauma and become functional again, at least temporarily. As a result, when Coin demands that Katniss and the other surviving victors vote on whether to hold a final Hunger Games featuring the children of those who supported Snow's regime, Katniss is able to think through the implications and ultimately takes action to prevent it, shooting Coin rather than Snow and thus ending the cycle of retribution that brought about the Games in the first place.

Killing Coin does not cure Katniss's PTSD, of course, or even improve her symptoms. On the contrary, she becomes suicidal, having nothing left to live for now that Prim is no longer there to be protected and her death has been avenged. Filled with loathing not only for herself but all of humanity, she loses interest in eating, soon becoming thinner and more fragile than she has ever been (377). At this point, it seems, Katniss has become a victim in Orgad's sense of the term, being entirely passive. She continues to live only because others take action to save her: once her trial is over, people come to feed and rehydrate her and then carry her "like a rag doll" to a waiting hovercraft, which takes her back to District 12.

The intervention by others proves critical: upon returning to District 12, Katniss slowly begins to recover. Although she remains inactive, withdrawn, and emotionally numb, she begins to eat again and makes no effort to kill herself even though she now has the opportunity to do so (381). Moving only between the kitchen and the bathroom for the most part, she converses with no one, ignoring the phone, leaving her letters unopened, and making no effort to contact her mother. Eventually she ventures quietly down the hallway, afraid "to awaken the ghosts," and in the study she finds her father's hunting jacket, the handwritten book of edible plants her parents made, and various other objects, including her old bows. Seeing these things seems to trigger something in her, and though she leaves the other objects untouched, she puts on the jacket, moves to the living room, and falls asleep on the sofa. The fact that she does not return to the kitchen to stare into the fire is significant: she is beginning to move forwards rather than remain in stasis.

Even the "terrible nightmare" that follows — a nightmare involving being buried alive beneath shovelfuls of ash thrown by everyone she has ever known who is now dead — signals that she is moving towards recovery. Although the nightmare ends darkly, with her mouth being filled with ash so that she cannot speak, when, upon awakening she can still hear the scraping of the shovel, she takes action, rushing outdoors to "scream at the dead" (382). As it turns out, the scraping of the shovel is caused not by the dead trying to bury her but by Peeta, who has returned to District 12 and is planting primroses outside of her window in honor of Prim. The suggestion that shovels can be used to plant as well as bury seems to have a positive effect upon Katniss, helping her to realize that life and death are interconnected and that renewal is always possible. Whatever the case, the encounter with Peeta prompts Katniss to take further action: "Trembling with weakness and anxiety," she runs upstairs, removes the odiferous white rose Snow put there to torment her, and throws it into the embers in the fireplace, where it bursts into flames. "Fire beats rose again," she observes, and then she washes for the first time in weeks, burns the clothes she has been wearing, has breakfast with Greasy Sae, and decides to go hunting (383).

Recovery from severe trauma is no simple matter, of course, and Katniss has a setback after seeing workers gathering the remains of those who were killed in the bombing the previous summer. Reflecting upon everyone she has lost — not just to death but to circumstances — she is overcome again and has to be taken home in one of the carts used to transport the dead and helped to the sofa, where she sits in a stupor. Being a survivor involves both resilience and perseverance, of course, something her sister's cat, Buttercup, reminds her of when he suddenly appears in the house and hisses at her, having somehow made it all the way back from District 13. As Jennifer Lynn Barnes observes, Buttercup serves as a mirror image of Katniss, not only because he is at once "strand-offish" and "protective" but because he is self-reliant and because he loves Prim (21–2). With this in mind, it should not be too surprising that upon seeing Buttercup, she speaks to him as if she were addressing herself, insisting that Prim is dead, that there is nothing left for him in District 12, that Prim is "never coming back here again!" (386). As she confronts him, a "new sound, part crying, part singing" comes out of her, "giving voice" to her "despair," prompting Buttercup "to wail as well." The mutual release of emotion proves therapeutic, Katniss realizing that she wants to survive, even though doing so "will require previously unthinkable acts" (386). The next morning the two again cry together, but this time they "comfort each other," and "[o]n the strength of this," Katniss is finally able to call her mother on the phone "and weep with her as well" (386–7). Addressing the trauma that results from the loss of her sister directly finally enables Katniss to begin moving beyond it, just as finally grieving for her father allowed her to come to terms with his loss earlier. Whereas before she grieved by herself, however, this time she shares her pain and thus is able to receive support from others and help them in turn.

As Katniss's mental state improves, she is able to take further steps towards recovery, celebrating the lives of those she has lost rather than just mourning their passing. With Peeta's help she creates a book that records "all of the details it would be a crime to forget," such as "Lady licking Prim's cheek," her "father's laugh," and Rue with her arms outstretched as if "about to take flight" (387). By representing the dead as they were in life — idealizing them even — Katniss is able to make them "dead survivors," to borrow Lawrence Langer's term, that is, people who preserved their agency until their death, never becoming victims in Orgad's sense of the term (Langer 6). Rather than make those Katniss mourns objects of pity, the books represents them as people to be admired, much like *The Diary of a Young Girl* presents Anne Frank. Ultimately, the project proves cathartic, she and Peeta crying over it as they write it and promising "to live well" in order to honor those who have died. Although still damaged, Katniss is able to move on with her life and find some measure of happiness, the book helping to remind her that life "can be good again" (388).

Trauma, Narrative, and Society

Katniss can only fully recover from the trauma she has undergone when she finds a way to narrate it, such storytelling being, as Kalí Tal notes, a "reconstitutive" act, that is, an act that enables people to reconstruct traumatic experiences in ways that gives them mastery over them, helping them to become whole again. It can also be reconstitutive on a social level, enabling a community to not only come to terms with shared trauma but to work towards "prevent[ing] the enactment of similar horrors in the future" (Tal 121). Indeed, as Orgad indicates, survivors are expected to tell their stories: "Talking about the suffering is framed not only as therapeutic and essential to personal recovery, but also as a political and moral responsibility: breaking the silence is the foundation from which to challenge denial and avoid repetition of past horrors" (154). Katniss, of course, meets this societal expectation by putting her experiences on record in the extended first-person narrative that comprises the *Hunger Games* trilogy. Telling her story does not heal her so much as help her move forward, trauma being a "transformative experience," in the sense that those who undergo it "can never entirely return to a previous state of innocence" (Tal

119). This seems to be true on a societal level as well, as evidenced by the consequences of events ranging from the Holocaust to the terror inflicted upon Iranians by SAVAK during the reign of Mohammad Reza Shah: as for individuals, for societies there is no possibility of returning to the past, only the possibility of reconciling itself with it. In order to achieve the latter, the past must be addressed directly, something Truth Commissions have attempted to do in South Africa and other places by publicizing accounts of both perpetrators and survivors, the latter being "a crucial component of reconciliation, posttraumatic justice and nation building," as Philipa Rothfield notes. In order for healing to occur on a societal level, people must come forward with their story just as Katniss does and give voice to their experiences.

CHAPTER EIGHT

Make of It What You Will (Remix)

The Hunger Games *Trilogy as Digital Text*

"[T]he goal of literary work (of literature as work) is to make the reader no longer a consumer, but a producer of the text."
— Roland Barthes, *S/Z: An Essay*, 4

"More and more, storytelling has become the art of world building, as artists create compelling environments that cannot be fully explored or exhausted within a single work or even a single medium."
— Henry Jenkins, *Convergence Culture: Where Old and New Media Collide*, 116.

As Alan Kirby argues in *Digimodernism: How New Technologies Dismantle the Postmodern and Reconfigure Our Culture*, with the advent of digital technology, textuality has changed in a fundamental way. According to him, digimodernism — that is, digital modernism —"has decisively displaced postmodernism to establish itself as the twenty-first century's new cultural paradigm," a paradigm characterized, among other things, by people's expectation that they can take an active role in the meaning-making process (1). In the case of literature, the change involved not only the ways in which texts are written but also the ways they are received by readers, who increasingly contest the author's authority over a text. Rather than simply try to discern an author's meaning — decoding it as it were — or rely upon critics and commentators to decode for them, readers assert meanings themselves, both individually and as part of fan collectives, the latter occurring in venues ranging from book clubs to online forums. Even established texts such as Jane Austen's *Pride and Prejudice* are being reformulated by readers, as evidenced by both the more than 1,700 pieces of Austen fan fiction archived at Fanfiction.net and by professional productions such as Guy Andrew's *Lost in Austen*, a 2008 British miniseries in which a young woman from the present exchanges places with Elizabeth Bennet, and Seth Grahame-Smith's *Pride and Prejudice and Zombies*, a novel that incorporates much of Austen's original text into a modern day zombie narrative (Flood). As these reformulated versions of *Pride and Prejudice* suggest, many readers are coming to regard texts not as static, fixed objects but as constructs that can be entered into, participated in, extended, and even changed. Such readers do not read texts so much as interact with them, almost as if they were playing video games like *World of Warcraft* or *Skyrim*, entering into a world that not only registers their presence but is also affected by it.

Writers, too, have been affected by digital culture, adapting their work to new media so as to better reach their audience. Readers want texts they can enter into and writers provide them, engaging in world-building almost as if they were writing video game software. For example, the incredible popularity of J.K. Rowling's *Harry Potter* series can be attributed in part to her skill in creating an immersive imaginative space or universe that people could enter into independent of any particular character or storyline: children can "play" Harry Potter without pretending to be Harry Potter or any other established character or reenacting the stories presented in the books. And it's not just children who immerse themselves in the *Harry Potter* universe: people of all ages write *Harry Potter* fan fiction, creating their own characters and situations and publishing them online so they can be shared with others. The *Hunger Games* trilogy seems to be the same sort of text, being as much about the place in which it is set as anything else, and so allowing for others to enter into it in a variety of ways. Like all dystopian novels, which by definition involve creating an alternative space for rethinking our own world (Ricoeur 16–7), Collins's trilogy provides readers with an imaginary space that they can enter into independently of any particular character or situation. Accordingly, the trilogy has generated a tremendous amount of online discussion and fan fiction: readers, it seems, are able to immerse themselves in Collins's world, not only exploring it but co-creating it by creating their own *Hunger Games* narratives.

Fandom Communities Past and Present

Fan communities existed long before the internet, going back not just to *Star Trek*— considered by many to be the fan community *par excellence*— but to the mid-nineteenth century at least, when increasing literacy rates and the serialization of longer texts in magazines such as *Bentley's Miscellany* and *The Cornhill Magazine* made it possible for novelists such as Charles Dickens and Anthony Trollope to acquire massive followings (Law 22–5). Dickens's tours of the United States were major media events, for example, and the eagerness with which installments of works such as *Oliver Twist* and *The Old Curiosity Shop* were awaited is comparable to that which occurred just before the release of the later volumes of series such as *Harry Potter, Twilight,* and the *Hunger Games*. It is not just that the works like those of Dickens and Trollope were widely read and enjoyed: readers came together forming interpretive communities, reacting to works, discussing them, and even offering up ideas to authors on how stories might be developed in the future (O'Gorman 117). Like Rowling, Stephenie Meyer, and Suzanne Collins, popular nineteenth century writers were cognizant of their fans' desires and some even responded to them in their work. Dickens, for example, sent the title character of *Martin Chuzzlewit* to America in an effort to increase sales as the novel was being serialized, and in his autobiography Trollope reports that he killed off Mrs. Proudie in *The Last Chronicle of Barset* because of reader complaints that he "reintroduced the same characters" into his novels too often (Morgentaler 349; Trollope 275).

One critical difference between present fan communities and past ones is fan fiction, nineteenth-century fans having little opportunity to circulate their own writings because self-publishing was prohibitively expensive. It is only when affordable offset printing, mimeographing, and photocopying became available to the general public in the 1960s that fan fiction — that is, stories that employ settings and/or characters created by other writers — began to be widely disseminated at fan meetings and conventions or through the mail. Although fans of the television show *The Man from U.N.C.L.E.,* which ran from 1964 to 1968, were the first to produce what today is known as fan fiction, according to Lev Grossman, *Star Trek* fans were the ones who made it a culturally significant phenomenon, with more than one hundred publications being available by the mid-1980s (Grossman; Jenkins 2006, 42). As Grossman notes, what these two shows — and most other sources of fan fiction — have in common is the fact that they are set in compelling, alternative worlds into which fans could enter imaginatively. In this sense *The Man from U.N.C.L.E.*'s secretive world of espionage and *Star Trek*'s interstellar civilization resemble Dickens's London and Trollope's Barchester, the difference being twentieth-century fans could not only imagine living in these worlds but set their own stories in them.

With the advent of the internet, self-publishing not only became easier but writers could also engage in back-and-forth exchanges with other fans on a much wider scale. Standards also became more relaxed since, in theory at least, anyone could publish anything from brief fragments to lengthy novels, assuming they had access to a computer and access to the web. Fan fiction is not the only thing that changed, of course: fan communities themselves evolved into what Pierre Levy calls "knowledge communities," that is, "expansive, self-organizing groups focused around the collective production, debate, and circulation of meanings, interpretations, and fantasies in response to various artifacts of contemporary popular culture" (Levy 217; Jenkins 2006, 137). In effect, fans began to function as collectives rather than individuals, not only generating new content but also according it legitimacy (Levy 217). Writing in 1997, Levy predicted that with the emergence of such knowledge collectives, textuality itself would change: "The distinction between authors and readers, producers and spectators, creators and interpretations will blend to form a reading-writing continuum," with each constituency "helping to sustain the activities of the others" (121).

As Jenkins observes, Levy's prediction appears to have been largely correct: although many individuals and corporations continue to regard cultural production as property, other people are increasingly coming to regard it as a public one, as evidenced by the proliferation of fan communities that make free use of existing material, copyrighted or not, adapting it to their own needs (Jenkins 2008, 185–7). Incorporating other people's work into one's own is nothing new, of course, Virgil's *Aeneid*, for example, being a sequel of sorts to Homer's *Iliad* and Shelley Jackson's *Patchwork Girl* being a reworking of Mary Shelley's *Frankenstein* and L. Frank Baum's *The Patchwork Girl of Oz*. Indeed, one could argue that stories are never absolutely original since they are defined by conventions established by other stories. With the implementation of copyright law in the early eighteenth century and the development of intellectual property as a legal concept, however, originality came to be valued almost as if it was an aesthetic quality (Vermazen 266). Although this expectation largely holds true today, original art generally being valued more than work that is obviously derivative, with advances in mass production a new aesthetic has emerged, one that valued the use of existing material in new ways. William S. Burroughs, for example, famously experimented with what he later termed "the cut-up method" in *The Nova Trilogy,* tearing apart and recombining works by Shakespeare, Jack Kerouac, and Joseph Conrad, among others, into a new narrative so as to demonstrate that one can create original works of existing ones (Knickerboker), and Andy Warhol painted Campbell's soup cans and Coca-Cola bottles, at once celebrating and decrying the commercialization of culture. Not surprising, perhaps, as new technologies made it easier for people to both produce and disseminate their works, what was once *avant garde* became commonplace: rip-offs, sampling, mash-ups, remixes, and crossovers were increasingly recognized as a legitimate means of expressing oneself artistically. Although individuals and corporations holding trademarks and copyrights initially resisted the appropriation of property to which they held legal title, they quickly discovered that, by and large, such appropriation could not be stopped (Jenkins 2008, 196). For example, in what came to be known as the "Potter Wars," Warner Bros. Entertainment acquired the rights to *Harry Potter* and then attempted to assert control over their property by forcing unauthorized *Harry Potter* websites to shut down. Ultimately, however, doing so proved impossible, not only because of the bad publicity generated when they threatened children who were using their property for non-commercial use but because there were simply too many websites to police effectively. Eventually, the company changed its policy, tolerating non-commercial sites that were not otherwise objectionable (Lessig 206–12). At present, an equilibrium of sorts appears to have been established between fans and corporations: the free use of copyrighted materials is generally tolerated by corporations so long as those materials are not being used for profit or are damaging the brand, and fans, in turn, generally provide disclaimers, acknowledging that they do not hold rights to the materials they draw from.

The Hunger Games *Fan Community*

The Hunger Games had a fan community even before the first volume was published, Scholastic Books having circulated advance copies long in advance of its release in order to generate interest (Sellers 2008). As John Sellers noted in an article that appeared in *Publishers Weekly* months before the first volume of the trilogy was released, the early copies drew "raves, particularly online, where commentary ... lit up blogs and listserves." Based on the success of its pre-publication marketing campaign, Scholastic increased the initial printing of the novel from 50,000 copies to 200,000, and critics speculated that it would be the next "breakout" success (Sellers 2008). As it turned out, they were correct: *The Hunger Games* remained on the *New York Times* bestseller list for more than two years.

Because a large, active fan community already existed when the second volume of the trilogy was released, Scholastic was able to market *Catching Fire* to young fans directly, building excitement by sponsoring a writing contest in which children were asked to write about how they would survive the Hunger Games were they tributes: prizes included advance reading copies of *Catching Fire* (Sellers 2009). At the behest of booksellers, Scholastic also moved up the book's release date so that it would be available to children before the school year started, and printed 350,000 copies in its initial run to ensure that it was widely available (Sellers 2009; Springen 2009). In promoting *Mockingjay*, which had an initial print run of 1.2 million, Scholastic again engaged with fans directly, enlisting prominent bloggers to participate in a 13 District Blog Tour featuring readings, discussions, and giveaways (Springen 2010). It also employed social media to reach younger fans, creating an official Facebook page, and licensed official *Mockingjay* t-shirts, bracelets, and posters.

One question that needs to be addressed is why, of all the outstanding YA titles released in 2008, it was the *Hunger Games* trilogy that was so quickly and warmly embraced by fan communities. The most obvious answer is that it was a dark book for a dark time, appearing in September 2008 as the world entered the Great Recession: as Mike Meaney and Mathew Hoyt observe in Georgetown University's newspaper, *The Hoya*, "Where adolescents once craved stories of social conflict and escape, they now want tales about something more instinctive: survival." It was also timely in another sense, the market for young adult fiction having already been expanded by earlier series such as Philip Pullman's *His Dark Materials*, J.K. Rowling's *Harry Potter*, and Stephenie Meyer's *Twilight*: as Lana Whited argues, because such series appeal to such broad audiences, young adult novels are no longer marketed automatically as kids' books or genre fiction (6). Although its timeliness in both senses were certainly important factors in the *Hunger Games'* immediate success, neither fully explains why a vibrant fan community developed so quickly: after all, not every dark YA series with a broad appeal that appears during difficult times develops such fan communities. As a quick search of the fan fiction archive at Fanfiction.net reveals, *The Hunger Games* trilogy has generated at least ten times as many fan stories as the highly-acclaimed and widely popular *His Dark Materials* series, and more than thirty times more stories than *The Uglies*. Such numbers suggest that perhaps *The Hunger Games* and its sequels were timely in an additional sense, being written in a way that is particularly appealing to contemporary readers — that is, readers accustomed to digital texts.

Reading in the Digital Age

According to Alan Kirby, digimodernist texts are fundamentally different from those that preceded them in that they are interactive, multi-authored, open-ended, and haphazard. Rather than approach them as fixed objects, readers tend to approach digimodernist texts as processes, helping to shape them not only by contributing to interpretive communities but by adding to texts materially through fan fiction, video responses, and other forms of textual production (Kirby 51). In some cases, digital technology has made it possible to alter published text themselves by inserting commentary, making modifications, adding new material, and extracting parts so that they can be combined with other materials or utilized independently. Indeed, because of technologies associated with Web 2.0, people using computers, tablets, smart phones, and the like have become accustomed to interactive texts. As interactivity has increasingly become the norm, people's expectations with regards to texts have changed: people expect not only to be able to respond to texts by participating in fan communities, online discussions, and the like but also to participate in textual production. This is true even with television, a medium traditionally thought of as passive. In recent years interactive television has enabled people to do more than just vote for favorites on *American Idol*. Anyone who has followed the various official and unofficial blogs associated with reality shows like *Survivor* can see how viewers participate as authors, creating not just heroes and villains but narratives themselves. As Kirby points out, in *Big Brother*, viewers take a leading role in transforming hundreds of hours of footage into a collectively-authored story (195). Video and computer games have also developed into interactive narratives, as evidenced by games such as *Bioshock* and *Skyrim* in which players shape the stories of their own characters, no two games being entirely the same even when players assign their characters the same attributes. Massively Multiplayer Online Role-Playing Games (MMORPGs) are particularly interesting in this regard since, as the name suggests, they are multi-authored texts without discernible beginnings, middles, and ends, and therefore might be considered "post-narrative" (Aarseth 362): using MMORPGs as an example, one could argue, as Kirby, Espen Aarseth, and Don Tapscott do, that textuality itself has changed almost beyond recognition with the advent of digital technology.

Another important characteristic of digital texts is that they are open-ended — that is, incomplete, changing, growing. As Kirby notes, responses to texts are often incorporated into them, the original texts growing by accretion. The Survivorsucks.com, which was created in 2000, is comprised of hundreds of thousands of posts, representing an ever-growing cultural history of *Survivor* and other reality programs that invites users to participate in the meaning-making process. Fan fiction works in a similar way: with each addition to *Harry Potter* fan fiction archives at sites such as HarryPotterFanFiction.com, MuggleNet.com, fanfiction.net, the Potterverse grows, more than half a million stories being archived at fanfiction.net alone. Not surprisingly, perhaps, not every author is happy about fans making free use of their characters and settings: George R.R. Martin, for example, author of the highly successful *A Song of Fire and Ice* series, frequently speaks out against fan fiction, not only because in his view it violates his intellectual property rights but because he regards his characters as his children and does not "want people making off with them." J.K. Rowling, in contrast, actively supports fan fiction so long as it is not sexually explicit or otherwise inappropriate and is not being used for profit (Waters; Jenkins 2008, 185). For her part, Suzanne Collins has had very little to say about fan fiction one way or the other to date, her silence perhaps signaling acquiescence if not approval. Certainly, she has not made of point of criticizing it as Martin, Anne Rice, and Orson Scott Card do (Grossman; Pauli).

In addition, digimodernist texts are marked by what Kirby terms "haphazardness," meaning that the stories contained therein can move in multiple directions and develop in unpredictable ways (52). In part this is because contemporary texts are often multi-authored, various contributors pulling the story or stories in various directions. The open-endedness that marks many contemporary texts also seems to contribute to their haphazardness: because they lack defined boundaries, digimodernist texts have the potential to continually grow and change, reflecting new ideas and circumstances. It is not that that digimodernist texts lack structure but rather that the structure itself is subject to change. Potential storylines may be introduced but never developed — or development might be deferred until later, possibly by another author. Although some readers may find such haphazardness disconcerting or even troubling, to others it increases the sense of verisimilitude since life itself can be chaotic and develop in ways that cannot be easily predicted.

One way to explain how textuality has changed in recent years is by thinking of texts as introducing readers to new worlds rather than presenting those worlds in their entirety. As Henry Jenkins notes, storytelling has increasingly become a matter of world building "as today's artists create compelling environments that cannot be fully explored or exhausted within a single work or even a single medium" (Jenkins 2008, 116). Because the possibilities of these environments are not exhausted by the writers that present them, readers have an opportunity to make their own contributions, published or not: they are "writerly" rather than "readerly" in Roland Barthes's sense of the terms in that the reader takes an active role in creating meaning (5). As Barthes predicted more than fifty years ago, contemporary readers have increasingly come to expect participating both in the making of meaning and in textual production.

The Hunger Games *Trilogy as a Writerly Text*

The *Hunger Games* trilogy has been enormously successful by almost any measure: it has been acclaimed by both critics and educators, it has sold tens of millions of copies, and it has prompted a lively, continually growing fan community. More than that, though, it is a text that has helped transform young adult fiction, dark dystopias coming to displace fantasy and horror as the most important subgenre (Cart). Much of the series' success can be attributed to its timeliness and to its literary qualities — strong characterization, careful plotting, dramatic structure, and evocative writing. Its generic qualities as a dystopian novel should be taken into account as well, however, dystopias involving by definition the sort of world building that has become so important in contemporary storytelling. As Paul Ricoeur indicates in *Lectures on Ideology and Utopia*, dystopia has "a *constitutive* role in helping us *rethink* the nature of our social life": by providing us with a "leap outside" of the world that we inhabit every day, dystopia helps us develop "new, alternative perspectives" on the worlds in which we live (16). Rather than just tell readers how things might be, dystopia helps us imagine it, engaging us in ways that are active rather than passive.

Collins sets up her world as an alternative space in the very first chapter by having Katniss make references to things such as "reaping day" and "District 12" as if readers were a part of her world and would know what these terms refer to. Rather than provide detailed information about Panen, however, the novel begins *in medias res* as Katniss awakens and heads out to the woods to hunt: using the present tense, she describes things as they happen, providing information about her world only incidentally. Because the novel does not begin with a description of what Katniss's world is like, how it came into being, and how it relates to our own world, readers experience a certain amount of disorientation as details about what Katniss's world is like emerge slowly from her narrative. In effect, readers are immersed in Katniss's world and have to sort through clues in order to figure out when and where the story takes place and what its rules are. In this it very much resembles video games such as *Bioshock* and *Skyrim* where player-characters begin in a fully-realized, internally-consistent world of which they only have partial knowledge: readers of *The Hunger Games* explore Katniss's world, as it were, figuring out its parameters for themselves. Only at the end of the first chapter does Katniss provide information about how things came to be, and then only briefly, describing Panem only as "the country that rose up out of the ashes of a place that was once called North America" and then adding a few sentences about how environmental degradation led to a "brutal war" that resulted in the establishment of the current totalitarian regime.

As the novel and its sequels proceed, readers must continually learn new things about Panem — again, much as those playing video games might — the new information sometimes supplementing what is already known and at other times superseding it. As a result, readers must continually reconsider their understanding of Collins's fictive world, updating it as new information becomes available. In *The Hunger Games*, for example, we learn through Katniss that District 13 led a rebellion against the Capitol nearly a century earlier and was destroyed as a result; Katniss presents this information as fact, having seen the smoldering ruins on news broadcasts and having no reason to doubt its veracity. In *Catching Fire*, however, Katniss meets two refugees in the woods who are heading towards District 13, firmly believing that it still exists, and in the end of the novel we discover they are correct: it has, indeed, survived the war and is now leading a second uprising against the Capitol. In *Mockingjay* we learn more about District 13, much of the novel being set there. The knowledge of it with which we are provided continues to be highly unstable, however: over the course of the book we gradually learn, as Katniss does, that what appears to be an utopian society is, in fact, a totalitarian one, its leader hoping to overthrow the government of Panem only so that she can rule it herself. By constructing the text in such a manner, Collins induces readers to do just what Katniss does — treat knowledge as contingent, continually subjecting it to critique so as to refine it. According to Barthes, performing such work is one of the central pleasures texts offer readers: Collins's texts are "writerly" in the sense that the reader becomes not just a "consumer ... but a producer of the text," a co-author as it were (4–5).

World Building in the Hunger Games *Trilogy*

In addition to providing readers with an alternative space and making them think, The *Hunger Games* trilogy presents readers with an internally-consistent, fully-realized world that they can enter into imaginatively. Collins facilitates entry into this world by using the familiar to prevent readers from being overly discomfited by the unfamiliar and therefore resistant. Accordingly, the opening chapter of *The Hunger Games* presents readers with little that is likely to be unknown to them, Katniss's world being comprised of things such as bows and arrows, the woods, school, a coal mine, electric fences, a town square, a lottery, and television screens.

The types of people and relationships between them are likely to be familiar: Katniss is a loner with a widowed mother, a sweet, innocent younger sister, a friend who wants to be more than friends, and another boy who admires her from afar. Because all of these things are familiar, readers are less likely to be estranged from the narrative by the unusual way in which these things are combined or other aspects of Katniss's post-apocalyptic world: although Collins's readers are unlikely to know what it is like to live surrounded by electric fences, for instance, they probably know what electric fences are and how they are used, if only because they have seen *Jurassic Park*, and they are most likely familiar with the concept of being "fenced in." As a result, while initially disorienting, readers of the trilogy can generally right themselves and identify with the characters and situations strongly and even participate in the story vicariously. In contrast to narratives such as Philip K. Dick's *A Scanner Darkly* and Joanna Russ's *The Female Man*—that is, narratives that, by design, continually disorient and confuse readers, keeping them at a distance—the *Hunger Games* trilogy allows readers "in" as it were, the story being open rather than closed.

As suggested earlier, such openness is characteristic of what Kirby terms digimodernist texts: The *Hunger Games* trilogy proffers a fictive world that readers can not only engage with but enter into, supplementing it with their own imaginings as they fill in gaps or develop suggestions and possibilities that are left open by the text. The idea of readers realizing the text by filling in the gaps is nothing new, of course, Joseph Conrad, for one, having observed that "one writes only half the book; the other half is with the reader" (370); indeed, the ways in which readers actualize meanings has become a reader-response theory and has long been an important area of inquiry in disciplines ranging from literary studies to neuropsychology. What is new — or at least newer — is the focus on how knowledge communities actualize meanings collectively by transforming "personal reaction into social interaction, spectatorial culture into participatory culture" (Jenkins 2006, 40). Writing primarily about *Star Trek* fandom, Henry Jenkins observes:

> One becomes a "fan" not by being a regular viewer of a particular program but by translating that viewing into some kind of cultural activity, by sharing feelings and thoughts about the program content with friends, by joining a "community" of other fans who share common interests. For fans, consumption

naturally sparks production, reading generates writing, until the terms seem logically inseparable ... [Jenkins's ellipses].

There is, of course, an important difference between *Star Trek* fandom and *Hunger Games* fandom. Whereas the original Trekkies had to rely upon photocopying, snail mail, and face-to-face meetings in order to exchange ideas, *Hunger Games* fans can instantly access other people's responses to the trilogy through the internet and publish their own reactions, further collapsing the distinction between consuming texts and producing them. The internet also facilitates collaboration, enabling readers to collectively analyze each volume as it appeared on discussion boards and in chat rooms, anticipate coming volumes, and try to map the location of each district by together weighing evidence Collins provides both in the texts and in interviews. In addition it enabled a new, particularly broad form of fan fiction known as SYOTs, which stands for "submit your own tribute." In SYOTs, the primary author or authors ask fans to submit characters to be incorporated into the story of a particular Hunger Games; as the story proceeds, the author/s continuously solicit ideas from readers, including those who submitted characters. These SYOTs show just how capacious the *Hunger Games'* fictive world is: since the trilogy provides detail about only three Hunger Games competitions, the two that Katniss participated in and the Quarter Quell that Haymitch won, the other 72 Hunger Games present readers with the opportunity to create new stories, as do the infinite number of Hunger Games that could conceivably take place after the trilogy closes, hypothetical Games that have generated numerous stories themselves. The trilogy has also generated a variety of slash fiction, that is, erotic stories featuring same-sex couples such as Peeta and Cinna or Katniss and Madge Undersee, and crossover fiction, that is, stories that blend the *Hunger Games* with other fictional universes such as the ones featured in *Buffy: The Vampire Slayer* and *Percy Jackson & the Olympians*. Collins's fictive world, it seems, can accommodate just about anything, at least in the minds of readers.

Sampling, Remix and Intertexuality

Another reason why digital age readers might find the *Hunger Games* trilogy appealing is because of the way Collins incorporates other stories into her own, borrowing characters and situations from sources ranging from Plutarch's *Lives of the Noble Grecians and Romans* to *Extreme Makeover.* Like many of her readers, Collins seems to be less concerned with being original than she is with conveying her ideas through her work however she can. Although in her interviews Collins typically cites the myth of Theseus and contemporary reality television like *Survivor* as her primary sources, she has also acknowledged Plutarch's *Lives*, Stanley Kubrick's *Spartacus*, Émile Zola's *Germinal*, and Thomas Hardy's *Far from the Madding Crowd* as sources at various times. *Robin Hood* also appears to have been an influence as has the story of Mulan, William Golding's *Lord of the Flies*, and possibly Tacitus's account of Queen Boudica in *On the Life and Character of Julius Agricola.* In effect, she remixes existing narratives, borrowing names from some, and storylines, subplots, themes, and characters from others, creating not so much a pastiche as a hybrid, that is, a combination of existing elements that, together, becomes something new. In many ways the *Hunger Games* trilogy is as much a work of crossover fiction as the fan stories that put Kirk and Spock in Panem or Katniss in *Glee.* Indeed, the plot of *The Hunger Games* can be described in one of the stories Collins incorporates into her text: make Robin Hood a teenage girl and put her in a post-apocalyptic future rather than the past, a future where a corrupt Capitol based on ancient Rome controls the populace through bread and circuses, the primary circus being a reality show like *Survivor* where people have to fight to the death, only the contestants are tributes like the ones King Minos demanded of ancient Athens. The main character, Katniss Everdeen, named for a Thomas Hardy character who refuses to marry the person everyone thinks she should because she wants to remain independent, is selected as one of the tributes from a community very much like the coal mining town in *Germinal* and is sent to the decadent Capitol, where she is prepared for the games as if she were an *Extreme Makeover* contestant. Then she is sent into the arena — which combines *Lord of the Flies*, Theseus and the Minotaur, and *Survivorman* — where she and the other tribute from her district fake a Romeo and Juliet–like double suicide and both get to emerge as victors in the Games. And that is just *The Hunger Games*: in the sequels Collins seemingly draws from the stories of Mulan, Spartacus, Boudica, Cincinnatus, and *The Lord of the Rings.*

Given the way Collins freely borrows from other stories, it would be difficult to argue that the *Hunger Games* trilogy is original, at least in the strict sense of the term. As suggested earlier, however, originality is no longer valued in the way it used to be, if only because borrowing, sampling, and remixing are increasingly accepted as a legitimate means of artistic expression: readers today seem to be more interested in a story's overall effect than whether it is derivative. Many readers have observed, for example, the premise of *The Hunger Games*—that is, children forced to fight to the death by an oppressive government — very much resembles the premise of Koushun Takami's *Battle Royale*. Few *Hunger Games* fans seem to care very much, however, recognizing that the trilogy amounts to much more than just an Americanized version of Takami's novel. Moreover, as one fan points out in an online debate about *The Hunger Games* and *Battle Royale*, Takami himself seems to use Stephen King's *Running Man* as source for his novel, something he appears to acknowledge by naming the town his child-warriors come from after the town of Castle Rock, which King frequently uses as a setting for his stories; ironically, King himself reportedly named Castle Rock after Jack's bastion in *Lord of the Flies* (Heather and Agent Z).

Of course, not everyone agrees where the line is between borrowing and stealing, between plagiarism and intertextuality; there seems to be some agreement among media theorists, however, that those growing up in the digital age are more open to make free use of other people's work than those who came before them, if only because doing so has become the norm (Lessig xvii). Indeed, one could even argue that to digital readers, utilizing existing material to new effect is just as much a creative act as creating an original work, if such a thing is even possible. According to German author Helene Hegemann, "Originality doesn't exist anymore ... only genuineness" (Funck). To Hegemann, who, a high school student at the time, incorporated material taken from blogs into her novel, *Axolotl Roadkill*, redeploying existing material is not "stealing" so long as "the material [is put] into a completely different and unique context" (Miller 2010): the only way she could genuinely express what she needed to was by employing the expressions of others. Although many of Collins's readers might not agree with Hegemann's privileging of genuineness over originality, many others presumably would since it seems to reflect the tenets of remix culture, tenets which value direct, honest expression above all else.

The Hunger Games *Trilogy as Digital Text*

That the *Hunger Games* trilogy qualifies as a digital text is difficult to dispute, if only because all three volumes have been on eBook bestseller lists continuously for more than two years. Whether it can be said to have the same aesthetic qualities as video games, blogs, and other interactive media is harder to ascertain since, as Kirby notes, digital media are changing our ideas about both texts and textuality. Traditionally written texts have been regarded as fixed, verbal representations of people's cultural lives — that is, of their thoughts, feelings, ideas, and actions as well as their relationships to other people and to social and political institutions. As physical objects, a text's form is literally set, and therefore, according to this view, the text of the *Hunger Games* trilogy is the particular arrangement of words on a page that one acquires when one purchases a copy of the book. Even an electronic version of the trilogy could be thought of as a text in the traditional sense if it corresponds exactly to the physical version: texts are traditionally viewed as static objects.

If, however, we define written texts not as words set upon pages but as representations of people's cultural lives that acquire meaning only when actualized by readers, both as individuals and as part of knowledge communities, then, by definition, all written texts are interactive, multi-authored, open-ended, and haphazard: as co-creators, readers actively participate in the meaning-making process, drawing upon their own knowledge and experience as they establish understandings of texts, understandings that, in many cases, could not possibly have been anticipated. According to this view, the fact that Aeschylus could not possibly have intended his play, *The Persians*, to be understood by audiences 2,500 years later as an implicit critique of the U.S. invasion of Iraq has no bearing on validity of such an interpretation (Donelan): audiences ultimately determine the meanings of texts for themselves. Having said that, texts facilitate understandings in different sorts of ways, some being more restrictive than others in terms of the types of stories they allow or enable. Texts that are relatively open — that is, texts that are constructed so as to invite readers to be active rather than passive — might be described as being "participatory," a term associated with the digital aesthetic, since, like video games, blogs, and other new forms, they allow for and even encourage user participation in the meaning-making process. Judging by the vibrant fan community that developed around it, the *Hunger Games* trilogy can be regarded as this sort of text. Collins, it seems, has created a fictive world that is not only compelling but is also one that readers can enter into imaginatively and participate in, sometimes by publishing *Hunger Games* stories of their own. She is not the first writer to create such a world, of course; rather, she is a leading member of a generation of writers that employs the digital aesthetic as a matter of course. In this sense she is very much a twenty-first century writer, a writer who regards readers as creative partners, constructing narratives that can accommodate the narrative desires of others.

Appendix A

Glossary of Terms

arena   The Hunger Games are set in outdoor soundstages so that tributes can be seen and heard continually. Arenas, which can be many miles across and feature any sort of terrain, are enclosed within force fields. Typically they center around a giant cornucopia containing weapons and sometimes other equipment. The physical environment is entirely controlled by the Gamemakers, who can create things such as earthquakes, landslides, fires, rainstorms. The Gamemakers also control flora and fauna, often introducing artificial creatures, or "mutts," that are specially designed to terrorize tributes. Once the Games are complete, arenas become tourist attractions.

Avox   Prisoners whose tongues are disabled so that they can no longer speak. Considered traitors by the Capitol, they are used for menial labor, working in the sewer systems or serving as personal attendants.

beauty base zero   A term used by Katniss's prep team to describe a physical state in which someone has been fully prepared for a fashion remake. For girls and women this involves conditioning the hair, depilation, skin treatments, a manicure, and the like. For men the process is much less involved, focusing on the face.

black goo   A toxic, tarlike substance released by one the Capitol's pods in so great a volume that it can drown people.

The Block   The nickname for a special military training area designed to train District 13 soldiers for street combat in the Capitol.

bloodbath   Intense combat that usually takes place at the beginning of the Games as tributes fight for whatever weapons and supplies are available at the Cornucopia.

The Book   A compendium of edible and medicinal plants compiled by Katniss's parents. Also known as the "plant book," it serves as a model for the book Katniss, Peeta, and Haymitch make to honor the dead at the end of the trilogy.

breads   Each District has a distinctive type of bread, often characteristic of the district's primary industry. Loaves from District 4, for example which produces seafood, are shaped like fish and contain seaweed. District 12 is symbolized by traditional Appalachian drop biscuits.

buttercup A poisonous plant that most livestock know to avoid. It features bright yellow, cup-shaped flower. Prim names her cat "Buttercup" because of the color of his fur.

The Capitol A large city located in the Rocky Mountains that serves as Panem's capital. The term "Capitol" is often used to refer to the government itself just as the term "Washington" is often used to refer to the United States government.

career pack Tributes from Districts 1, 2, and 4 typically work together as a pack, at least initially, slaughtering other tributes in the bloodbath at the beginning of the Games, taking control of the supplies, and then hunting down other tributes systematically.

careers A nickname for tributes from Districts 1, 2, and 4 who have been specially trained to become tributes. Careers are physically strong, adept at fighting, and have been conditioned to kill, giving them a distinct advantage in the Hunger Games.

City Circle A large open space in the Capitol's center used for public gatherings, including the filming of pre–Game ceremonies. The Circle is bordered by grand buildings, including the president's mansion.

Command District 13's high-tech war room, featuring communications equipment, maps, computers, and control panels.

communicuff Communications device worn on arm by important military personnel in District 13.

Community Home An orphanage of sorts for children of District 12 without parents to care for them.

cornucopia Modeled on the Horn of Plenty associated with the harvest, in the arena the cornucopia is a large golden metal horn filled with weapons and sometimes other supplies.

dandelion A small plant with edible leaves that is identifiable by its bright yellow flower, which later becomes a parachute ball, enabling seeds to be distributed by air. In *The Hunger Games*, seeing the first dandelion of the year reminds Katniss that she can forage for food and thus provide for her family.

Dark Days The name used by the Capitol for a previous uprising of the districts against it. District 13 was largely destroyed during the conflict.

dungeon   A detention center located in lower levels of District 13. Katniss's team is held there in shackles.

feast   A term used to denote a special event held in the arena during the Games; Gamemakers typically use feasts, which offer food or other necessities, to draw tributes together so they will fight.

force field   Energy fields that function as barriers. Some are invisible and others have mirror-like surfaces; some merely repel objects and others burn them. Both types have weakness or "chinks" that can sometimes be spotted visually.

The Gamemakers   The team of people responsible for running the Hunger Games. In addition to designing the arenas, they evaluate and rank tributes and oversee the Games once they begin. They wear deep purple robes, marking their high status.

gesture of District 12   A rarely used signal of admiration and respect. The gesture is made by putting the three middle fingers of the left hand to the lips and then holding them out towards the person being honored.

gifts   Supplies provided to tributes by sponsors while the former are in the arena. Gifts are delivered by silver parachutes.

"The Hanging Tree"   A song about a lover who beseeches another to join him in death. Katniss learns the song from her father as a girl but is forbidden to sing it because of its macabre subject matter. It serves as a motif in *Mockingjay*.

Harvest Festival   A usually modest gathering to celebrate the harvest in District 12; in *Catching Fire*, it corresponds with Katniss and Peeta's official appearance in the District during their victory tour. New Year's Day is the only other holiday mentioned in the trilogy.

Head Gamemaker   The person responsible for staging the Hunger Games. A fur-trimmed collar marks the Head Gamemaker's rank.

healer   A layperson who uses local flora and traditional medicine to treat the sick and injured.

hijacked   A term used to describe the use of tracker jacker venom to implant false memories and associate them with fear in order to condition people.

The Hob   An illegal market housed in a converted warehouse in District 12.

The Holograph   A three-dimensional map of the Capitol that includes pod locations; it is also referred to as the "Holo."

hovercraft   Silent, low-flying aircraft used by both the Capitol and District 13 for transportation and combat. They are equipped with sight shields, making them invisible.

jabberjay   A muttation created by the Capitol during the first Rebellion for intelligence purposes, jabberjays are able to repeat human conversations in their entirety. The Capitol released these exclusively male birds into rebel areas, where they memorized conversations so that they could be analyzed later by the government. Once the rebels learned how jabberjays were being used, they started using them to provide the Capitol with misinformation.

Justice Building   The government building in each District, where official business is conducted. The Justice Building in District 11 may once have been a state capitol building since it has a dome.

katniss root   A water flower with starchy, potato-like tubers. Katniss is named after the plant, her father telling her once, "As long as you can find yourself, you can never starve" (*Hunger Games* 52).

lamb stew   A dish Katniss first encounters in the Capitol that becomes her favorite. She mentions it in her interview with Caesar Flickerman before her first Hunger Games, receives it from a sponsor while in the arena, and has it again while part of the Star Squad in *Mockingjay*.

the lightning tree   A large artificial tree in the Quarter Quell arena that is struck by lightning at noon and midnight, marking the beginning of an electrical storm.

lizard mutts   Part-human, part-reptilian monsters that hiss Katniss's name as they pursue her through the sewers under the Capitol. The fact that they smell of roses suggests that they have been specifically designed to terrorize Katniss, who has been conditioned to associate that smell with President Snow.

mayor   The official title of each district's political leader. The fact that they are called "mayor" even though they are appointed rather than elected suggests that the Capitol represents itself as governing in the interests of the people.

The Meadow   A scruffy field located between the Seam and the woods in District 12. It serves as a place of temporary refuge when District 12 is bombed and later is used as a mass grave.

mentor   Past winners of the Hunger Games who prepare the tributes from their district for the Games.

merchants Shop owners and tradespeople who live in town. In District 12, members of the merchant class tend to have lighter hair and skin and hold themselves above those living in the Seam.

mockingjay A small black, crowned bird with a bit of white on its wings that proliferated when the jabberjays created by the Capitol to spy on the rebels during the Dark Days bred with mockingbirds, creating a new species. Although they cannot enunciate words as jabberjays do, the can reproduce melodies and mimic human vocal sounds.

mockingjay pin A circular golden pin that Madge Undersee gives to Katniss to wear as a District token while in the arena. The mockingjay is connected to the ring surrounding it only by its wing tips. Previously it had belonged to Maysilee Donner, a tribute who died in the second Quarter Quell.

monkey mutts Aggressive monkey-like mutts that attack *en masse* in the Quarter Quell. They are orange and about half the size of an adult human.

morphling A highly-addictive analgesic derived from morphine, this medication is generally available only to those in the upper echelons of society in the districts and in the Capitol. The drug can cause hallucinations. The term "Morphling" is also used in reference to people who are addicted to the medication, such as the tributes from District 6 in *Catching Fire.*

muttations (aka mutts) Animal mutations created by the Capitol to terrorize its enemies. Mutts often have both human and animal characteristics so as to unsettle their victims.

nightlock A poisonous berry that closely resembles an edible variety. Katniss encounters nightlock both in the woods outside of District 12 and the arena. In Mockingjay, "nightlock" is the name given to a suicide pill designed by District 13 scientists. The word "nightlock" is also used to trigger the Holo's self-destruct function.

The Nut An important Capitol base located in a hollowed out mountain in District 2. It is nicknamed "the Nut" after Plutarch describes it as a "tough nut to crack."

Panem The nation that emerges in North America following a global ecological catastrophe which involves the destruction of the upper atmosphere and rising sea levels. Panem is seemingly named after the Latin word for bread, as in *panem et circenses*, but may also reference

Pan-America, suggesting that the national boundaries extend beyond the former United States. In interviews, Suzanne Collins pronounces "Panem" with the accent on the last syllable.

panem et circenses   Latin phrase meaning bread and circuses. It was first used in Juvenal's Tenth Satire.

pods   Anti-personnel devices used by the Capitol to booby trap urban areas. The fact that they kill in so many different ways make them not only difficult to defend against but also terrifying.

prep team   Beauty specialists devoted to making tributes presentable as participants in the Hunger Games and related events such as processions and interviews.

The President's Mansion   President Snow's residence, located in the Capitol at the City Center.

primrose   Medieval Latin for "first rose."

propos   "Propaganda spots" produced in District 13 and broadcast to the other districts as well as the Capitol in support of the rebellion.

Quarter Quell   A special version of the Hunger Games, held every 25 years. In the first Quarter Quell, the districts were forced to elect tributes in order to remind people of the costs of having elected to rebel 25 years earlier. In the second Quarter Quell, twice the number of tributes were selected from each district to remind people that twice as many rebels died as loyalists. In the third Quarter Quell, tributes are drawn from previous victors in order to remind people that even the strongest cannot resist the Capitol's power.

reaping   A public ceremony held in each District at which the year's tributes are determined by lottery.

Remake Center   A facility located in the Capitol where the tributes' prep teams groom and dress them for public appearances.

rue   An evergreen shrub that features large numbers of small, yellow flowers.

Rue's song   A four-note tune Rue sings in District 11 when she sees the flag signaling the end of the workday. Mockingjays take up the tune, indicating to all the workers that they can stop. Rue uses the tune in the 74th Hunger Games to signal to Katniss that she is okay.

The Seam   An area in District 12 near the coal mines that is inhabited by workers and their families. Denizens of the Seam are generally looked down upon by people who live in town.

showmance An portmanteau of the words "show" and "romance" that came into usage with the advent of reality television in the 1990s. Showmances are on-camera romances that may or may not have a real basis.

sight shield Cloaking devices that make hovercrafts invisible. They do not operate when cargo doors or bomb bays are open.

silver parachutes Devices used to deliver gifts to tributes while they are in the arena.

Spartacus A 1960 Stanley Kubrick film based on the novel by Howard Fast. The film focuses on a gladiator, Spartacus, who leads a slave revolt in the first century B.C.E. Collins cites the film as greatly influencing the story arc of the *Hunger Games* trilogy.

Special Defense A facility located in District 13 where special weapons are designed and tested.

spile A tool used to penetrate the tree bark so that fluids beneath it can be tapped.

Sponsor People who purchase gifts for delivery for tributes while they are in the arena. Sponsors are often affluent citizens who spend money on their favorite tributes and/or those they have bet on. Groups sometimes sponsor tributes' from their district as well. Sponsors are recruited by the tributes mentors, who also organize the distribution of gifts.

Squad Four-Five-One (aka "Star Squad") A special military squad comprised of former victors, sharpshooters, and a camera crew. The number "451" is apparently a reference to Ray Bradbury's novel, *Farenheit 451.*

The Square A central area of many districts including District 12 where events such as the Reapings and other gatherings take place

stylist As leaders of the tributes' prep teams, stylists are responsible for creating and projecting the media personae of their tributes. Cinna, for example, presents Katniss as "the girl who was on fire," while Rue's stylist presents her as a bird, dressing her in a winged, gossamer gown.

tesserae A system which makes it possible for children to acquire extra grain and oil for their families by entering their names multiple times in annual Hunger Games lotteries, thereby increasing the odds that they will be selected for the Games.

Theseus A mythic Greek king, Theseus is considered the founder of Athens and one of the greatest heroes of ancient Greece. According to Collins, the story of his battle with the minotaur greatly influenced her conception of the Hunger Games. Like King Minos, who demanded Athens send tributes into the Labyrinth in order to face the minotaur as part of their war reparations, the Capitol demands that the districts send tributes to the Games. Katniss resembles Theseus in that, like him, she volunteers to be a tribute and ultimately takes decisive action, making it so that no more children have to be sacrificed.

toasting   An informal marriage ceremony that involves the sharing of bread. In District 12, couples do not consider themselves married until they have undergone the ceremony.

token   A small, innocuous object that tributes are allowed to bring with them into the arena. Tokens are typically related to a district's principle industry. Glimmer, for example, the tribute from District 1, which manufactures luxury items, chooses a ring as a token, only to have it rejected by a review board because twisting the gemstone causes a poisoned spike to pop out.

tracker jacker   A genetically-enhanced wasp that is extremely aggressive, attacks in swarms, and has a particularly deadly venom that induces hallucinations.

tracker jacker venom   A deadly substance extracted from tracker jackers that creates fearsome hallucinations, pain, and sometimes death. The Capitol uses the venom both to torture prisoners and to condition them.

Training Center   A building in the Capitol where tributes come together to practice fighting and learn survival techniques; the center also affords tributes the opportunity to meet each other and form alliances before entering the arena.

tributes   Children selected by lottery to participate in the annual Hunger Games. Each of the 12 districts is represented by one boy and one girl between the ages of 12 and 17.

Victors' Village   Large, luxurious homes assigned to the victors of past Hunger Games.

Victory Tour   A national tour organized by the Capitol for Hunger Games victors. The victors and their entourage visit every district, where they are feted as heroes. The Tour takes place in late fall, beginning in District 12 and ending in the victor's district.

volunteering   After tributes are selected by lottery, an eligible child may volunteer to participate in the Games, replacing the tribute of his or her sex.

white liquor   Hard liquor that is barely if at all aged, such as most moon-shine.

wolf mutts   Wolf-like creatures that have sharp claws and can stand on their hind legs. The wolf mutts that appear towards the end of the 74th Hunger Games are particularly terrifying because they appear to have the eyes and other features of tributes who have already died.

Appendix B

Glossary of Characters

Note: Characters are alphabetized by first name.

Alma Coin   The president of District 13 who has ambitions of becoming ruler of all of Panem.

Annie Cresta   A victor from District 4 who becomes mentally unstable during the Games after seeing a fellow tribute decapitated. She is selected for the third Quarter Quell but replaced by Mags, who volunteers for her.

Atala   A tall, athletic woman who is in charge of training tributes before the Games.

Beetee   An extremely intelligent middle-aged victor from District 3. Following his escape from the third Quarter Quell arena, he relocates to District 13 and works for the rebellion.

Blight   A victor from District 7 who dies in the third Quarter Quell by running into the force field surrounding the arena.

Boggs   A District 13 soldier who works closely with President Coin. He serves as one of Katniss's bodyguards when she becomes the Mockingjay and later commands the Star Squad.

Bonnie   A young woman who escapes District 8 along with her teacher, Twill, following an uprising, and tries to reach District 13.

Bristel   A member of Gale's crew in the mines of District 12.

Brutus   A victor from District 2 who volunteers to participate in the third Quarter Quell. He is over 40 years old but remains fit and is very aggressive in the arena.

Buttercup   Prim's cat, named for the bright yellow flower, the color of which, according to Prim, matches Buttercup's fur. Katniss tries to drown him when Prim first came home with him but relents because of her sister's tears.

Caesar Flickerman   The host of the Hunger Games and related programming.

Cashmere   A victor from District 1 who is selected for the third Quarter Quell along with her brother, Gloss.

Castor A District 13 videographer who, along with his brother, Pollux, films Katniss for propos.

Cato A brutish tribute from District 2. He is one of the favorites to win the 74th Hunger Games.

Cecelia A victor from District 8 who, when selected for the third Quarter Quell, has to leave her three children behind.

Chaff A one-armed victor from District 11, who is a good friend of Haymitch's. He is selected to participate in the third Quarter Quell.

Cinna Katniss's stylist, who decides to present her as "the girl who was on fire" in the 74th Hunger Games, making her a sensation both in the Capitol and the districts.

Claudius Templesmith The official announcer for Hunger Games.

Clove A sadistic career tribute from District 2 who fights in the 74th Hunger Games.

Coriolanus Snow The president of Panem. He is a white-haired man who smells of blood and roses. He secured his place as president by poisoning potential rivals.

Cray The Head Peacekeeper in District 12 until he is replaced by Romulus Thread for being too lax. As Head Peacekeeper, he is known for sexually exploiting young women.

Cressida The woman who directs a propaganda spot featuring Katniss that is filmed in District 8.

Dalton A cattle expert who escaped from District 10 and made his way to District 13 years before the rebellions starts. He participates in a focus group organized by Haymitch to strategize about how to present Katniss as the Mockingjay and later presides over Finnick and Annie's wedding.

Darius A young, friendly Peacekeeper from District 12 who becomes an Avox.

Delly Cartwright A classmate of Katniss's who knows Peeta well. She relocates to District 13.

Dr. Aurelius A District 13 psychiatrist responsible for Katniss's treatment. At one point he describes her as a mental Avox.

Effie Trinket District 12's escort for the Hunger Games. She has ambitions of being assigned to a better district.

Enobaria A victor from District 2 who volunteers to participate in the third Quarter Quell. She is notorious for having used her teeth to tear open the throat of another tribute in the Games that she won.

Finnick Odair   The victor of the 65th Hunger Games at age 14, Finnick, who comes from District 4, is extraordinarily attractive and known for his romantic exploits. He is selected to participate in the third Quarter Quell and becomes an ally of Katniss and Peeta.

Flavius   A member of Katniss's prep team, he takes primary responsibility for her hair.

Foxface   The nickname Katniss gives to the female tribute from District 5 in the 74th Hunger Games. She has a fox-like face, red hair, and is wily.

Fulvia Cardew   The calculating assistant of Plutarch Heavensbee.

Gale Hawthorne   Katniss's hunting partner in District 12 who becomes her close friend. He is literally tall, dark, and handsome.

Glimmer   A blonde-haired, green-eyed tribute from District 1 whom Katniss describes as being "sexy all the way."

Gloss   A victor from District 1 who is selected for the third Quarter Quell along with his sister, Cashmere.

The Goat Man   A sickly former miner who makes his living in District 12 selling goat milk. He sells Katniss an injured goat, which she gives to Prim.

Greasy Sae   A vendor at the Hob in District 12.

Greasy Sae's granddaughter   A developmentally disabled girl who is treated as a pet in District 12; she is described as living in her own world and may be autistic.

Haymitch Abernathy   Victor of the second Quarter Quell, which involved 48 tributes rather than the usual 24. He has since served as a mentor for District 12 and become an alcoholic.

Hazelle Hawthorne   Gale's mother, who, after losing her husband in the same mining accident that Katniss's father died in, began takes in laundry for money just one week after giving birth to a child.

Homes   A District 13 soldier who is assigned to the Star Squad because of his sharpshooting skills.

Jackson   A member of the Star Squad, second-in-command to Boggs.

Johanna Mason   An emotionally unstable victor from District 7 who won her first Hunger Games by feigning weakness. She allies herself with Katniss in the third Quarter Quell.

Katniss Everdeen   Born on May 8 to a mother from town and a father from the Seam. Following the death of her father in a mining accident, she provides for her family by hunting illegally in the woods outside District 12 and trading in the Hob.

Lady A nanny goat Katniss purchases for Prim. The goat, which is injured when Katniss buys it, is healed by Prim and her mother and goes on to produce a regular supply of milk.

Lavinia An Avox whom Katniss meets while in the Training Center. Upon seeing her there, Katniss realizes she is the same person she saw being captured in the woods outside of District 12.

Leeg 1 and 2 Two sisters from District 13 who look so much alike, Katniss can only tell them apart by their eyes. They are both members of the Star Squad.

Leevy A girl who lives several doors down from Katniss in the Seam, she survives the bombing of District 12 and relocates to District 13. She participates in a focus group organized by Haymitch to strategize about how to utilize Katniss in propaganda videos.

Lyme A victor from District 2, she is the rebel commander in charge of the siege of the Nut.

Madge Undersee The daughter of the mayor of District 12, she is one of Katniss's few friends, giving Katniss the mockingjay pin her aunt, Maysilee Donner, wore when she participated in the second Quarter Quell.

Mags An elderly victor from District 4 who volunteers to take Annie Cresta's place when she is selected for the third Quarter Quell.

Martin A developmentally-disabled boy from District 11 who is killed by Peacekeepers for stealing a pair of infrared glasses.

Marvel A tribute from District 1 who participates in the 74th Hunger Games. Katniss only learns his name when she visits District 1 in her Victory Tour.

Mayor Undersee The mayor of District 12, he is relatively lax in enforcing the Capitol's rules. His daughter, Madge, is one of Katniss's friends.

Maysilee Donner A tribute from District 12 who allies herself with Haymitch in the second Quarter Quell. She is Madge Undersee's aunt and the original owner of the mockingjay pin that Katniss wears in the arena.

Messalla An assistant to Cressida, the director of a propaganda spot featuring Katniss that is filmed in District 8.

Mr. Mellark Peeta's father, Mr. Mellark is the District 12 baker who was once romantically interested in Katniss's mother. He promises to make sure Prim has enough to eat when Katniss leaves for the Capitol to participate in the 74th Hunger Games.

Mitchell   A District 13 soldier who is assigned to the Star Squad because of his sharpshooting skills.

The Morphlings   A pair of victors from District 6 who participate in the third Quarter Quell. Both are morphling addicts.

Mrs. Everdeen   The daughter of a District 12 apothecary who marries a miner and moves to the Seam. When her husband dies in a mining accident, she falls into a deep depression, forcing Katniss to provide for the family and take responsibility of Prim. Once she recovers from her depression, she becomes a healer.

Mrs. Mellark   Peeta's mother, Mrs. Mellark is a harsh woman who chases Katniss from the garbage cans near her bakery and strikes Peeta for burning a loaf of bread.

Mrs. Undersee   Madge's mother, who has been traumatized by the loss of her sister, Maysilee Donner, in the second Quarter Quell.

Octavia   A member of Katniss's prep team whose entire body is dyed green.

Paylor   A rebel commander from District 8 who is later elected president of Panem.

Peeta Mellark   A baker's son from District 12 who participates in both the 74th Hunger Games and the third Quarter Quell. He is well-liked, ethically-aware, and a gifted communicator.

Plutarch Heavensbee   A Gamemaker for the 74th Hunger Games who becomes Head Gamemaker for the third Quarter Quell. He relocates to District 13.

Pollux   A District 13 videographer who, along with his brother Castor, films Katniss for propos. Pollux is an Avox.

Portia   Peeta's stylist for both the 74th Hunger Games and the third Quarter Quell.

Posy Hawthorne   Gale's 4-year-old brother. He survives the bombing of District 12 and relocates to District 13, along with the rest of his family.

Primrose Everdeen   Katniss's younger sister, whom Katniss goes to great lengths to protect. Prim is a healer like her mother.

Purnia   A District 12 Peacekeeper who intercedes on Gale's behalf when he is being whipped by Romulus Thread, possibly saving his life.

Ripper   A purveyor of white alcohol in District 12.

Romulus Thread   The Head Peacekeeper who replaces Cray in District 12. He quickly cracks down on the district, electrifying the fence that surrounds it 24 hours a day, shutting down the black market, and punishing people publically in the town square.

Rooba   A District 12 butcher who purchases game from Katniss and Gale.

Rory Hawthorne   Gale's 12-year-old brother. He survives the bombing of District 12 and relocates to District 13.

Rue   A Tribute from District 11 who reminds Katniss of her sister, Prim. The two become allies in the 74th Hunger Games.

Seeder   A 60ish victor from District 11 who is selected to participate in the third Quarter Quell.

Seneca Crane   The Head Gamemaker of the 74th Hunger Games.

Tax   A trainer assigned to the archery station in the Training Center.

Thom   A member of Gale's mining crew. He survives the bombing of District 12 and later returns there, helping to dispose of bodies.

Thresh   A tall, strong dark-skinned tribute from District 11 who refuses to ally with the Careers in the 74th Hunger Games. He appears to be survived only by a sister and an old woman, possibly his grandmother.

Tigris   The proprietor of furry underwear in District 13, she was once a well-known stylist for the Hunger Games. Too much plastic surgery has made her repellent, at least to Katniss.

Twill   A schoolteacher who leaves District 8 after her husband and many others are killed by the Capitol following an uprising. She and her companion, Bonnie, try to reach District 13.

Venia   A woman with brightly dyed hair and golden tattoos who is a member of Katniss's prep team.

Vick Hawthorne   Gale's 10-year-old brother. He survives the bombing of District 12 and relocates to District 13 along with his family.

Wiress   A middle-aged victor from District 3, she is a highly-intelligent inventor who has some difficulties in communicating.

Woof   An elderly victor from District 8 who is selected for the third Quarter Quell.

Questions
for Further Study

The Underland Chronicles

Gregor the Overlander was published in 2003, just months after the U.S. invaded Iraq. Discuss Collins's attitudes towards war as represented in the novel and consider how those attitudes change as Collins continued publishing volumes of *The Underland Chronicles* through 2007. Can the final volume, *Gregor and the Code of the Claw* be read as an anti-war novel in a way that *Gregor the Overlander* cannot?

At times Suzanne Collins describes *The Underland Chronicles* as books about family, and at other times she describes the series as books about war. Discuss the ways in which the two subjects — that is family and war — are represented in the series. How are the two interconnected?

After returning home to New York City after fighting in a brutal war against the rats in the Underland, Gregor watches the news and realizes that the same sorts of horrors occur in the Overland every day. Why do you think Collins ends the book this way? Are children reading *Gregor and the Code of the Claw* likely to be saddened by such a conclusion? Are they likely to look at war differently?

In a 2010 interview with Rick Margolis, Collins describes both *The Underland Chronicles* and the *Hunger Games* trilogy as war stories. Discuss the two series in relation to one another. Do they express similar attitudes towards war and violence? How else are they similar? How are they different?

Before becoming a children's author, Collins wrote scripts for children's programs such as *Clarissa Explains It All*, *Clifford's Puppy Days*, and *Wow! Wow! Wubbzy!* See if you can connect the types of stories that are presented in children's television to the type of story Collins relates in *The Underland Chronicles*. Do programs such as *Clifford's Puppy Days* address serious themes despite their apparent lightness? Do books like *Gregor the Overlander* offer children pleasure, entertainment, and even comfort?

The Hunger Games

The Hunger Games begins with Katniss donning her father's jacket, tucking her hair under her hunting cap, and heading into the woods to provide for her family, assuming a role traditionally identified with men. What is the significance of these actions? Is she a "female man" of sorts or is something else being suggested by Collins here with regards to women's capabilities and potential? Does she continue to cross traditional gender boundaries throughout the novel? Throughout the trilogy? What message might Collins be conveying and how does it relate to that of other contemporary narratives involving gender transgressions such as Disney's *Mulan* or *The Hunchback of Notre Dame*?

The premise of *The Hunger Games* is similar to that of Koushun Takami's *Battle Royale* (1999), a Japanese novel in which a repressive government forces schoolchildren to fight to the death over the course of several weeks. Both works remain extremely popular with young adult readers and others and have been adapted for film. What does the fact that two writers from very different cultures utilize very similar premises say about contemporary attitudes about government? About the entertainment media? About globalization? About youth culture?

In *The Hunger Games*, Katniss repeatedly refers to Peeta as "the boy with the bread." What does this phrase mean and what feelings is Katniss expressing when she uses it? What does bread symbolize in the story?

In 2008, *The Hunger Games* was named to the American Library Association's Amelia Bloomer list of recommended feminist fiction. In what ways might the book be considered a feminist novel? Be sure to consider not only Katniss and her relationships with Gale and Peeta but other characters and the way they are represented.

In his review published in *Entertainment Weekly*, Stephen King writes: "Reading *The Hunger Games* is as addictive (and as violently simple) as playing one of those shoot-if-it-moves videogames in the lobby of the local eightplex; you know it's not real, but you keep plugging in quarters anyway." Does King's comparison seem valid? In what ways is reading *The Hunger Games* like playing a video game? Does Collins provide her readers with a subject position within the text in the same way that first-person shooter games do?

Catching Fire

Catching Fire opens with Katniss sitting on a rock in the woods as the sun begins to rise. She reflects, "I can't fight the sun. I can only watch helplessly as it drags me into a day that I've been dreading for months." She dreads the coming day so much because it marks the beginning of the Victory Tour, which will entail visiting every district and celebrating her victory in the Games. Discuss Katniss's use of the rising sun as a conceit for her in the novel's opening paragraph and in the passages that follow. In what ways do her references to the sun play off of the line well-known Biblical line, "The sun also arises, and the sun goes down, and hastens to its place where it arose" (Ecclesiastes 1:5)? How does the conceit set the tone for the opening portion of the novel?

Katniss's mother behaves very differently in *Catching Fire* than she does in *The Hunger Games*, seemingly having recovered entirely from the depression that earlier paralyzed her. How are her activities as a healer connected to her recovery? What might Collins's message be about agency? About the importance of community?

Early on in *Catching Fire*, Cray, the head Peacekeeper, is replaced by Romulus Thread, who quickly begins a crackdown in District 12, closing the black market, strictly enforcing laws that had previously been ignored, and punishing people publicly. Discuss the effects his actions have upon the populace: to what extent do they succeed in intimidating the people and preventing them from offering resistance to the government? See if you can relate events that happen in District 12 under Thread to recent efforts by law enforcement to contain dissent in places like Egypt, Iran, and the United States. Is strict enforcement of the law an effective means of controlling populations?

In the second chapter of *Catching Fire*, Gale surprises Katniss by grabbing her by the face and kissing her. Discuss Katniss's response to this unwanted sexual attention. Why doesn't she kiss him back? Why does she compare his hands to snares? What does the involuntary noise she makes at the back of her throat suggest? Discuss whether the encounter affects their relationship in a permanent way.

Before she enters the Quarter Quell arena, Haymitch advises Katniss to remember who the real enemy is. Recalling his words at the climax of the story, she decides to try take down the force field surrounding the arena rather than kill Enobaria. Discuss the significance of her action, both in the context of *Catching Fire* and in the context of her relationship with Haymitch. If he wanted her help in taking down the force field — something that the rebels clearly planned in advance since they went to great lengths to ensure that the tools necessary to do so were available within the arena — then why didn't he inform her of the plan in advance? Is it important to Haymitch that Katniss decide for herself who the real enemy is, or does he simply not trust her with information about the plan?

Mockingjay

In Chapter 9 Katniss sings "The Hanging Tree," a song she learned from her father, to the mockingjays outside of District 13 so that Pollux can hear the beautiful music mockingjays make when they repeat songs. After singing the song, she tells the story of how she came to understand the lyrics of the song as she became older. Discuss what the song means and how Katniss's understanding of it changes over time. What does it mean to Katniss at the time she sings it, and why does the song keep coming back to her for the rest of the book?

In an interview with Rick Margolis (2010), Collins indicates that she thinks that "the concept of war, the nature of war, the ethical ambiguities of war are introduced too late to children." She adds that if "the whole concept of war were introduced to kids at an earlier age, we would have better dialogues going on about it, and we would have a fuller understanding." Such dialogues, she argues, could conceivably lead to an end to war, though admittedly this seems like "a far-off dream." Bearing Collins's comments in mind, discuss *Mockingjay* as an effort to introduce children to war. Can it be considered an anti-war text? Does it glorify war in any way? Is *Mockingjay* a significant contribution to dialogue on war? Are children likely to be influenced by the novel?

In *Mockingjay* Johanna Mason becomes addicted to morphling, going so far as to steal it from Katniss when the latter is hospitalized after being shot in District 2, and, after being severely burned in the bombing that kills Prim, Katniss becomes an addict herself. Discuss the ways in which drug use is represented in *Mockingjay*. What benefits do Johanna and Katniss derive from them? What are the costs? In what ways, if any, is the use of morphling represented as being any different from the use of alcohol? Is morphling worse? What lessons might Collins be conveying to her readers?

Toward the end of Chapter 16, Peeta confronts Katniss about her having kissed both him and Gale, insinuating that she was wrong to do so without getting their consent. When she retorts that she does not need anyone's permission, he calls her "a piece of work." Discuss the significance of Peeta's insult: what is he implying? Also, discuss Katniss's response: why does she find it so hurtful, particularly after she just defended her conduct?

In *Mockingjay,* both Katniss and Peeta have difficulty distinguishing "Real" from "not Real" because of the debilitating trauma they each undergo. Discuss the strategies the two of them employ in order to rebuild their worlds. How do their strategies differ? How well do they succeed? Is their inability to differentiate "real" from "unreal" permanently affected by their experiences? More importantly, do their realities themselves change?

The Hunger Games *Trilogy*

In "Why So Hungry for the Hunger Games?" Sarah Rees Brennan writes, "The message of the Hunger Games is that appearances are deceiving and vitally important." Explain what she might mean by this seemingly paradoxical statement. Does it pertain to the characters, the setting, or both? How do characters like Katniss avoid being deceived? What forms of deception do they practice? Is truth ever available?

Although Haymitch and Katniss never become friends, they do form a strong attachment and are able to communicate at times without speaking. Why might this be — is it because they are alike or for some other reason? Consider in particular the vote the surviving victors take about whether to reinstitute the Hunger Games: why, after voting "yes" and awaiting Haymitch's decision, does Katniss think that it is at this moment that she'll finally know if Haymitch really understands her? How does he end up voting and what is the significance of his decision?

In the *Hunger Games* trilogy, the environment has been seriously compromised. Identify the types of damage that have occurred and discuss their possible causes. Could things like those described really happen? Can the trilogy be read as a cautionary tale about the environment? If so, why doesn't Collins go in to more detail about the behaviors that led to the ecological disaster so as to mark certain behaviors as being reckless? Is her message about the environment more powerful because she is vague about what exactly happened?

In an interview with Rick Margolis, Collins indicates that although the Hunger Games themselves are based on the story of Theseus being sent by Athens to Thebes as a tribute to face the Minotaur, Spartacus "becomes more of a model for the arc of the three books, for Katniss." Discuss the ways in which Katniss's story resembles Spartacus's, referring to either "The Life of Crassus" from Plutarch's *Lives of the Noble Grecians and Romans* or Stanley Kubrick's film *Spartacus* (1960), both of which Collins cites as sources.

Global warming and other environmental issues have been receiving increasing attention as weather patterns appear to change and polar ice continues to melt, raising sea levels. Discuss the ways in which environmental degradation is represented in the *Hunger Games* trilogy. What has happened to the Earth in the 200 or so years that have passed since our own time? How has environmental change affected human society? Is the extinction of human beings presented as a real possibility? Do the people of Panem seem to be taking any steps to prevent further damage?

Discuss the ways in which science and technology are represented in *The Hunger Games Trilogy*. How important are things like muttations, hoverplanes, force fields, and advanced medications to the story itself? Do the books make technology a primary subject? Could the same story be told without references to future technology? Does it read like science fiction?

The Hunger Games *Film*

As Collins herself acknowledges, adapting a novel for the screen involves difficult choices. In the case of *The Hunger Games*, a number of characters were omitted from the film, including Madge Undersee, Katniss's only friend, other than Gale, when the story opens. Discuss the significance of this omission. Why do you think Madge was included in the first place and why was she cut? How does it affect your understanding of the story?

In a podcast with the *New York Times Review of Books*, Suzanne Collins expressed both interest and concern about how the film might be viewed. In particular, she worried that audience members would "be caught up in the Capitol's game," enjoying it in the same way audiences enjoyed gladiator games in ancient Rome. How valid were her concerns? Does the film present violence as a spectacle to be enjoyed? Be sure to discuss your own experience of viewing the film — both your response and the response of those around you.

Discuss how Katniss and her world as they are realized in the film. Is she as you imagined her? Be sure to consider not only how she looks and acts but her relationships with other people, as well as her place in the District 12 community. Is she essentially the same character in both the book or film? Discuss both similarities and differences.

In the novel, Suzanne Collins employs cliffhangers at the end of each chapter to generate suspense and keep the reader engaged: even the final chapter ends with a cliffhanger, creating a tension that is only resolved when the reader begins *Catching Fire*. Filmmakers general resort to other means to generate tension. Discuss what these means are and how the film employs them. Does the film depend upon suspense to the same extent that the novel does?

According to the director of *The Hunger Games*, Gary Ross, it was very important to him that the film convey the same sense of immediacy that the book does and that a first-person perspective be maintained to the extent possible. With this in mind, discuss Ross's cinematic style. How does he induce viewers to perceive the world from Katniss's perspective? How does he maintain this perspective in scenes in which Katniss is absent?

Bibliography

Primary Texts

THE UNDERLAND CHRONICLES

Gregor the Overlander. New York: Scholastic, 2003. Print.
Gregor and the Prophecy of Bane. New York: Scholastic, 2004. Print.
Gregor and the Curse of the Warmbloods. New York: Scholastic, 2005. Print.
Gregor and the Mark of the Secret. New York: Scholastic, 2006. Print.
Gregor and the Code of the Claw. New York: Scholastic, 2007. Print.

THE *HUNGER GAMES* TRILOGY

The Hunger Games. New York: Scholastic, 2008. Print.
Catching Fire. New York: Scholastic, 2009. Print.
Mockingjay. New York: Scholastic, 2010. Print.

ADDITIONAL WRITINGS

Fire Proof: Shelby Woo #11. New York: Aladdin, 1999. Print.
When Charlie McButton Lost Power. Illustrated by Mike Lester. New York: Puffin, 2005. Print.

Secondary Texts

Aarseth, Espen. "Quest Games as Post-Narrative Discourse." *Narrative Across Media: The Languages of Storytelling.* Ed. Marie-Laurie Ryan. Lincoln: University of Nebraska Press, 2004. 361–76. Print.
Addison, Paul. *Churchill on the Homefront, 1900–1955.* London: Pimlico, 1993. Print.
Aronson, Marc. "Coming of Age: One Editor's View of How Young Adult Publishing Developed in America." *Publisher's Weekly.* 11 February 2002. 82–6. Print.
_____. *Exploding the Myths: The Truth About Teenagers and Reading.* London: Scarecrow, 2001. Print.
Atwood, Margaret. *The Handmaid's Tale.* New York: Everyman's Library, 2006. Print.
_____. *Oryx and Crake.* New York: Anchor, 2004. Print.
Austen, Jane. *Pride and Prejudice.* Ed. Donald Gray. New York: Norton, 2000. Print.
Austin, John. *How to Do Things with Words.* Ed. J.O. Urmson and Marina Sbisa. Cambridge: Harvard University Press, 1975. Print.
Baird, Jane. "Mockingjay." *School Library Journal.* 31 August 2010. Web.

Bibliography

Barnes, Jennifer Lynn. "Team Katniss." *The Girl Who Was on Fire: Your Favorite Authors on Suzanne Collins's Hunger Games Trilogy.* Ed. Leah Wilson. Dallas, TX: Benbella, 2011. 13–27. Print.

Barthes, Roland. *S/Z: An Essay.* Trans. Richard Miller. New York: Hill and Wang, 1975. Print.

Bartter, Martha. "Normative Fiction." *Science Fiction, Social Conflict, and War.* Ed. Philip John Davies. New York: Manchester University Press, 1990. 169–185. Print.

Baum, L. Frank. *The Patchwork Girl of Oz.* New York: Harper Collins, 1995. Print.

Beauvoir, Simone de. *The Second Sex.* Trans. Constance Borde and Sheila Malovany-Chevallier. New York: Vintage, 2011. Print.

Bird, Elizabeth. "Review of the Day: *The Hunger Games* by Suzanne Collins." *School Library Journal.* 28 June 2008. Web.

Bjorkman, Edwin. "An Interview: Pragmatism — What It Is." *New York Times.* 3 November 1907. Web.

Blasingame, James. "An Interview with Suzanne Collins." *Journal of Adolescent & Adult Literacy* 52.8 (2009): 726–7. Print.

"Book Review Podcast: Suzanne Collins." *New York Times Review of Books.* 27 August 2010. Web.

Booth, John. "*Mockingjay* Emerges Victorious." Geekdad. *Wired.* 2 September 2010. Web.

Borsellino, Mary. "Your Heart Is a Weapon the Size of a Fist." *The Girl Who Was on Fire: Your Favorite Authors on Suzanne Collins's Hunger Games Trilogy.* Ed. Leah Wilson. Dallas TX: Benbella, 2011. 29–40. Print.

Bratton, J.S. "British Imperialism and the Reproduction of Femininity in Girl's Fiction, 1900–1930." *Imperialism and Juvenile Literature.* Ed. Jeffrey Richards. New York: Manchester University Press, 1989. 195–215. Print.

Brennan, Sarah Rees. "Why So Hungry for the Hunger Games?" *The Girl Who Was on Fire: Your Favorite Authors on Suzanne Collins's Hunger Games Trilogy.* Ed. Leah Wilson. Dallas, TX: Benbella, 2011. 1–12. Print.

Bucher, Katherine, and M. Lee Manning. *Young Adult Literature: Exploration, Evaluation, and Appreciation.* Upper Saddle River, NJ: Pearson, 2006. Print.

Burgess, Anthony. *A Clockwork Orange.* New York: W.W. Norton, 2011. Print.

Butler, Judith. *Bodies that Matter: On the Discursive Limits of "Sex."* New York: Routledge, 1993. Print.

_____. *Gender Trouble: Feminism and the Subversion of Identity.* New York: Routledge, 1990. Print.

Carpenter, Susan. "Book Review: *Mockingjay.*" *Los Angeles Times.* 22 August 2010. Web.

Cart, Michael. *From Romance to Realism: 50 Years of Growth and Change in Young Adult Literature.* New York: Harper Collins, 1996. Print.

Chafe, Wallace. *Discourse, Consciousness, and Time: The Flow and Displacement of Conscious Experience in Speaking and Writing.* Chicago: University of Chicago Press, 1994. Print.

"Children's Review: *Mockingjay.*" *Publishers Weekly.* 23 September 2010. Web.

Clark, Terri. "Crime of Fashion." *The Girl Who Was on Fire: Your Favorite Authors on Suzanne Collins's Hunger Games Trilogy.* Ed. Leah Wilson. Dallas, TX: Benbella, 2011. 127–140. Print.

Cole, Pam B. *Young Adult Literature in the 21st Century.* New York: McGraw Hill, 2009. Print.

Bibliography

Conrad, Joseph. *The Collected Letters of Joseph Conrad: Volume One, 1861–1897*. Ed. Frederick R. Karl and Laurence Davies. New York: Cambridge University Press, 1983. Print.

"A Conversation: Suzanne Collins." Scholastic. Scholastic.com. No date. Web.

Couldry, Nick. "Teaching Us to Fake It: The Ritualized Norms of Television's 'Reality' Game." *Reality TV: Remaking Television Culture*. Ed. Susan Murray and Laurie Ouellette. New York: New York University Press, 2004. 57–74. Print.

Cusey, Rebecca. "*The Hunger Games* Is a Blue-State Harry Potter." *The Daily Caller*. 29 August 2011. Web.

Davies, Philip John, ed. *Science Fiction, Social Conflict, and War*. New York: Manchester University Press, 1990. Print.

de Certeau, Michael. *The Practice of Everyday Life*. Trans. Steven F. Rendall. Berkeley: University of California Press, 1984. Print.

Defoe, Daniel. *Robinson Crusoe*. New York: Barnes & Noble, 2003. Print.

Derrida, Jacques. *Writing and Difference*. New York: Routledge, 2001. Print.

Despain, Bree. "Community in the Face of Tyranny." *The Girl Who Was on Fire: Your Favorite Authors on Suzanne Collins's Hunger Games Trilogy*. Ed. Leah Wilson. Dallas, TX: Benbella, 2011. 195–210. Print.

Dewey, John. *John Dewey: The Middle Works, 1899–1924*. Ed. Jo Ann Boydston. Edwardsville: Southern Illinois University Press, 1978. Print.

Dickens, Charles. *Martin Chuzzlewit*. Oxford: Oxford University Press, 2009. Print.

Dominus, Susan. "Suzanne Collins's War Stories for Kids." *New York Times*. 8 April 2011. Web.

Donelan, Charles. "A New Translation of *The Persians* Reinvents the Chorus: A Modern Ancient Tragedy." *Santa Barbara Independent*. 27 March 2008. Print.

Donnelly, Shannon. "Best YA Novels of 2010." *The Daily Beast*. 20 December 2010. Web.

Dunae, Patrick A. "New Grub Street for Boys." *Imperialism and Juvenile Literature*. Ed. Jeffrey Richards. New York: Manchester University Press, 1989. 12–33. Print.

Dunn, Steve. "Inspirational Patient Stories." CancerGuide. 12 December 2011. Web.

Dworkin, Andrea. *Woman Hating: A Radical Look at Sexuality*. New York: Dutton, 1974. Print.

Easthope, Anthony. "The Personal and the Political in Utopian Science Fiction." *Science Fiction, Social Conflict, and War*. Ed. Philip John Davies. New York: Manchester University Press, 1990. 50–67. Print.

Edinger, Monica. "It's All About the Horror of War in Suzanne Collins's *Mockingjay* and Patrick Ness's *Monsters of Men*." *The Huffington Post*. 30 August 2010. Web.

Egan, Kate. *The Hunger Games: Official Illustrated Movie Companion*. New York: Scholastic, 2012. Print.

Ellison, Ralph. "Recent Negro Fiction." *New Masses*. 40.6 (1940): 22–6. Print.

Eno, Brian. "A Big Theory of Culture." *Culture: Leading Scientists Explore Societies, Art, Power, and Technology*. Ed. John Brockman. New York: Harper Perennial, 2011: 57–69. Print.

Erritouni, Ali. "Apartheid Inequality and Postapartheid Utopia in Nadine Gordimer's *July's People*." *Research in African Literatures* 37.4 (2006): 68–84. Print.

Feminist Cupcake. "Currently, I'm Diggin' the Hunger Games." Feminist Cupcake. 28 January 2011. Web.

Flood, Alison. "Jane Austen in Zombie Rampage up the Book Charts." *The Guardian*. 9 April 2009. Web.

Franich, Darren. "The Hunger Games: How Reality TV Explains the YA Sensation." EW's Shelf-Life. *Entertainment Weekly*. 6 October 2010. Web.

Frank, Anne. *The Diary of a Young Girl*. New York: Everyman, 2010. Print.

Freedman, William. "The Literary Motif: A Definition and Evaluation." *Essentials of the Theory of Fiction*. Ed. Michael Hoffman and Patrick Murphy. Durham: Duke University Press, 1996. 200–12. Print.

Funck, Gisa. "Plagiarism Debate Irks Authors Who Claim Everything Is Derivative." *Deutsche Welle*. 24 February 2010. Web.

Garber, Marjorie. *Vested Interests: Cross-Dressing and Cultural Anxiety*. New York: Routledge, 1997. Print.

Gibbs, Anna. "Affect Theory and Audience." *The Handbook of Media Audiences*. Ed. Virginia Nightingale. New York: Wiley-Blackwell, 2011. 251–66. Print.

Gillespie, Tarleton. "Narrative Control and Visual Polysemy: Fox Surveillance Specials and the Limits of Legitimation." *Velvet Light Trap* #45 (Spring 2000): 36–49. Print.

Golding, William. *Lord of the Flies*. New York: Perigee, 2011. Print.

Gordimer, Nadine. *July's People*. New York: Penguin, 1982. Print.

Grahame-Smith, Seth. *Pride and Prejudice and Zombies*. Philadelphia: Quirk Books, 2009. Print.

Gramsci, Antonio. "State and Civil Society." *Selections from the Prison Notebooks of Antonio Gramsci*. Ed. and trans. Quentin Hoare & Geoffrey Nowell Smith. New York: International Publishers, 1971. Print.

Granger, John. "Suzanne Collins: Writing 'War Stories'?" Hogwarts Professor. 15 August 2010. Web.

Green, John. "Scary New World." Sunday Book Review. *New York Times*. 7 December 2008. Web.

Grossman, Lev. "The Boy Who Lived Forever." *Time*. 7 July 2011. Web.

Gurdon, Meghan Cox. "Darkness Too Visible." *The Wall Street Journal*. 4 June 2011. Web.

Heather and Agent Z. "*The Hunger Games* vs. *Battle Royale*." *The Galaxy Express*. 30 March 2010. Web.

Heinze, Rüdigeboutrer. *Ethics of Literary From in Contemporary American Literature*. New Brunswick, NJ: Transaction, 2004. Print.

Henderson, J. Maureen. "The Teenage Wasteland of Dystopian Fiction." *True/Slant*. 29 September 2011. Web.

Higgins, Brian, and Hershel Parker. *Herman Melville: The Contemporary Reviews*. New York: Cambridge University Press, 2009. Print.

Hintz, Carrie and Elaine Ostry, eds. *Utopian and Dystopian Writing for Children and Young Adults*. New York: Routledge, 2003. Print.

Hogan, Patrick Colm. *Colonialism and Cultural Identity: Crises of Tradition in the Anglophone Literatures of India, Africa, and the Caribbean*. Albany: State University of New York Press, 2000. Print.

Hollingdale, Peter. "The Adolescent Novel of Ideas." *Only Connect: Readings on Children's Literature*. Ed. Sheila Egoff et al. New York: Oxford University Press, 1996. Print.

Hollinger, Veronica. "(Re)reading Queerly: Science Fiction, Feminism, and the Defamiliarization of Gender." *Future Females, the Next Generation: New Voices and Velocities in Feminist Science Fiction Criticism*. Ed. Marleen Barr. New York: Rowman and Littlefield, 2000. 197–215. Print.

Homer. *The Iliad*. Trans. Bernard Knox. New York: Penguin, 2006. Print.

Hopkinson, Deborah. "A Riveting Return to the World of *The Hunger Games*." Book Page. No date. Web.

Hudson, Hannah Trierweiler. "Q & A with Hunger Games Author Suzanne Collins." Scholastic. 25 May 2011. Web.

Hughes, Monica. "The Struggle Between Utopia and Dystopia in Writing for Children and Young Adults." *Utopian and Dystopian Writing for Children and Young Adults*. Ed. Carrie Hintz and Elaine Ostry. New York: Routledge, 2003. 156–160. Print.

Hurston, Zora Neale. *Their Eyes Were Watching God*. New York: Harper and Row, 1990. Print.

Huxley, Aldous. *Brave New World*. New York: Harper Perennial, 2006. Print.

Italie, Hillel. "How Has 'Hunger Games' Author Suzanne Collins' Life Changed?" *Huffington Post*. 23 September 2009. Web.

Jackson, Shelley. *The Patchwork Girl*. Watertown, MA: Eastgate Systems, 1995. Print.

Jacobs, Harriet. *Incidents in the Life of a Slave Girl, Written by Herself*. Ed. Jean Yellin. Cambridge: Harvard University Press, 2000. Print.

James, Edward. "Violent Revolution in Modern American Science Fiction." *Science Fiction, Social Conflict, and War*. Ed. Philip John Davies. New York: Manchester University Press, 1990. 98–112.

James, P.D. *Children of Men*. New York: Knopf, 1993. Print.

James, William. "The Will to Believe." *The New World* 5 (1896): 327–347. Print.

Jameson, Fredric. "Then You Are Them." *London Review of Books*. 10 September 2009. 7–8. Print.

Jeffries, Sheila. *Beauty and Misogyny: Harmful Cultural Practices in the West*. New York: Routledge, 2005. Print.

Jenkins, Henry. *Convergence Culture: Where Old and New Media Collide*. New York: New York University Press, 2008. Print.

_____. *Fans, Bloggers, and Gamers: Exploring Participatory Culture*. New York: New York University Press, 2006. Print.

Johnson, Steven. *Everything Bad Is Good for You: How Today's Popular Culture Is Actually Making Us Smarter*. New York: Riverhead Trade, 2006. Print.

Jordan, Tina. "Suzanne Collins on the Books She Loves: *The Hunger Games* Author Talks about 'A Wrinkle in Time' and 'The Idiot.'" *Entertainment Weekly*. 13 August 2010. Web.

_____. "Suzanne Collins on Writing a 'Hunger Games' Movie: 'You Have to Let Things Go.'" *Entertainment Weekly*. 9 December 2010. Web.

Juvenal. *The Satires*. Trans. Niall Rudd. New York: Oxford University Press, 1999. Print.

Kafka, Franz. "The Hunger Artist." Trans. Ian Johnston. Johnstonia. 15 February 2012. Web.

King, Stephen. "The Hunger Games." *Entertainment Weekly*. 8 September 2008. Web.

_____. *The Running Man*. New York: Signet, 1999. Print.

Kirby, Alan. *Digimodernism: How New Technologies Dismantle the Culture and Reconfigure Our Culture*. New York: Continuum, 2009. Print.

Kirk, Robin. "Dark Materials in Young Adult Fiction." Open Salon. 14 April 2011. Web.

Klumpp, Jennifer. Comment. "The Hunger Games: Entry 1." The Book Club: New Books Dissected over E-Mail. *Slate Magazine*. 31 August 2010. Web.

Knickerbocker, Conrad. "William S. Burroughs, The Art of Fiction No. 36." *The Paris Review* (1965): 35. Web.

Bibliography

Knox, Olivier. "Politics Colored U.S. 'Terror Alert': Former Bush Aide." Agence France Press. 20 August 2009. Web.

Koepp, Stephen, Gisela Bolte, and Jon Hull. "Is the Middle Class Shrinking?" *Time.* 29 September 2011. Web.

Kress, Adrienne. "The Inevitable Decline of Decadence." *The Girl Who Was on Fire: Your Favorite Authors on Suzanne Collins's Hunger Games Trilogy.* Ed. Leah Wilson. Dallas TX: Benbella, 2011. 179–194. Print.

Lady G. "Collected Thoughts on the Hunger Games, Book 1: Team Katniss All the Way." Are We Feminists? Arewefeminists.wordpress.com. 31 August 2011. Web.

Langer, Lawrence. *Admitting the Holocaust: Collected Essays.* New York: Oxford University Press, 1995. Print.

Lansing, Alfred. *Endurance: Shackleton's Incredible Voyage to the Antarctic.* New York: Basic Books, 2001. Print.

Lavenne, Francois-Xavier, et al. "Fiction, Between Inner Life and Collective Memory: A Methodological Reflection." *New Arcadia Review* Vol. 3 (2005). Web.

Law, Graham. *Serializing Fiction in the Victorian Press.* New York: Palgrave Macmillan, 2001. Print.

Lee, Harper. *To Kill a Mockingbird.* New York: Harper, 2010. Print.

Lessig, Lawrence. *Remix: Making Art and Commerce Thrive in the Hybrid Economy.* New York: Penguin, 2008. Print.

Lessing, Doris. *The Memoirs of a Survivor.* New York: Vintage, 1988. Print.

Levy, Pierre. *Collective Intelligence: Mankind's Emerging World.* Cambridge, UK: Perseus, 1997. Print.

Lippmann, Walter. *Public Opinion.* New York: Harcourt, Brace, 1922. Print.

Littman, Sarah Darer. "The Politics of *Mockingjay.*" *The Girl Who Was on Fire: Your Favorite Authors on Suzanne Collins's Hunger Games Trilogy.* Ed. Leah Wilson. Dallas, TX: Benbella, 2011. 163–194. Print.

Locke, Alain. Review of *Their Eyes Were Watching God. Opportunity.* 1 June 1938. Print.

Lockwood, Cara. "Not So Weird Science." *The Girl Who Was on Fire: Your Favorite Authors on Suzanne Collins's Hunger Games Trilogy.* Ed. Leah Wilson. Dallas, TX: Benbella, 2011. 113–125. Print.

London, Jack. *The Iron Heel.* New York: Dover, 2009. Print.

Lorber, Judith. *Paradoxes of Gender.* New Haven: Yale University Press, 1994.

Lowry, Lois. *The Giver.* New York: Delacourt, 2007. Print.

Mahoney, Kathy. "Watching the Hunger Games." Tales of the Marvelous. Wordpress. 18 July 2011. Web.

Margolis, Rick. "A Killer Story: An Interview with Suzanne Collins, Author of *The Hunger Games.*" *The School Library Journal.* 30 June 2008. Web.

_____. "The Last Battle: With *Mockingjay* on Its Way, Suzanne Collins Weighs in on Katniss and the Capitol." *School Library Journal.* 1 August 2010. Web.

Markiewicz, Agnes. "The Feelings in the Arena: Subversion of Gender and Representation of Feelings in the *The Hunger Games* by Suzanne Collins." New York College English Association 2011 Conference: Literature and Feeling. Utica, New York. 1 October 2011.

Martin, George R. R. "Someone Is Angry on the Internet." *Not a Blog.* 7 May 2010. Web.

McCarthy, Cormac. *The Road.* New York: Knopf, 2006. Print.

Meaney, Mike, and Mathew Hoyt. "Young Adult Fiction Comes of Age: The State of Nature." *The Hoya.* 30 January 2012. Web.

Melville, Herman. *Moby-Dick: A Longman Critical Edition*. New York: Longman, 2009. Print.

Meyer, Stephenie. "Stephenie's Book of the Month for November." Twilightmoms.com. 17 October 2008.Web.

_____. *Twilight*. New York: Little Brown Books, 2008. Print.

Miller, Laura. "Fresh Hell: What's Behind the Boom in Dystopian Fiction for Young Readers?" *The New Yorker*. Newyorker.com. 29 September 2011. Web.

_____. "Plagiarism: The Next Generation." *Salon*. 16 February 2010. Web.

"*Mockingjay* Sells More than 450,000 Copies in the First Week." *Publishers Weekly*. 2 September 2010. Web.

Monbiot, George. "50 People Who Could Save the Planet." *The Guardian*. 5 January 2008. Web.

Morgentaler, Goldie. "*Martin Chuzzlewit*." *A Companion to Charles Dickens*. Ed. David Paroissien. Malden, MA: Blackwell, 2011. 348–57. Print.

Morrison, Kathy. "*Mockingjay* Ends Suzanne Collins' Trilogy with Disappointment." *St. Petersburg Times*. Tampabay.com. 26 September 2010. Web.

Neary, Lynn. "Edgy, Violent Thrillers for the Teen-Age Set." NPR Books. 1 September 2009. Web.

Nel, Philip. "The Trauma Games." Nine Kinds of Pie. 28 August 2010. Web.

O'Brien, Robert. *Z for Zachariah*. New York: Simon Pulse, 2007. Print.

Oetzel, Shawn. "*The Road* by Cormac McCarthy: A Writer's Perspective." Yahoo! Voices. 12 March 2010. Web. 251

O'Gorman. *A Concise Companion to the Victorian Novel*. Malden, MA: Blackwell, 2005. Print.

Orgad, Shani. "The Survivor in Contemporary Culture and Public Discourse: A Genealogy." *The Communication Review* 12.2 (2009): 132–61. Print.

Orwell, George. *Collected Essays, Journalism and Letters*. Vol. 1. Ed. Sonia Brownell Orwell and Ian Angus. New York: Harcourt Brace and World, 1970. Print.

_____. *1984*. New York: Signet, 1961. Print.

Palahniuk, Chuck. *Fight Club*. New York: W.W. Norton, 2005. Print.

Pauli, Michelle. "Fan Fiction." *The Guardian*. 4 December 2002. Web.

Paulsen, Gary. *Hatchet*. New York. Simon & Schuster, 2007. Print.

Pearson, Jacqueline. "Where No Man Has Gone Before: Sexual Politics and Women's Science Fiction." *Science Fiction, Social Conflict, and War*. Ed. Philip John Davies. New York: Manchester University Press, 1990. 8–25. Print.

Peirce, C.S. *Charles S. Peirce: The Essential Writings*. New York: Prometheus, 1998. Print.

Pfeffer, Beth. *Life as We Knew It*. New York: Harcourt, 2006. Print.

Plotz, David. "*Mockingjay* Left Me Sated, Not Satisfied." *Slate*. 30 August 2010. Web.

Plutarch. *Lives of the Noble Grecians and Romans*. Trans. John Dryden. New York: Modern Library, 1932. Print.

Pratt, Annis. *Archetypal Patterns in Women's Fiction*: Bloomington: Indiana University Press, 1982. Print.

Prinzi, Travis. Comment upon "Suzanne Collins: Writing 'War Stories.'" Hogwarts Professor. 16 August 2010. Web.

Probst, Jeff. *Survivor: Redemption Island, Episode 13*. Jeffprobst.com. 19 May 2011. Web.

Pullman, Philip. "Carnegie Medal Acceptance Speech." Randomhouse.com. 27 November 1996. Web.

_____. *The Golden Compass*. New York: Scholastic, 1995. Print.

Bibliography

"Q and A with Suzanne Collins." "After Words: Suzanne Collins's *Gregor the Overlander*." *Gregor the Overlander*. New York: Scholastic, 2003. Print.

Rapp, Adam. *Copper Elephant*. New York: HarperTempest, 2002. Print.

Rees, Elizabeth. "Smoke and Mirrors." *The Girl Who Was on Fire: Your Favorite Authors on Suzanne Collins's Hunger Games Trilogy*. Ed. Leah Wilson. Dallas TX: Benbella, 2011. 41–65.

Reese, Jennifer. "Author Interview." Scholastic. Scholastic.com. No date. Web.

_____. *"Catching Fire." Entertainment Weekly*. 28 August 2009. Web.

Richards, Jeffrey. "Introduction." *Imperialism and Juvenile Literature*. Ed. Jeffrey Richards. New York: Manchester University Press, 1989. 1–11.

Ricoeur, Paul. *Lectures on Ideology and Utopia*. Ed. George H. Taylor. New York: Columbia University Press, 1986. Print.

Riordan, Rick. *The Lightning Thief*. New York: Puffin, 2005. Print.

Ristuccia, Michelle. "YA Report: *The Hunger Games Trilogy*, by Suzanne Collins." Science Fiction and Fantasy Writers Chat. 12 September 2011.

Roiphe, Katie. "Survivor." *New York Times*. 8 September 2010. Web.

Roth, April L. "Contrived Television Reality Survivor as a Pseudo-event." *Survivor Lessons: Essays on Communications and Reality Television*. Ed. Mathew J. Smith and Andrew F. Wood. Jefferson, NC: McFarland, 2003. 27–36. Print.

Rothfield, Philipa. "Surviving Reconciliation, from the Social to the Singular." *Radical Psychology* 6.1 (2007). Web.

Rowen, Michelle. *Demon Princess: Reign Check*. New York: Walker's Children, 2010. Print.

Rowling, J.K. *Harry Potter and the Sorcerer's Stone*. New York: Scholastic, 1999. Print.

Ryan, Carrie. *The Forest of Hands and Teeth*. New York: Delacorte, 2010. Print.

_____. "Panem and Circenses." *The Girl Who Was on Fire: Your Favorite Authors on Suzanne Collins's Hunger Games Trilogy*. Ed. Leah Wilson. Dallas, TX: Benbella, 2011. 99–111. Print.

Safire, William. "Besotted with Potter." *New York Times*. 27 January 2000. Web.

St. John, Graham. "Introduction." *Victor Turner and Contemporary Cultural Performance*. Ed. Graham St. John. New York: Berghahn, 2008. 1–37. Print.

Salinger, J.D. *The Catcher in the Rye*. Boston: Back Bay Books, 2001. Print.

Sambell, Kay. "Presenting the Case for Social Change: The Creative Dilemma of Dystopian Writing for Children." *Utopian and Dystopian Writing for Children and Young Adults*. Ed. Carrie Hintz and Elaine Ostry. New York: Routledge, 2003. 163–178. Print.

Scarry, Elaine. *The Body in Pain: The Making and Unmaking of the World*. New York: Oxford University Press, 1985. Print.

"Season Finale." *Survivor Borneo*. Aired on 23 August 2000.

Selby, Nick. *Herman Melville: "Moby-Dick."* New York: Columbia University Press, 1993. Print.

Sellers, John. "A Dark Horse Breaks Out: The Buzz Is on for Suzanne Collins's YA Series Debut." *Publishers Weekly*. 9 June 2008. Web.

_____. "Hungry? The Latest on *The Hunger Games*." *Publishers Weekly*. 12 March 2009. Web.

Shakespeare, William. *Othello*. New York: Simon & Schuster, 2004. Print.

_____. *Romeo and Juliet*. New York: Simon & Schuster, 2004. Print.

Shelley, Mary. *Frankenstein*. Ed. D.L. Macdonald and Kathleen Scherf. Toronto: Broadview, 1999. Print.

Bibliography

Simon, Ron. "The Changing Definition of Reality Television." *Thinking Outside the Box: A Contemporary Television Genre Reader*. Ed Gary R. Edgerton and Brian G. Rose. Lexington: University Press of Kentucky, 2005. 171–200. Print.

Simpson, Joe. *Touching the Void: The True Story of One Man's Miraculous Survival*. New York: Perennial, 2004. Print.

Sinfield, Alan. *Literature, Politics, and Culture in Postwar Britain*. Berkeley: University of California Press, 1989. Print.

Smith, Betty. *A Tree Grows in Brooklyn*. New York: Harper Perennial, 2006. Print.

Smith, Dinitia. "The Times Plans a New Best-Seller List." *New York Times*. 24 June 2000. Web.

Springen, Karen. "Counting Down to *Catching Fire*." *Publishers Weekly*. 21 August 2009. Web.

_____. "Marketing *Mockingjay*." *Publishers Weekly*. 5 August 2010. Web.

_____. "This Isn't Child's Play." *The Daily Beast*. 4 September 2008.

Stowe, Harriet Beecher. *Uncle Tom's Cabin*. New York: W.W. Norton, 2010. Print.

Tacitus. *The Annals & The Histories*. New York: Modern Library, 2003. Print.

Takami, Koushun. *Battle Royale*. San Francisco: Haika Soru, 2009. Print.

Tal, Kalí. *Worlds of Hurt: Reading the Literatures of Trauma*. New York: Cambridge University Press, 1995. Print.

Tapscott, Don. *Grown Up Digital: How the Net Generation is Changing Your World*. New York: McGraw-Hill, 2008. Print.

Tatar, Maria. "No More Adventures in Wonderland." *New York Times*. 9 October 2011. Web.

Taylor, Jim. "Reality TV Is Not Reality." Huffpost Health. *Huffington Post*. 31 January 2011. Web.

Thussu, D.K. *News as Entertainment: The Rise of Global Infotainment*. London: Sage, 2007. Print.

Tompkins, Jane. *Sensational Designs: The Cultural Work of American Fiction, 1790–1860*. New York: Oxford University Press, 1985. Print.

Totaro, Rebecca Carol Noel. "Suffering in Utopia: Testing the Limits in Young Adult Novels." *Utopian and Dystopian Writing for Children and Young Adults*. Ed. Carrie Hintz and Elaine Ostry. New York: Routledge, 2003. 127–138. Print.

Trollope, Anthony. *An Autobiography*. Oxford: Oxford University Press, 2009. Print.

Valby, Karen. "Team 'Hunger Games' Talks: Author Suzanne Collins and Director Gary Ross on Their Allegiance to Each Other, and Their Actors." *Entertainment Weekly*. 7 April 2011. Web.

Vermazen, Bruce. "The Aesthetic Value of Originality." *Midwest Studies in Philosophy* 16.1. (1991): 266–79. Print.

Virgil. *The Aeneid*. Trans. Robert Fagles. Penguin: New York, 2010. Print.

Vizzini, Ned. "Reality Hunger." *The Girl Who Was on Fire: Your Favorite Authors on Suzanne Collins's Hunger Games Trilogy*. Ed. Leah Wilson. Dallas, TX: Benbella, 2011. 81–98. Print.

Washington, Mary Helen. "Foreword." *Their Eyes Were Watching God*. New York: Harper and Row, 1990. vii–xiv. Print.

Waters, Darren. "Rowling Backs Potter Fan Fiction." BBC News. 27 May 2004. Web.

Waugh, Evelyn. *Brideshead Revisited: The Sacred and Profane Memories of Captain Charles Ryder*. New York: Back Bay Books, 2008. Print.

Welch, Rollie. "'Catching Fire' Brings Back Suzanne Collins' Kindhearted Killer: Young Readers." *The Plain Dealer*. 6 September 2009. Web.

Bibliography

Wells, H.G. *The Time Machine*. New York: W.W. Norton, 2008. Print.

West, Candace, and Don Zimmerman. "Doing Gender." *Gender and Society* 1.2 (1987): 125–151. Print.

White, Mimi. "Ideological Analysis and Television." *Channels of Discourse, Reassembled*. Ed. Robert C. Allen. Chapel Hill: University of North Carolina Press, 1992. 181–7. Print.

Whited, Lana. *"Harry Potter*: From Craze to Classic?" *The Ivory Tower and "Harry Potter."* Ed. Lana Whited. Columbia: University of Missouri Press, 2002. Print.

Wilkinson, Lili. "Someone to Watch Over Me." *The Girl Who Was on Fire: Your Favorite Authors on Suzanne Collins's Hunger Games Trilogy*. Ed. Leah Wilson. Dallas TX: Benbella, 2011. 67–79. Print.

Wilson, Leah, ed. *The Girl Who Was on Fire: Your Favorite Authors on Suzanne Collins's Hunger Games Trilogy*. Dallas, TX: Benbella, 2011. Print.

Wittig, Monique. "One Is Not Born a Woman." *The Straight Mind and Other Essays*. Boston: Beacon Press, 1992. 9–20. Print.

Wolf, Naomi. *The Beauty Myth*. New York: Doubleday, 1991. Print.

Woolston, Blythe. "Bent, Shattered, and Mended." *The Girl Who Was on Fire: Your Favorite Authors on Suzanne Collins's Hunger Games Trilogy*. Ed. Leah Wilson. Dallas, TX: Benbella, 2011. 141–162. Print.

Wright, Chauncey. *The Philosophical Writings of Chauncey Wright: Representative Selections*. Ed. Edward H. Madden. New York: Liberal Arts Press, 1958. Print.

Wright, Christopher J. *Tribal Warfare: Survivor and the Political Unconscious of Reality Television*. New York: Lexington Books, 2006. Print.

Wright, Richard. "Between Laughter and Tears." *The New Masses*. 5 October 1937. 22–3. Print.

Zevin, Gabrielle. "Constant Craving." *New York Times*. 9 October 2009. Web.

Zola, Émile. *Germinal*. New York: Oxford University Press, 2008. Print.

Index

Index

Index

Index